D0022857

The Eleanor Houston and Lawrence M. C. Smith

Cartographic Collection

TOM JONES PHOTO, BRUNSWICK, MAINE

Eleanor Houston Smith (1910-1987) and Lawrence Meredith Clemson Smith (1902-1975) on 30 July 1968 at the ceremonies transferring their ownership of environmentally significant Popham Beach, Maine, to the state of Maine as a state park.

Maps, Globes, Atlases and Geographies Through The Year 1800

THE ELEANOR HOUSTON AND LAWRENCE M. C. SMITH

CARTOGRAPHIC COLLECTION

at the

Smith Cartographic Center, University of Southern Maine

———•———

Catalogued by JAMES E. MOONEY *with Foreword by* KENNETH NEBENZAHL

Introduction by PHILIP CHADWICK FOSTER SMITH

Published by the University of Southern Maine Library

PORTLAND, MAINE · 1988

© 1988 by The Renfrew Group, P.O. Box 617, Freeport, Maine 04032

All Rights Reserved

Library of Congress Cataloguing in Publication Data

Mooney, James E.
Maps, Globes, Atlases and Geographies Through The Year 1800
The Eleanor Houston and Lawrence M. C. Smith Cartographic Collection

Bibliography: p.
Includes index.
I.   Cartography — History
II.   The Renfrew Group
III.   Nebenzahl, Kenneth, foreword
IV.   Smith, Philip Chadwick Foster, introduction
V.   Title
VI.   Numbers

ISBN 0-939561-03-4

Library of Congress Catalog Card Number 88-92267

THE UNIVERSITY OF SOUTHERN MAINE LIBRARY

WISHES TO THANK THE RENFREW GROUP

FOR PERMISSION TO PUBLISH

THIS SPECIAL EDITION

CONTENTS

ILLUSTRATIONS

FOREWORD

ECENTLY I was recalling people who have made strong, positive impressions on me since I became a dealer in rare books thirty years ago. Among the first to come to mind were Mr. and Mrs. L. M. C. Smith, whom I met early in my career. Eleanor and Sam Smith had a combination of grace, charm, warmth, and boundless intellectual curiosity that made knowing them a wonderful experience. As collectors they personified a truism in my profession: the personal associations that a rare-book dealer is privileged to have are often as attractive as the pleasure of dealing with the books, manuscripts, maps, globes, and prints themselves.

When Sam Smith telephoned concerning items in one of the early issues of *The Compass for Map Collectors,* he also invited me to stop by when next in Philadelphia. Soon after, I had my first visit to 3460 School House Lane. This great nineteenth-century rambling frame house, once the home of Mayor Henry of Philadelphia, was full of books which the Smiths had "accumulated" over the years, before they began to "collect" books more formally and purposefully.

When we looked at books together, I had never experienced such enthusiasm and direct expression of curiosity and interest —equally strong with both collectors. This last point is remarkable for its unusualness. There are many gentlemen collectors, and quite a few lady collectors, but a husband-wife collecting team with both parties of equal strength is indeed rare.

I visited Germantown a number of times over the years and experienced the generous hospitality of the Smiths, epitomized in my recollection by the candelabra-lit dinners presented and served as in a by-gone era. Mr. and Mrs. Smith continued to develop their wonderful collection of maps, atlases, globes, and books on geographical subjects, pursuing this interest assiduously for years. Their wide-ranging intellectual curiosity and enthusiasm never waned with the passage of time. They became increasingly more knowledgeable in the history of cartography and related subjects. One of the ways great collectors can be identified is by their reference libraries of sources for their fields of collecting. The Smiths' collection of reference books not only grew, but showed appropriate signs of wear.

The University of Southern Maine is very fortunate to have been selected as the location of the Smith collection, with its many rarities from the fifteenth through the nineteenth centuries, many now improcurable. I know that Mrs. Smith derived great pleasure from seeing the collection remain together at the University of which she was very fond, where it will always be available for scholars of every sort to consult and find inspiration as well as information.

KENNETH NEBENZAHL

PREFACE

THE six hundred entries in this catalogue include nearly twenty thousand maps and geographies collected by the Smiths with enthusiasm and good taste over a period of two decades. These examples of three centuries of mapmaking through the year 1800 have great value not only to the students and scholars of geography but to the interested general public which has in its number more lovers of maps, true cartophiles, than often is thought. The catalogue is intended for use by both groups, and the illustrations give a sample of the beauty and utility of such maps, globes, atlases, and geographies.

The arrangement of the material in this catalogue is chronological and, within each year, alphabetical by name of mapmaker or geographer. Each entry is under the year of publication without brackets if the date is printed on the item or within brackets when the year of publication is known but not printed. The date is followed by a question mark when authorities disagree or the date is a guess, and the date followed by the character § when the item is a reproduction or facsimile. The entry begins with the name of the mapmaker or geographer with dates of birth and death where known from Tooley, Mansell, Shipton-Mooney, and other sources. The second line has the short title of the item taken from the title page or cartouche. Next in the entry is information on the place where it was published, its printer and publisher, and its date. The next line begins the description of the item as an object and it includes the format, its height in inches for all items except globes, where the measurement is of the diameter, and information on binding for books and atlases, on margins for maps, and the like. The next area of the entry has the cartographical content of the item and it is designed to help the reader to learn more about the piece by being referred to such standard sources as those listed among Selected References. It is here also that the place of the piece in cartographic history and other information is included.

In the Introduction to his study of English county atlases, R. A. Skelton wrote that "the compiler of such a work as this depends to a very large extent on the labours of his predecessors in the field, and he must be ready to confess, like John Speed, 'I have put my sickle into other men's corne'." The reader will note that the truth of this confession applies especially here, for the alternative to calling the reader's attention to the work of such predecessors as Koeman and Phillips and Sabin and others would be to add immensely to the heft of this catalogue by slavishly copying their findings here.

The period covered by this catalogue is only three hundred of the five hundred years since Columbus sparked European interest in the new world of the Americas by his discoveries. The two centuries not included here are represented within the collection at the Smith Center where there are, for example, many nineteenth-century globes included in Yonge's list under the names of Bardin, Cary, Loring, Newton, Wilson, and others. References in the entries to Donald H. Cresswell are to his written appraisal of the complete collection, a copy of which is at the Center. His help to me was significant as was the typing of the manuscript by Elaine Cohen of Kreda Secretarial Services in Philadelphia. The cataloguing was done in the Map Room of the Smiths' former home in Germantown where members of the staff were very helpful, especially Mrs. Elbert J. Taylor. The chief support was given freely by the late Mrs. L. M. C. Smith following the suggestion of a daughter and son-in-law that the catalogue be prepared as a complement to the presentation of the collection to the Center. I am grateful to all who helped in this most interesting work, but to none more than to Eleanor Houston Smith for sharing the joy of the work.

In the seventeenth century, Robert Burton wrote in his *Anatomy of Melancholy* that a study of maps was a good antidote for melancholy: "What greater pleasure can there now be, than to view those elaborate maps of Ortelius, Mercator, Hondius, &c.? To peruse those books of cities put out by Braunus and Hogenbergius?" What, indeed? This catalogue then may be your guide to travel at the lowest price and least discomfort to that new world contained within these maps.

JAMES E. MOONEY

INTRODUCTION

EARLY on in their forty-two-year marriage, Lawrence Meredith Clemson ("Sam") Smith (1902-1975) and his wife, Eleanor Houston Smith (1910-1987), developed an unique *modus operandi* for collecting. Their method applied equally to all areas of their wide-ranging, eclectic interests, and it smoothed their way immeasurably while assembling the cartographic archive they themselves and, now, their six children still refer to as the "MAPA" collection.

Their technique was to enter an antique shop, browse casually for a time, and then ask the proprietor if, perchance, any "wooden tea sets" might be found there. Sleepy dealers, or those intent upon closing up shop for the day, suddenly brightened and invariably engaged the Smiths in lively conversation. At the proper moment, Sam and Eleanor Smith got to the point.

By rights and by original intent, this Introduction should have been written by Eleanor Houston Smith herself; not by a son-in-law of the same surname. Yet a son-in-law can be sufficiently far removed from center stage to take objective notice of many things neither she nor any one of her children would have thought meet to chronicle on their own.

Nevertheless, before she died on 29 August 1987 Mrs. Smith had had the pleasure for several years to work closely—not only in Philadelphia but also from her summer home in Maine —with the distinguished compiler/editor of this work, Dr. James E. Mooney, and to see much of the printer's composition reach page proof stage. Concurrently, she was able to observe the maturing plans for an opening of the Smith Cartographic Center in the library of the University of Southern Maine.

Lawrence M. C. Smith was born in Philadelphia to an old Philadelphia and Delaware County family, educated at the Haverford School, the University of Pennsylvania, and Oxford. By profession a lawyer, he became many other things as well—conservationist, collector, farmer, to name but a few—and yet he preferred to think of himself as a "generalist." He practiced law in Philadelphia for five years before moving, with his new bride of 1933, to Washington, D.C.

His bride was the former Eleanor Houston, also from an old Philadelphia family with Pennsylvania roots going back to the days of William Penn. She was the daughter of Samuel Frederic Houston, developer of the delightful Chestnut Hill area of the city and granddaughter of Pennsylvania Railroad executive Henry Howard Houston. From the day they were married until Sam Smith's death in 1975 they worked as a team in all things —with foresight, fervor, and joy.

In Washington, as part of the Franklin D. Roosevelt Administration, L. M. C. Smith served, successively, for more than a dozen years as general coordinator of the legal division of the National Recovery Administration, associate counsel for investigation and study of investment trusts at the Securities and Exchange Commission, and, during World War II, chief of the special war policies unit of the Department of Justice, chief of the economic mission to French West Africa, and head of the United States purchasing mission in Switzerland. For his wartime services, he became a Chevalier of the Légion d'honneur of France and was awarded Brazil's Order of the Southern Cross.

After the war, the Smiths returned to Philadelphia, whence he became active in UNESCO, of which he was national vice-chairman for ten years preceding his death. In Philadelphia he served as chairman of the Board of Trade and Conventions for nearly a decade and for his work there was honored with the Order of the British Empire. He was also a founder of the local chapter of Americans for Democratic Action, the Human Relations Commission, and the Housing Association. At the same time, Sam and Eleanor Smith together founded Philadelphia's first classical music station, WFLN-FM, and created the Schuylkill Valley Nature Center in the city's Roxborough section.

In 1946, they purchased the nucleus of what was to become a saltwater organic beef farm on Wolfe's Neck, Freeport, Maine. There, with Casco Bay sparkling on one side and the Harraseeket River ebbing and flowing on the other, the Smith family has summered to the present day.

It was against this background, with a succession of worthy projects yet to come, that the Smiths became infatuated with ancient maps, globes, and atlases.

During the twelve years between the death of her husband and her own, Mrs. Smith had jotted down an occasional memorandum concerning the acquisition and scope of their map collection. Once, she had even attempted a draft introduction to a private index of it, but her memories made it too painful to complete. "There is something very sad about this now," she scribbled in a note to herself in 1978, having reviewed her words. "How simple & not very educated these remarks are &

how sad that years of enjoyment & fulfillment are now mine alone."

"Our interest started with the development of maps having to do with the New World," she stated in 1966. "As the sixteenth century went into the seventeenth and eighteenth centuries, our field narrowed down to the Northeast Coast from Maine to Virginia." It was a spring Sunday morning of 1956 in a quaint English village when the scope of their map collecting suddenly came into focus. The Smiths, accompanied by one or two of their daughters, tapped on the door of a closed antique shop, used the "wooden tea set" ploy on the resident owner, and were granted immediate, jovial entry. There, much to their surprise, they discovered an ancient map of Maine. It struck a chord. Why not in the future concentrate on maps depicting the northeast coast of America? After all, their farm in Maine was their second home. It all added up.

The policy of restricting themselves to a regional focus, she wrote in her draft of 1966,

has been hard to stick to as maps turn up that are of great interest for some reason or other, and so we take in other fields. This emerging into wider interests had its greatest impact when we realized the beauty of the atlas as a whole. So, for the moment, let us talk about only our books and atlases, some of which are facsimiles.

Because we have come to the game late, many of the originals, if available, are way beyond our means, and thus we settle for the content which is to be found in the very beautiful facsimiles which are being made today, especially in Amsterdam.

I say "we have come to the game," for when we innocently made our first purchases, we really didn't know that it was a game; especially is it so at auctions where many of these treasures are found.

There we discovered how many others besides ourselves had found map collecting a fascinating and rewarding game (I don't mean rewarding in the sense of cash) and discovered also at the very start of 1956 that the really interesting things were already expensive. Let us start with some of the earliest and follow on through our collection [as it stood in 1966]:

We begin with a short discussion about the first engraved atlas of the world: The *Cosmographia* of Claudius Ptolemy, Bologna 1477, written by Edward Lynam, Superintendent of the Map Room in the British Museum. We feel lucky that Nico Israel, our first-visited bookseller of note, in Amsterdam, is issuing a series of atlases in facsimile, Theatrum Orbis Terrarum, of which this Ptolemy of 1477 is the first. Thus, we can really see and enjoy this first edition along with the discussion as well as the edition of 1482, each with biographical notes and beautifully printed folio, without owning the original.

It is interesting to remember that Ptolemy lived in Egypt around 150 A.D., that his thinking was still on the basis of this first engraved atlas printed by others under his name, which was again corrected and enlarged in 1482, and that Columbus must have spent some hours with these maps. Because we have been able to add Yale's book, *The Vinland Map and the Tartar Relation,* we feel that the early explorations of America are beginning to be covered on our shelves.

We start our voyages to America in 1507. Each map is, of course, nothing more than the setting down on paper of some explorer-captain's description of the lands he had sailed to and by, or a combination of a number of descriptions. Each of those in the sixteenth century made the route of the *Mayflower* so much easier to attempt.

In 1507 Martin Waldseemüller wrote his geographical introduction *Cosmographiae Introductio* with an account of the four voyages of Amerigo Vespucci. This included ten maps: a plane projection of the world, on which for the first time appeared the use of the word "America," obviously because he had written of Vespucci's voyages, and a globe in elliptical segments (an original copy selling in 1960 at Sotheby-Parke-Bernet for £12,500; a fun item of ours is the illustrated catalogue for this sale).

Two Jesuits, who did much research on Waldseemüller, have given us a facsimile and English translation. We have, in fact, two copies of this, one large and one small.

And so, immediately, we plunge into controversy as Henry Stevens discusses in 1928 this and other early maps. Which is the first to show America? This volume, nicely printed, makes an interesting question mark on our shelf.

Our first original volume—individual maps will come later—is a most wonderful treasure. Ptolemy's *Geographia* of 1513, printed in Strassburg and the most important of all editions of Ptolemy. Because of the many added "new" maps, this becomes "in effect the first modern Atlas," says [R. V.] Tooley in *Maps and Map Makers.* The Italian leather binding has, alas, only broken catches.

Our first original small volume is 1520, Solinus's Polyhistor—with the earliest map in a printed book to use the name "America," the map being drawn by Apianus. The book has stains, but some of the printing is quite beautiful, and, of course, the world map is of the greatest interest. The vellum binding is simple, and the two ties are still there.

For 1546 we have Ortelius's own copy of Pincius, an historical work actually used by him as shown by his added margin notes. A present to me [from her husband], the card reads, "To Eleanor Houston Smith (née Ortelius) who believes so in the continuity of the world—from that Map Collector in her life." The "née" is because E[leanor] H[ouston] S[mith] could be connected to him, though by 1500, the records of Dutch forebears are rather vague!

1548—Vadianus—lovely little woodcut maps showing South America and vague islands to the north, and with a charming merman on a strange fish playing a harp.

Then we skip thirty years to when in Antwerp in 1578 de Jode made his *Speculum Orbis Terrarum,* our first folio illustrated atlas and a rare one (with very poor coloring). The Theatrum Orbis Terrarum of [Nico] Israel has provided us with a facsimile.

Again, this series helps us as we also have the Waghenaer works of 1584-1585 [, Spieghel der Zeevaerdt,] and of 1592, *Thresoor Der Zeevaert,* two very early sea chart atlases, which do much to prove that the old sea captains really sailed "by guess and by God"!

The earliest atlas devoted entirely to America is Wytfliet's *Descriptionis Ptolemaicæ [Augmentum],* printed in [Louvain in] 1598. The text gives the history of discovery, and the maps show the knowledge of the New World up to that date.

Another volume of the sixteenth century is *Opusculum Geographicum Rarum* by Joannes Myritius in 1590, a penciled note in the front says "No sale of any copy in America since 1916, though there are copies in the Library of Congress and the John Carter Brown Library." This is an old and worn copy, which, to me, seems so romantic. Who used it so much, and to what use did he put the knowledge he gained, and in what cold and damp room did he sit for his study?

Alas, we have no original Ortelius folio, though the facsimile of the Theatrum Orbis Terrarum makes us hope to find one! We do have two small volumes of Ortelius, one the miniature edition of his famous atlas, *Epitome Theatri Ortliani* of 1595. Various owners have inscribed their names, and one had his marked in the vellum. Among its woodcut maps are [eight] of America.

The other charming little vellum-bound volume is *Le Miroir du Monde,* a French version printed by Plantin in Antwerp in 1579.

A little larger, thin and very worn volume by Ortelius, with no texts and uncolored maps, as preferred by him, is an historical atlas of ancient geography—*Veteris Geographiae Tabulae.* Its very poor condition testifies to all who have studied with it. Here, again, how I would love to know who and where!

Then to our first real book on a part of America, de Bry's *Florida,* a part of his "Grand Voyage," full of views of the life of the Indians and a large map of Florida.

With this we have the modern two-volume copy of the John White drawings done in part by our friend, Professor [David] Quinn. These are beautifully reproduced books.

In commemoration of the 450th anniversary of Mercator's birth in 1512, Bibliothèque Royale of Belgium printed a facsimile of his *Atlas Sive Cosmographicæ,* which starts off with a lovely portrait of Mercator holding a globe.

One final facsimile in this sixteenth century is Livio Sanuto's *Geografia. . . . dell'Africa,* important because of the trade routes round Africa to the Far East.

The other original works bring us to the close of the sixteenth century by Ramusio and van Meteren. The third volume of the Navigation and Voyages of Ramusio deals with the New World and shows details in maps and pictures of Cartier, New France, and the Indians. Theatrum Orbis Terrarum Publishing Company has just announced a facsimile of the Ramusio *Navigationi et Viaggi* and calls it "the greatest source book for the history of discovery." The introduction by [R. A.] Skelton, and other statements in this reprint, will be most interesting. Van Meteren's *Historia Belgica [Nostri Potissimum Temporis]* is the first Latin edition with interesting pictures of the most important contemporary source of Dutch history, written by the man who was the Consul of the Dutch merchants in London, a cousin of Ortelius, and perhaps an ancestor of E[leanor] H[ouston] S[mith].

At the turn of the century, the map makers became more flowery, adding ships and animals and fish, as well as decorative cartouches. The opportunities of study and enjoyment are endless, with all these different aspects of the cartographer's work. I hope that we can enable a wider public to know and enjoy these treasures.

As I read this I can see how very superficial the facts are, but this is done as merely a beginning to show you our interest and really deep appreciation of these treasures, and with the hope of many quiet hours to delve more deeply into their various aspects.

The above words Eleanor Houston Smith wrote in 1966 while her beloved Sam was still at her side, sharing the excitement of the search. The two continued to collect, their enthusiasm never flagging and their knowledge of maps and atlases ever increasing despite other occupations with a multitude of projects and enterprises both in Maine and in Philadelphia.

During this period, and for nearly another ten years of joint collecting, they together nurtured their organically raised Angus beef herd at Wolfe's Neck Farm, experimented with alternative agricultural methods, and fought successfully in court for Maine property owners to have the right to prevent Central Maine Power from spraying their land with chemical defoliants.

They gave a portion of their farm to the state for public use as Wolf[e] Neck State Woods, a parcel of nearby land for the Maine Audubon Society's Mast Landing Sanctuary, the early nineteenth-century Pettengill house and farm to the Freeport Historical Society, and the historic Percy & Small Shipyard in Bath, Maine, to the Maine Maritime Museum. They also enabled the preservation of the ecologically important Popham Beach as a state park.

In Philadelphia, they continued to foster the growth of classical radio station WFLN-AM/FM, contributed more woodlands to the Schuylkill Valley Nature Center, participated in the donation of land to Fairmount Park for the Andorra Natural Area, pursued interests in UNESCO, ADA, civic and political issues, held institutional trusteeships, and annually entertained at Christmastime as many as 300 foreign students, all lonely and far from home, a tradition the Smiths had initiated during their days in Washington.

Mrs. Smith tried to pick up her draft introduction to the "MAPA" index the year after her husband died but could not bring herself to complete it.

And now it is 1976 [she wrote]. These ten years became busy ones, a great load of business problems and that "map collector in my life" feeling less and less well. So we never finished this, but even so I think it shows you the enormous pleasure we had, and we had it to the end, spending many an evening enjoying the beauty and the content of all we had collected.

Buying became less and less of a pleasure as prices went higher and higher, though we were tempted from time to time.

Though I hope these things we have loved will find libraries where they will be of use, I realize that we were not as particular in our buying as some people would expect and that we really do not have much of great importance or top quality. It is sometimes hard to explain the romance of a very used old book, but I am sure that in our own way we had as much deep and lasting pleasure with our "maps, atlases, globes, and related books" as the most fastidious scholar would have had with only the most important and the best.

In the eleven years remaining to her, Eleanor Houston Smith pursued the course she and her "hubby," as she was wont to speak of him, had set for themselves years before. She donated the bulk of her Wolfe's Neck Farm to the American Farmland Trust, to be administered by the University of Southern Maine, and gave her summer home to the same institution for its eventual use as a conference center.

The map collection presented special problems for her. She shied away from placing it in any existing map repository of note

—such as the Library of Congress, the New York Public Library, Harvard, the Clements Library, or the John Carter Brown Library—lest it be anonymously absorbed or portions of it become liable to deaccessioning as duplicative. After investigating a few more agreeable possibilities, the enthusiastic response she received from the then University of Maine Chancellor Patrick McCarthy and USM's President Robert Woodbury, subsequently a successor to McCarthy as Chancellor, persuaded her to choose the University of Southern Maine as the collection's future guardian. There, in the Smith Cartographic Center, her hope that it would prove to be useful to others will certainly be fulfilled.

Once prompted to commit the collection's content to a scholarly catalogue, she engaged her longtime friend, James E. Mooney, to undertake the work of compilation. He and Donald Cresswell of The Philadelphia Print Shop spent many an hour in the map vault at her Germantown home, he cataloguing and Cresswell evaluating and appraising each individual item. Meanwhile, in South Portland, Maine, another of Mrs. Smith's friends of long standing, Harry Milliken, a letterpress master printer of more than four decades' experience, was in the process of setting up a new shop, The Shagbark Press. To him and his colleague, David Wolfe, went the job of composition and printing of the text, the offset illustrative plates to be done by the respected Meriden-Stinehour Press of Meriden, Connecticut.

Eleanor Houston Smith was, and would have continued to have been, extraordinarily grateful to all those people for the culmination of her dreams. It is a pity that she and her husband could not have lived to see the flower they watered so assiduously burst into brilliant bloom.

PHILIP CHADWICK FOSTER SMITH

The Eleanor Houston and Lawrence M. C. Smith

Cartographic Collection

[THE VINLAND MAP — A World Map of about 1440.]

Map, 15¼″ high overall at map plus English title and margins, uncolored.

Forty-percent enlargement with text and translation published by Rand McNally & Company. The history of this controversial map may be found in many cartographical journals and newspapers. Its history from publication as *The Vinland Map and the Tartar Relation* in 1965 through publication of *Proceedings of the Vinland Map Conference* of 1966 is outlined by Wilcomb E. Washburn in his Preface to the *Proceedings,* published in 1971. Yale admitted in January 1974 that it was a forgery, but Barbara McCorkle, Curator of Maps at Yale, wrote in the catalogue of the 1985 exhibition honoring Alexander O. Vietor that Yale now reserves judgment.

1477§

PTOLEMY, CLAUDIUS, 87-150.

COSMOGRAPHIA.

Bologna, Domenico de'Lapi, 1477.

Folio, 17⅜″ high, bound in modern cloth, stamped.

Facsimile published by Theatrum Orbis Terrarum, Amsterdam, 1963, as Volume I of the First Series. This is the first atlas, the printing and dating of which is discussed by R. A. Skelton in the Introduction. The twenty-six maps do not relate to America. Sabin 66471 lists the maps and discusses the dating and suggests 1482.

1477§

PTOLEMY, CLAUDIUS, 87-150.

COSMOGRAPHIA.

Bologna, Domenico de'Lapi, 1477.

Folio, 17″ high, bound in modern cloth, stamped, with map pocket at back cover.

Facsimile of three maps, numbers 1, World; 7, Italy; and 15, Africa, in the List by Edward Lynam, published by the George H. Beans Library of Jenkintown in 1941 as Publication Number Sixteen. Sabin 66471 discusses typesetting and printing in Bologna. See also the comments at PTOLEMY 1477.

1478§

PTOLEMY, CLAUDIUS, 87-150.

COSMOGRAPHIA.

Rome, Conrad Sweynheym and Arnold Buckinck, 1478.

Folio, 17⅜″ high, bound in modern cloth, stamped.

Facsimile published by Theatrum Orbis Terrarum, Amsterdam, 1966, as Volume VI of the Second Series. The twenty-seven engraved maps do not relate to America, but it was this Rome, 1478, edition which Columbus owned and annotated. Sabin 66470 notes that this edition "contains the first printed atlas and the first collection of maps engraved on copper," a point discussed by Skelton and Lynam in each entry at PTOLEMY 1477, and discussed in the Introduction here by Skelton.

1482 §

BERLINGHIERI, FRANCESCO DI NICOLA, 1440-1501.

GEOGRAPHIA.

Florence, Nicolaus Laurentii, 1482.

Folio, 17⅝″ high, bound in modern cloth, stamped.

Facsimile published by Theatrum Orbis Terrarum, Amsterdam, 1966, as Volume IV of the Third Series. The thirty-one engraved maps do not relate to America. Sabin 66500 lists the maps in this Italian verse edition and dates it [1480?]. Sabin 66501 describes the second issue.

1482 §

PTOLEMY, CLAUDIUS, 87-150.

COSMOGRAPHIA.

Ulm, Lienhart Holle, 1482.

Folio, 17¼″ high, bound in modern cloth, stamped.

Facsimile published by Theatrum Orbis Terrarum, Amsterdam, 1963, as Volume II of the First Series. The thirty-two woodcut maps do not relate to America, except for that of the northern countries, which includes Greenland, at map number eight. Sabin 66472 notes that the redrawn maps mention Engronelant and Norbegia and that they were done by the Benedictine Nicolaus Donis.

[1492 §]

BEHAIM, MARTIN, 1459-1507.

ERDAPFEL.

[Nuremberg, 1492.]

Globe gores, 23″ high, on four folding sheets, colored.

Facsimile printed to serve as part of E. G. Ravenstein, *Martin Behaim His Life and Globe,* London, George Philip & Son, Ltd., 1908. This book deals with many aspects of Behaim and reproduces a number of maps of his period. The globe summarizes the Renaissance knowledge of the world at the moment when Columbus set sail for the land which, thanks to Behaim, came to be called America.

[1507 §]

WALDSEEMÜLLER, MARTIN, 1470-1521.

[THE WORLD MAPS OF 1507 AND 1516.]

[Strassburg? 1507.]

Folio, 20½″ high, bound in modern cloth.

Facsimile published in 1903 in Innsbruck by Wagner, edited by Joseph Fischer, S.J., and Franz von Wieser. Also here is Monograph Four of the United States Catholic Historical Society, *The Cosmographiae Introductio of Martin Waldseemüller,* of 1907 and the London, Henry Stevens, Son and Stiles, *The First Delineation* of 1928. Waldseemüller is discussed by Sabin at 101017 where he notes these facsimile editions of von Wieser and the Society. The following numbers through 101026 discuss Waldseemüller.

1513

PTOLEMY, CLAUDIUS, 87-150.

GEOGRAPHIA [edited by Jacobus Eszler and Georgius Ubelin].

Strassburg, Johann Schott, 1513.

Folio, 18¼″ high, bound in contemporary full leather, blind-tooled with missing clasps.

Wilberforce Eames and others before and since have agreed that this is the most important edition of Ptolemy's geographies, and Sabin 66478 calls it "this grand and important edition." The first part has twenty-six double-page woodcut maps and one single-page map. The *Supplementum* is the first modern world atlas based upon new facts. It has twenty woodcut maps. The first has the New World represented by two named islands, "Isabella" and "Spagnolla," and five mainland points on a rough representation of South America. The second map is titled "Tabula Terre Nove," also called the Admiral's map, which identifies more islands and more of the mainland of North and South America. All of the maps are double-page, except the last which is printed in three colors on a single page. Martin Waldseemüller did the maps. In the editors' comments to the reader, the maps of the New World are credited as compiled from facts gotten from "the Admiral," which all since have believed to be Columbus. This is described in Sabin 66478, and Harrisse *B.A.V.* 74 gives references.

See PLATE 1

1513§

PTOLEMY, CLAUDIUS, 87-150.

GEOGRAPHIA.

Strassburg, Johann Schott, 1513.

Folio, 17¾″ high, bound in modern cloth, stamped.

Facsimile published by Theatrum Orbis Terrarum, Amsterdam, 1966, as Volume IV of the Second Series. Three maps of the *Supplementum* relate to America and they are listed by title at Phillips 359 as numbers [28], [29], and [35]. See notes to PTOLEMY 1513 above.

SOLINUS, CAIUS JULIUS.

JOANNIS CAMERTIS MINORITANI.

Vienna, Johann Singrenius for Lucas Alantse, 1520.

Folio, 12½″ high, bound in limp vellum with ties.

This is the first edition to contain the map of the world by Apianus, Peter Apian of Leisnig, done on a cordiform projection, the second map ever made on which the word "America" appears, and the first such map in a book. It was preceded only by the large Waldseemüller map of 1507. The printer's and publisher's devices are on either side of the index. Sabin 86390 notes that this edition is "the first to have any American interest," and supplies the full scholarly apparatus. Harrisse *B.A.V.* 108 mentions another edition while describing this one.

See PLATE 2

1523§

SCHOENER, JOHANN, 1457-1547.

... A REPRODUCTION OF HIS GLOBE OF 1523 LONG LOST ... BY HENRY STEVENS.

London, Stevens & Son, 1888.

Quarto, 7⅜″ high, bound in modern cloth with gold-stamped leather label on spine.

This facsimile volume includes globe gores and other material in the case. They are listed at pages 205 and 206, and those relating to America are: The Cantino Map of 1502, The Hunt-Lenox Globe of 1506, The Globe Gores for the Boulonger *Cosmographia* of 1514, and Schoener's Globes of [1515?], 1520, and 1523. Sabin 77798 gives his birthdate as 1477. The reproductions are discussed in 77800 through 77804.

1528§

BORDONE, BENEDETTO, 1460-1531.

LIBRO . . . DE TUTTE L'ISOLE DEL MONDO.

Venice, Nicolo Zoppino, 1528.

Quarto, 12⅜″ high, bound in modern cloth, stamped.

Facsimile published by Theatrum Orbis Terrarum, Amsterdam, 1966, as Volume I of the Third Series. Of the hundred and eleven woodcut maps in the text, nine relate to America: 3, World; 12, Temistitan or Mexico; 13, Jamaiqua Spagnola; 14, Spagnola; 15, Jamaiqua; 16, Cuba; 17, S. Maria Antica; 18, Guadalupe; and 19, Matinina. Sabin 6417 describes this edition as does Harrisse *B.A.V.* 145 where a short biography of Bordone is included.

1533

MARTYR, PETER D'ANGIERI, 1459-1526.

. . . DE REBUS OCEANICIS & ORBE NOVO.

Basel, Johann Bebel, 1533.

Quarto, 11¾″ high, bound in contemporary full leather, gold-tooled also at page edges.

The first edition of 1516 was the first to use the Latin words for New World and Western Hemisphere. Martyr was in Spain when Columbus sailed and when he returned. In addition to the voyages of Columbus, it contains the first references in print to both Cabot's voyages and Balboa's discovery of the Pacific. Sabin 1557 notes that this contains "Decades I., II., III., and an abridgment of Decade IV.," and Harrisse *B.A.V.* 176 notes that this "may captivate the attention of the reader curious of novelties."

[1537?]

BORDONE, BENEDETTO, 1460-1531.

ISOLARIO . . . NEL QUAL SI RAGIONA DI TUTTE LE ISOLE.

Venice, Francesco di Leno [, 1537?].

Quarto, 11⅝″ high, bound in contemporary vellum with gold-tooling on spine.

Contains eight double-page maps, one full-page map of Western Europe, and 106 smaller woodcut maps including twelve relating to America. They are the world map following signature mark DD and maps on verso and recto of leaves X through XIIII. Text contains the earliest authentic report of Pizarro's conquest of Peru, for Bordone was one of the best cartographers of Venice. Sabin 6420 dates [1537] as does Harrisse *B.A.V.* 221.

See PLATE 3

1540§

MÜNSTER, SEBASTIAN, 1489-1552.

GEOGRAPHIA UNIVERSALIS.

Basel, Heinrich Petri, 1540.

Folio, 12½″ high, bound in modern cloth, stamped.

Facsimile published by Theatrum Orbis Terrarum, Amsterdam, 1966, as Volume V of the Third Series. Of the forty-eight woodcut maps called for at Phillips 365 and 3388 those relating to America are listed as numbers 1, 41, and 45. Sabin 66484 notes this as a "new and important edition" of Ptolemy by Münster who "designed the maps anew," and he describes the maps, especially those of America. Harrisse *B.A.V.* 231 also describes this.

[1540]

[MÜNSTER, SEBASTIAN, 1489-1552.]

TABULA ASIAE III.

[Basel, Heinrich Petri, 1540.]

Map, 9⅞″ high plus title and margins, colored.

On verso is printed in Latin a description of the map and the folio 19, within a decorative border. This is not exactly the same as in the Theatrum Orbis Terrarum facsimile of 1966 though the map is the same and shows Armenia in the area between the Black and Caspian Seas. Phillips 365 describes the Basel 1540 edition of Ptolemy's *Geographia,* and Sabin 66484 notes that the maps of Asia are from 17 through 28. Harrisse *B.A.V.* 231 discusses the edition.

[1542]

[MÜNSTER, SEBASTIAN, 1489-1552.]

TYPUS UNIVERSALIS.

[Basel, Heinrich Petri, 1542.]

Map, 10⅛″ high plus title and margins, colored.

On verso printed in Latin is a description of the map, "Orbis Universalis Descriptio." Phillips discusses at 365, 367, and 368. A 1545 variant of this woodcut is illustrated by Tooley in his dictionary at Münster. Sabin 66486 describes this second edition as having maps "the same as those in the 1540 edition, having been printed from the same blocks." Harrisse *B.A.V.* 231 describes the edition. Shirley 76 terms this the first edition of Münster's modern world.

See PLATE 4

[1545]

[MÜNSTER, SEBASTIAN, 1489-1552.]

NOVAE INSULAE XXVI NOVA TABULA.

[Basel, Heinrich Petri, 1545.]

Map, 10″ high plus title and margins, uncolored.

The first printed map of the Western Hemisphere to show North and South America connected by an isthmus. Ptolemy's *Geographia* published at Basel in 1540, Phillips 365, has this map with numerals XVII. Numerals as here appear in 1545 edition, Phillips 368, as number 54. On verso printed in Latin is a description of the map. *Imago Mundi,* XVI, 84-97, has a full survey of the Münster maps in various editions, and Sabin 66487 discusses the 1545 third edition and identifies this as number 54. Harrisse *B.A.V.* 231 cites the 1545 edition among others.

See PLATE 5

1546

PINCIUS, JANUS PYRRHUS.

... DE VITIS PONT[IFICUM] TRID[ENTINORUM] LIBRI DUODECIM.

Mantua, Venturini Rufinelli, 1546.

Folio, 12″ high, bound in blind-tooled full leather, a contemporary Antwerp binding.

This is Abraham Ortelius's copy, signed on title page and with marginal notes and underlinings of text. Nebenzahl translates Brunet at Pincius, "this history which goes to the year 1539, is rare," and adds, "it is apparent that this volume was a source for Ortelius in his work and possible that he even planned a subsequent edition. Notice his underlining of passages and numbering in the margins for reorganization."

See PLATE 6

7

1548

PTOLEMY, CLAUDIUS, 87-150.

... LA GEOGRAFIA.

Venice, Nicolo Bascarini for Giovanni Baptista Pedrezano, 1548.

Octavo, 6⅝″ high, bound in contemporary full vellum.

First edition of Ptolemy in Italian with sixty maps drawn by the cartographer Giacomo Gastaldi, described in Phillips 369 which calls for colophon following leaf 214, present here. Phillips commented that "a whole series of plates of the New World is here met with, for the first time, and some of them are of no slight interest to the history of geography." They are maps number 54, "Tierra Nova," through number 60. Also described at Sabin 66502 where the maps are listed, and Harrisse *B.A.V.* 285 describes this edition.

See PLATE 7

1548

VADIANUS, JOACHIM, 1484-1551.

EPITOME TRIUM TERRAE PARTIUM, ASIAE, AFRICAE, ET EUROPAE.

Zurich, Christoffel Froschauer, 1548.

Sixteenmo, 6¼″ high, bound in contemporary vellum with missing ties.

Map of world dated 1546 shows South America but differs radically from map of world in first edition of 1534. The other map relating to America in the twenty-eight pages of maps is the globe at leaf a2. Sabin 98282 dates this cordiform map of the world [154–?].

1549

HONTER, JAN CORONENSIS, 1498-1549.

RUDIMENTORUM COSMOGRAPHICORUM. ... LIBER I [-IV].

Zurich, Christoffel Froschauer, 1549.

Octavo, 6¼″ high, bound in modern full leather, gold-stamped on spine.

Contains ten maps of which the first, a globe, and second, cordiform world map, relate to America. Tooley mentions this latter map at page iii of his *Maps and Mapmakers*. Sabin 32794 describes this edition, quoting Muller, "this book is interesting for America ... containing an atlas of the world." Harrisse *B.A.V.* 287 describes this edition.

1550§

MÜNSTER, SEBASTIAN, 1488-1552.

COSMOGRAPHEI.

Basel, Heinrich Petri, 1550.

Octavo, 13⅜″ high, bound in modern full leather, stamped.

Facsimile published by Theatrum Orbis Terrarum, Amsterdam, 1968, as Volume V of the First Series on Urbanization. Of the fifty-three maps and views, only the first map, that of the world, and the fourteenth, that of the new world, relate to America. Sabin 51387 calls for fourteen maps, as does Harrisse *B.A.V.* 294 where the quality is noted with the comment that "this edition is the best for the admirers of ancient good woodcuts."

RAMUSIO, GIOVANNI BATTISTA, 1485-1557.

DELLA NAVIGATIONI ET VIAGGI RACCOLTE DA . . . IN TRE VO-
LUMI.

Venice, Lucantonio Giunti Heirs [, 1556-1613].

Folios, 12″ high, bound in contemporary full leather, gold-stamped
on spines and labels.

Volume One is the sixth edition dated 1613 with four maps; Volume
Two is the third edition dated 1583 with no maps; and Volume Three
is the first edition dated 1556 with nine woodcut maps including one
of Mexico City facing page 309, one of Cuzco on page 412, one of "La
Nuova Francia" on page 425, one of Brazil on page 428, one of
Montreal on page 447, and one of the Western Hemisphere on page
456. The map of Montreal shows Jacques Cartier being greeted by
Hurons, reproduced as fig. 52, page 93, in Skelton's *Explorers' Maps*.

See PLATE 8

[1561]

RUSCELLI, GIROLANEO, 1504?-1566.

TIERRA NUEVA.

[Venice, 1561.]

Map, 7⅛″ high plus margins and title.

On verso printed in Latin is a description of the map and the folio 59.
This map is from the edition of Ptolemy's *Geografia* of 1561. Phillips 371 has as number XXXII, as does Sabin 66503.

[1563-1603§]

RAMUSIO, GIOVANNI BATTISTA, 1485-1557.

PRIMO VOLUME [OF THREE], & TERZA EDITIONE DELLE NAVI-
GATIONI ET VIAGGI.

Venice, Lucantonio Giunti Heirs [, 1563-1603].

Octavos, 12½″ high, bound in modern cloth stamped.

Facsimile published by Theatrum Orbis Terrarum, Amsterdam,
1970, as Volumes II-IV of the First Series of Mundus Novus. Volume
Three relates to America with maps of Hispaniola at leaf 36, Mexico
City at leaf 258, Cuzco at leaf 344, Northeast Coast of North America
at leaf 354, Brazil at leaf 357, New France at leaf 380, and Western
Hemisphere at leaf 385. Sabin 67732 describes the edition.

[1565?]

BERTELLI, FERNANDO, fl. 1556-1572.

[CHART SHOWING AMERICA FROM LABRADOR TO BRAZIL.]

[Venice, Fernando Bertelli, 1565?]

Map, 9½″ high plus margins, uncolored.

Phillips 258, number 183, dates this as "about 1565," and Sabin 5000
describes an imperial folio edition of 1558-1580. A very early depiction of a great lake near the location of the Great Lakes of North
America.

See PLATE 9

1566

ZALTIERI, BOLOGNINO, fl. 1550-1580.

IL DISEGNO DEL DISCOPERTO DELLA NOVA FRANZA.

Venice, Bolognino Zaltieri, 1566.

Map, 10½″ high plus directions and margins closely trimmed, uncolored.

This is the earliest map showing triangular shape of North America and the Straits of Anian. Phillips 3392 has as number 64, published in Antonio Lafreri's *Geografia Tavole Moderne* of Rome of [1575?]. Schwartz and Ehrenberg have at plate 30.   *See* PLATE 10

[1570]

ORTELIUS, ABRAHAM, 1527-1598.

AMERICAE SIVE NOVI ORBIS, NOVA DESCRIPTIO.

[Antwerp, 1570.]

Map, 14½″ high plus margins, colored.

On verso printed in Latin is a description of the map. *Atlantes* Ort 1A has as number (2), a new map, in the 1570 *Theatrum*. This is the first edition with the bulge in the western coast of South America and the first state, with the ghost off the coast of Brazil, the hyphenation of "S. Iaco-mo" island in the Cape Verde group, and the redundant "Carthago" in present-day Colombia.   *See* PLATE 11

[1570]

[ORTELIUS, ABRAHAM, 1527-1598.]

INDIÆ ORIENTALIS INSULARUMQUE ADIACIENTIUM TYPUS.

[Antwerp, 1570.]

Map, 13¾″ high plus margins, colored.

On verso printed in French is a description of the map and the folio 109. America is shown in part. *Atlantes* Ort 1A has as number (48), a new map, in the *Theatrum* of 1570. Also present in the collection is a reproduction of slightly reduced size.

[1570]

[ORTELIUS, ABRAHAM, 1527-1598.]

RUSSIAE, MOSCOVIAE ET TARTARIAE DESCRIPTIO. AUCTORE ANTONIO JENKENSONO ANGLO.

[Antwerp, 1570.]

Map, 14″ high plus margins, colored.

On verso printed in Latin is a description of the map and the folio 117. This is the first map of Russia by an Englishman. *Atlantes* Ort 1A has as number (46), a new map, in the *Theatrum* of 1570.

[1570]

[ORTELIUS, ABRAHAM, 1527-1598.]

TARTARIAE SIVE MAGNI CHAMI REGNI TYPUS.

[Antwerp, 1570.]

Map, 14⅞″ high plus margins, colored.

On verso printed in French is a description of the map and the folio 106. America is shown just east of Japan with California as a cape. *Atlantes* Ort 1A has as number (47), a new map, in the *Theatrum* of 1570.

1570§

ORTELIUS, ABRAHAM, 1527-1598.

THEATRUM ORBIS TERRARUM.

Antwerp, Gillis van Diest, 1570.

Folio, 16″ high, bound in modern cloth, stamped.

Facsimile published by Theatrum Orbis Terrarum, Amsterdam, 1964, as Volume III of the First Series. Phillips 374 lists the fifty-three maps, of which numbers 1, 2, 5, 45, 47, and 48 relate to America. In addition to discussion there, see *Atlantes,* III, 25-35. Sabin 57693 notes that the maps are engraved by Hogenberg.

[1570]

ORTELIUS, ABRAHAM, 1527-1598.

TYPUS ORBIS TERRARUM . . . FRANCISCUS HOGENBERGUS SCULPSIT.

[Antwerp, 1570.]

Map, 13¼″ high plus margins, colored.

On verso printed in German is a description, "Die Gantsche Welt." *Atlantes* Ort 1A has as number (1), a new map, in the *Theatrum* of

1570. This was the basis from which other cartographers' world maps came for many years. It is also the earliest issue before the hump on the West Coast of South America was removed. Phillips, *Maps,* page 1087, lists editions. Also present in the collection is a facsimile 14½″ high, colored, and dated 1590. Shirley 122 notes as the first state with crack at lower left corner just beginning.

1571

ARIAS, MONTANO BENITO, 1527-1598.

. . . SACRAE GEOGRAPHIAE TABULAM.

Antwerp, 1571.

Map, 12⅜″ high plus margins, uncolored.

This world map is from the *Biblia Polyglotta,* printed at the Plantin Press in 1572, and the depiction of America in the left hemisphere resembles that of Giacomo Gastaldi of Venice. Shirley 125 notes as second state.

See PLATE 12

[1572]

PORCACCHI, TOMASO, 1530-1585.

CANDIA INSULA, OLIM CRETA.

[Venice, 1572.]

Map, 5″ high plus margins and text on small folio page.

From one of the great Italian isolarios, *L'Isole piu Famose del Mondo,* this map of Crete was engraved by Girolamo Porro.

1572-1618§

BRAUN, George, 1541-1622, and
HOGENBERG, Frans, 1535-1590.

CIVITATES ORBIS TERRARUM [in six books].

Antwerp, Philippe Galle, and Cologne, George Braun and Frans Hogenberg, 1572-1618.

Three portfolios of unbound folded sheets, 17¼″ high, uncolored.

Facsimile published by World Publishing Company of Cleveland and New York in 1966. These were Volumes One, Two, and Three in the First Series of "Mirror of the World, a series of early books on the history of urbanization." The preface by R. V. Tooley and the introduction by R. A. Skelton provide biographical and bibliographical information. Of the 546 maps, only the last two in the first book, Cuzco and Mexico, relate to America, and Sabin 7448 notes these two maps. This is in Phillips at 59 with a general description repeated at 3292 with a list of contents. This Latin text is in *Atlantes* as B&H 1 through B&H 6. Loose in the first portfolio are colored maps, with blank versos, of London, Cologne, Amsterdam, Paris, Venice, and Stockholm.

1575

BRAUN, George, 1541-1622, and
HOGENBERG, Frans, 1535-1590.

CANTABRIGIA.

[Cologne, George Braun and Frans Hogenberg,] 1575.

Map, 13″ high plus margins, uncolored.

Verso has Latin text with date "pridi Pentecostes, M.D.LXXV." This appeared originally in *Civitates Orbis Terrarum,* Sabin 7448.

1575

ORTELIUS, Abraham, 1527-1598.

THEATRUM ORBIS TERRARUM.

Antwerp, Aegidius Radeus, 1575.

Folio, 18″ high, bound in contemporary leather, gold-tooled.

When the first edition was published in 1570, it was the first modern atlas and it inaugurated the golden age of Dutch cartography, according to Nebenzahl. Tooley wrote that it "was the first uniformly sized, systematic . . . modern atlas." This volume has an engraved allegorical title page in color and seventy colored mapsheets, is listed in *Atlantes* as Ort 13, and the maps are as in the 1574 Latin edition, Ort 12. Phillips 328 also has 106 names in the "Catalogus Auctorum," as here.

[1578]

JODE, Gerard de, 1509-1591.

SPECULUM ORBIS TERRARUM [title page volume one], SPECULUM GEOGRAPHICUM TOTIUS GERMANIÆ [title page volume two with both volumes in one].

Antwerp, Gerard Smits for Gerard de Jode [, 1578]. Two volumes in one.

Folio, 16¾″ high, bound in contemporary vellum.

This is the first edition of the rarest of all atlases, and is the only one known in color. Van Ortroy knows of only eight copies, two of them incomplete, none in color. For a listing and description of the sixty-four maps, see *Atlantes* Jod. 1. This copy has blank verso of title page. Phillips has at 383 with numbers 1, 2, and 4 relating to America. Sabin lists only the 1593 edition which contained the first printing of de Jode's separate map of North America.

See PLATE 13

12

1578§

JODE, GERARD DE, 1509-1591.

SPECULUM ORBIS TERRARUM [title page volume one], SPECULUM GEOGRAPHICUM TOTIUS GERMANIÆ [title page volume two with both volumes in one].

Antwerp, Gerard Smits for Gerard de Jode, 1578.

Folio, 17¼" high, bound in modern cloth, stamped.

Facsimile published by Theatrum Orbis Terrarum, Amsterdam, 1965, as Volume II of the Second Series. Of the sixty-four maps, those relating to America are listed in Phillips 383 as numbers 1, 2, and 4. All maps are listed in *Atlantes* Jod. 1. In his introduction R. A. Skelton states that "both editions of the *Speculum* are of great rarity."

1579

ORTELIUS, ABRAHAM, 1527-1598.

LE MIROIR DU MONDE.

Antwerp, Christopher Plantin for Philippe Galle, 1579.

Oblong twenty-fourmo, 5½" high, bound in contemporary vellum.

This first French edition is lightly colored in its seventy-one maps and single engraved frontispiece as in the 1577 Dutch edition. The "typus orbis terrarum" of 1574 called for in Phillips 385 is missing. *Atlantes* Ort 48 calls for seventy-two maps. America appears at numbered leaf 3, a part of Brazil is on the map of Africa at leaf 5, and a part of Greenland on the folding map of Europe at leaf 6. Part of America appears on the map of Tartary at leaf 64 and on the map of India on

leaf 65. On verso of last leaf is a contemporary manuscript map of "LE NOUVEAU MONDE."

1579

ORTELIUS, ABRAHAM, 1527-1598.

CULIACANAE, AMERICAE REGIONIS DESCRIPTIO [at upper map cartouche], HISPANIOLAE, CUBAE, ALIARUMQUE INSULARUM CIRCUMCIENTIUM, DELINEATIO [at lower map cartouche].

[Amsterdam, Abraham Ortelius,] 1579.

Map, 14" high plus margins, colored.

On verso printed in Latin is a description of the area and the folio 8. *Atlantes* Ort 14B has as number (2) of the *Additamentum* of 1580 where it is a new map.

[1580]

ORTELIUS, ABRAHAM, 1527-1598.

ROMANI IMPERII IMAGO.

[Antwerp, Abraham Ortelius, 1580.]

Map, 13¾" high plus margins, colored.

On verso printed in French is a description of the map and the folio 118. The map includes the area south of the twentieth to north of the fifty-eighth parallels, from the Canaries to the area east of the Caspian Sea. *Atlantes* Ort 14B describes the *Additamentum* of 1580, of which this is number (22), a new map. The French edition of 1585 is Ort 20.

13

1582§

HAKLUYT, RICHARD, 1553?-1616.

DIVERS VOYAGES.

London, Thomas Woodcocke, 1582.

Quarto, 7½″ high, bound in modern cloth, stamped.

Facsimile published by Theatrum Orbis Terrarum, Amsterdam, 1967, as Volume I in the First Series of Mundus Novus. Contains two maps, World facing page [45] and America facing page [58]. Sabin 29592 calls it "a tract of excessive rarity."

1582

MELA, POMPONIUS, first century A.D.

. . . DE SITU ORBIS LIBRI TRES.

Antwerp, Christopher Plantin, 1582.

Twelvemo, 7¾″ high, bound in paste-paper boards.

Contains one double-page map of Europe, Africa, and Asia by Ortelius, dated 1582. Sabin 63955 through 63961 discuss his work in various editions.

1583§

SAXTON, CHRISTOPHER, 1542?-1606.

BRITANNIA INSULARUM.

[London, Augustine Ryther?,] 1583.

Folio, 19⅛″ high, bound in modern cloth, stamped.

Facsimile published by Nico Israel, Amsterdam, 1974, as Supplement Six for *Imago Mundi,* where it is noted by R. A. Skelton that this is the earliest known wall map engraved and printed in England.

[1584]

ORTELIUS, ABRAHAM, 1527-1598.

PERUSINI AGRI; EXACTISSIMA NOVISSIMAQUE DESCRIPTIO: AUCTORE EGNATIO DANTE.

[Antwerp, Abraham Ortelius, 1584.]

Map, 13″ high plus margins, colored.

On verso printed in French is a description of the map and the folio 73. *Atlantes* Ort 18 has as number (9), a new map, in the *Additamentum* of 1584.

[1584]

ORTELIUS, ABRAHAM, 1527-1598.

PERUVIAE AURIFERÆ REGIONIS TYPUS. DIDACO MENDEZIO AUCTORE. LA FLORIDA. AUCTORE HIERON. CHIAVES. GUASTECAN REG.

[Antwerp, 1584.]

Map, 13⅜″ high plus margins, colored.

On verso printed in Latin is a description of the three maps and the folio 9. *Atlantes* Ort 18 has as number (10), a new map, in the *Additamentum* of 1584. A break in the lower left corner of the plate indicates a later impression.

[1584]

[ORTELIUS, ABRAHAM, 1527-1598.]

TERRA SANCTA A PETRO LAICSTAIN PERLUSTRATA, ET AB EIUS
ORE ET SCHEDIS A CHRISTIANO SCHROT IN TABULAM REDACTA.

[Antwerp, Abraham Ortelius, 1584.]

Map, 14½″ high plus margins, colored.

On verso printed in Latin is a description of the map which has in its cartouche three scenes from the life of Christ and a depiction of Jonah and the whale in the sea. *Atlantes* Ort 18 has as number (13), a new map in the *Additamentum* of 1584.

1584-1585§

WAGHENAER, LUCAS JANSZ, 1533-1606.

SPIEGHEL DER ZEEVAERDT.

Leyden, Christopher Plantin, 1584-1585.

Folio, 17¼″ high, bound in modern cloth, stamped.

Facsimile published by Theatrum Orbis Terrarum, Amsterdam, 1964, as Volume IV of the First Series. Of the forty-four charts described at *Atlantes,* IV, 465-478, all are concerned with the navigation of European waters.

[1584-1624]

ORTELIUS, ABRAHAM, 1527-1598.

[ABRAHAMI ORTELII THEATRI ORBIS TERRARUM PARERGON;
SIVE VETERIS GEOGRAPHIAE TABULAE.]

[Antwerp, 1584-1624.]

Folio, 16¾″ high, bound in full leather with gold-stamped leather labels on spine with "Veteris Geographiae Tabulae Orteli Antuerpiae 1584-1624."

Using list of maps in *Atlantes* Ort 46, the order here is:

49, 8, 1-7, 39, 9-11 (all text missing including that called for at map numbers 12, 14, 16, 20), 13, 17-19, 23 (map of Philip Cluver, "Italia Antiqua," of 1603), 24, 25, 36, 26-30, 32, 34, 31, 36, 37, 40, 39, 42, and 48.

The binding is broken and the maps are wonderfully worn, and uncolored as Ortelius preferred. Sabin 57697 calls for twelve maps in the *Parergon.*

1585

FAVOLI, HUGO, 1523-1585.

THEATRI ORBIS TERRARUM ENCHIRIDION, MINORIBUS TABULIS.

Antwerp, Christopher Plantin for Philippe Galle, 1585.

Twelvemo, 8″ high, bound in contemporary vellum.

Phillips 391 notes eighty-three maps with only numbers 1 and 2 relating to America. Also relating to America are numbers 4, 5, 72, 74, and 75. Included in *Atlantes* at Ort 51, and Sabin has at 23935 where he terms it a "curious poetical work." Favoli did this Latin verse translation of Pieter Heyns's *Spieghel der Werelt,* but this first issue does not contain Heyns's name and is not oblong.

1585§

WHITE, JOHN, 1545?-1606?

[THE AMERICAN DRAWINGS OF . . . 1577-1590 . . . BY PAUL HUL-
TON AND DAVID BEERS QUINN.]

Folios, 15¼″ high, bound in modern cloth, gold-stamped.

Facsimile produced by the British Museum in 1964 containing manuscript maps at plates 58 and 59 and plans of fortifications at plates 2
and 3. These are described in the introduction by Hulton and Quinn.

1587

ORTELIUS, ABRAHAM, 1527-1598.

AMERICA SIVE NOVI ORBIS, NOVA DESCRIPTIO.

[Antwerp,] 1587.

Map, 14″ high plus margins, colored in outline in map but full in
cartouches and spandrels.

On verso printed in Dutch is a description of America. The hump of
the 1570 map has been altered, and *Atlantes* Ort 22 has as a re-
newed map, number 5, replacing old no. [2]. Shirley 158 notes as
first state.

1587

ORTELIUS, ABRAHAM, 1527-1598.

TYPUS ORBIS TERRARUM.

[Antwerp,] 1587.

Map, 14″ high plus margins, colored.

On verso printed in Latin is a description of the map, "Orbis Terrarum." Listed in *Atlantes* Ort 22 as number (1), replacing old number 1. The southwestern hump in South America on the earliest issue
of 1570 has been corrected.   *See* PLATE 14

1588§

SANUTO, LIVIO, 1520-1576.

GEOGRAFIA. . . . DELL'AFRICA.

Venice, Damianus Zenaro, 1588.

Folio, 17⅝″ high, bound in modern cloth, stamped.

Facsimile published by Theatrum Orbis Terrarum, Amsterdam,
1965, as Volume I of the Second Series. This first published atlas of
Africa contains twelve maps, none of which relates to America, although Sabin lists at 76897 with a biographical comment.

1588§

WAGHENAER, LUCAS JANSZ, 1533-1606.

THE MARINERS MIRROUR.

London, John Charlewood [for Henry Haslop], 1588.

Folio, 17¾″ high, bound in modern cloth, stamped.

Facsimile published by Theatrum Orbis Terrarum, Amsterdam,
1966, as Volume II of the Third Series. Of the forty-five engraved
charts listed in Phillips 3981, none relates to America.

[1588]

WAGHENAER, LUCAS JANSZ, 1533-1606.

THE SEA CARDE OF BRITAYNE. . . . THEODORE DE BRY SCUL.

{London, Lucas Jansz Waghenaer, 1588.}

Map, 12⅝″ high plus margins, colored.

On verso printed in English is a description of the coast of Brittany and the folio 7, for the *Mariners Mirrour,* described at *Atlantes,* IV, Wag 13, with this at number (7). Sabin 100950 cites the Arnold study of Waghenaer.

[1588-1628]

MÜNSTER, SEBASTIAN, 1489-1552.

DIE ERST GENERAL TAFEL.

Basel, Sebastian Petri, 1588.

Map, 12¼″ high plus title and margins, uncolored.

A crude woodcut with the general features of the Ortelius World of 1570 including the hump on the West Coast of South America, removed by the 1587 edition. On verso is German text describing the map, "Die erste Land-tafel begreifft in sich der gantze Erd-kugel. . . ." Shirley 163 discusses this map in editions from 1588 to 1628.

[1588-1628]

PETRI, SEBASTIAN.

AMERICAE SIVE NOVI ORBIS, NOVA DESCRIPTIO.

{Basel, Sebastian Petri, 1588-1628.}

Map, 12¼″ high plus title and margins, uncolored.

On verso is another title, "America. Die Neue Welt." Shirley 163 discusses this map in editions from 1588 to 1628. Two copies of this woodcut map are in the collection.

1589§

HAKLUYT, RICHARD, 1553?-1616.

THE PRINCIPALL NAVIGATIONS.

London, George Bishop and Ralph Newberie for Christopher Barker, 1589.

Octavo, 11½″ high, bound in modern cloth, stamped.

Facsimile published in Cambridge by the Hakluyt Society in 1965 as Extra Series No. XXXIX. The only map is that of the World facing page 1, and Sabin 29594 comments on the map.

1590

MYRITIUS, JOANNES.

OPUSCULUM GEOGRAPHICUM RARUM.

Ingolstadt, Wolfgang Ederi, 1590.

Quarto, 12⅜″ high, bound in contemporary vellum.

This is the first edition, complete with curious large folding woodcut world map, the last of the Mercator and Ortelius type, combining Asia on the north with America and indicating a vast Antarctic continent in the south. Among other woodcuts are a large armillary sphere on the title page and in the text, geographical tables, and diagrams. Chapters Twenty and Twenty-one relate to the New World. Sabin 51650 describes the maps. The portrait of the author is at the end.

1590-1602

BRY, THEODORE DE, 1528-1598.

ADMIRANDA NARRATIO FIDA TAMEN . . . VIRGINIÆ. . . . AMERI-CÆ [in nine parts in three volumes].

Frankfort on the Main, Johann Wechel and Matthew Becker for Theodore de Bry and Heirs, dates below.

Folios, 13½″ high, with seventeenth-century gold- and blind-tooled leather boards and spine.

Sabin 8784 has a long description. The parts and dates of publication and major maps follow:

Part One, 1590, two of Virginia by John White;
Part Two, 1591, eight of Florida by Jacques LeMoyne de Morgues;
Part Three, 1592, America;
Part Four, 1594, Caribbean;
Part Five, 1595, New Spain;
Part Six, 1596, America;
Part Seven, 1599, None;
Part Eight, 1599, two of the world, one each of Guiana, Atlantic, Hispaniola, Cartagena, and St. Augustine; and
Part Nine, 1602, Tierra del Fuego.

1592

[GIRAULT, SIMON, b. 1535.]

GLOBE DU MONDE CONTENANT UN BREF TRAITÉ DU CIEL & DE LA TERRE.

Langres, Jean des Preyz, 1592.

Quarto, 8¼″ high, bound in contemporary full leather, gold-tooled with modern spine, blind-tooled.

This is the unrecorded first issue of the first edition without the author's name on title page, not recorded in the bibliographies of America except Mansell where copies are located at DLC, NNH, and NN. Contains seventy-six woodcut maps and globes printed in text including four maps, the last of which, on verso of leaf 80, relates to America.

See PLATE 15

1592§

WAGHENAER, LUCAS JANSZ, 1533-1606.

THRESOOR DER ZEEVAERT.

Leyden, Francis Raphelengen for Lucas Jansz Waghenaer, 1592.

Quarto, 10″ high, oblong, bound in modern cloth, stamped.

Facsimile published by Theatrum Orbis Terrarum, Amsterdam, 1965, as Volume III of the Second Series. Of the twenty-two double-page charts in this first edition listed in *Atlantes,* IV, Wag 16, none relates to America.

[1593]

JODE, CORNELIS DE, 1568-1600.

QUIVIRAE REGNU[M].

[Antwerp, de Jode Widow and Heirs, 1593.]

Map, 13½″ high at plate marks plus margins, colored.

One of the earliest separate maps of the west coast of North America from Cape Blanco to the North Pole. Among decorative features is the early illustrations of the American bison and of Indians. *Atlantes* Jod 2 has as number (13).

Presented to the Philadelphia Maritime Museum in May 1984.

1593

JODE, CORNELIS DE, 1568-1600.

AMERICÆ PARS BOREALIS, FLORIDA, BACCALAOS, CANADA, COR-
TEREALIS.

Antwerp, Cornelis de Jode, 1593.

Map 14¼″ high plus margins, uncolored.

On verso printed in Latin is a description of the map. *Atlantes* Jod 2 has as number (12) in the *Speculum* of 1593.

[1593]

NORDEN, JOHN, 1548-1625?

MIDDLESEX OLIMA TRINOBANTIBUS.

[London, 1593.]

Map, 10¾″ high plus margins, colored.

On verso is description in Latin, signature mark Hh2, and folios 299 and 302. This map is from Part One of *Speculum Britanniae,* which is discussed by Tooley in his *Maps and Mapmakers* at page 66.

1593

NORDEN, JOHN, 1548-1625?

SPECULUM BRITANNIAE. THE FIRST PARTE . . . MIDDLESEX.

[London,] 1593.

Twelvemo, 7¾″ high, bound in modern vellum.

Contains three double-page maps of Middlesex, Westminster, and the City of London, and engraved by "Pieter Vanden Keere" of Amsterdam.

1594§

BOUGUEREAU, MAURICE, d. 1597?

LE THÉATRE FRANÇOYS.

Tours, Maurice Bouguereau, 1594.

Folio, 17¼″ high, bound in modern cloth, stamped.

Facsimile published by Theatrum Orbis Terrarum, Amsterdam, 1966, as Volume V of the Second Series. This first national atlas of France contains sixteen maps, none of which relates to America.

1594

ORTELIUS, ABRAHAM, 1527-1598.

AENEAE TROIANI NAVIGATIO AD VIRGILII SEX PRIORES AENEI-
DOS.

Antwerp, Abraham Ortelius, 1594.

Map, 13½″ high plus margins, colored.

On verso printed in Latin is a description of the map and the folio XXV. *Atlantes* Ort 29 describes the *Additamentum* of 1595, where this is no. (16), a new map.

1595 §

MERCATOR, GERARD, 1512-1594.

ATLAS.

Duisburg, Albertus Busius of Dusseldorf for Rumold Mercator, 1595.

Folio, 16⅛″ high, bound in modern full leather, stamped.

Facsimile published by Culture et Civilisation in Brussels with one hundred and seven maps. Only the first six in the last section, Atlantis Pars . . . Totius Mundi, relate to America, and they are listed and described at *Atlantes* Me 12 as numbers [74], [75], [76], [77], [78], and [79], all new maps.

[1595]

MERCATOR, MICHAEL, 1567?-1600.

AMERICA SIVE INDIA NOVA. . . . PER MICHAELEM MERCATOREM DUYSBURGENSEM.

[Duisburg, 1595.]

Map, 14¼″ high plus margins, colored.

Atlantes Me 12 has as number 5, in the 1595 edition as does Sabin 47882. On verso is title "America" and two massings of printer's flowers. It keeps the southwestern hump of South America first published by Ortelius in 1570 but corrected by him in 1587. Phillips, *Maps,* page 104, lists as published in the eleventh edition of the *Atlas.*

See PLATE 16

[1595]

MERCATOR, GERARD, 1512-1594.

SCOTIA REGNUM.

[Duisburg, Gerard Mercator, 1595.]

Map, 13¾″ high plus margins, colored.

On verso printed in French is a description of Scotland, folios 105 and 108, and a catchword for the missing and inexplicable 106. The text is longer but the map the same as in the great atlas of 1795. *Atlantes* Me 12 has as number (9), a new map.

1595

ORTELIUS, ABRAHAM, 1527-1598.

EPITOME THEATRI ORTLIANI. . . . NOVA EDITIO.

Antwerp, Arnold Coninx for Philippe Galle, 1595.

Thirty-twomo, 4½″ high, oblong, bound in ink-stamped vellum.

Engraved frontispiece and 109 maps in this Latin edition of the earlier Ortelius folio atlas of 1570. This is described at *Atlantes* Ort 56 and in Phillips 402 where he lists those maps relating to America as numbers 1, 2, 4, 5, 97, 99, and 101. Map number 3 also shows America.

1595

ORTELIUS, ABRAHAM, 1527-1598.

ALEXANDRI MAGNI MACEDONIS EXPEDITIO.

[Antwerp,] Abraham Ortelius, 1595.

Maps, 14⅛″ high plus margins, colored.

On verso of each of two maps is printed in Latin a description of the map, the folio xxxiiii, and a catchword. *Atlantes* Ort 28 describes the *Additamentum* of 1595 where this is number (15), a new map.

1597

BRY, THEODORE DE, 1528-1598.

ROMANAE URBIS TOPOGRAPHIAE . . . BOISSARDO [three parts in one volume].

Frankfort on the Main, Johann Feyrabend [Part One], Salamon Saurij [Part Two], and Abraham Faber [Part Three], for Theodore de Bry, 1597.

Quarto, 11¾″ high, bound in contemporary full vellum with gold-stamped leather label on spine.

Maps are of Italy, one in Part One, and Rome, three maps and street plan in many parts in Part Two. Colophon for Part Three, at page 42, is dated 1595.

1597

PTOLEMY, CLAUDIUS, 87-150.

GEOGRAPHIAE UNIVERSAE.

Cologne, Petrus Keschedt, 1597.

Octavo, 8⅞″ high, bound in contemporary full leather, blind- and gold-tooled with page edges gold-tooled.

Among the sixty-two colored maps are a Ptolemaic world map on the verso of the engraved title page of the second part, a double-page world map following leaf 28 and a single-page world map on the verso of the next leaf, both showing the New World. A part of North America appears on the map at leaf 95 (actually 89), on the map at leaf 184 (actually 176), on the map at leaf 229 (actually 225), and on the map at leaf 251 (actually 247). There is a map entitled "America" at leaf 278 (actually 274), and America appears on a world map at leaf 291 (actually 287). This copy lacks the colophon at the second part called for in Phillips 404. Sabin 66493 notes as the second edition of Magini's Ptolemy.

1597 §

WYTFLIET, CORNELIUS, d. 1597.

DESCRIPTIONIS PTOLEMAICÆ AUGMENTUM.

Louvain, Jan Bogaert, 1597.

Folio, 11⅝″ high, bound in modern cloth, stamped.

Facsimile published by Theatrum Orbis Terrarum, Amsterdam, 1964, as Volume V of the First Series. This is the first separately published atlas relating exclusively to America in its nineteen maps. They are listed in *Atlantes* Wyt 1A and more briefly at Phillips 1140. Sabin discusses them at 105696-105701.

[1598?]

METEREN, EMMANUEL VAN, 1535-1612.

HISTORIA BELGICA NOSTRI POTISSIMUM TEMPORIS.

[La Haye?, 1598?]

Folio, 12⅜″ high, bound in contemporary leather, blind- and gold-tooled.

First Latin edition contains map of Low Countries, the most important contemporary source on Holland in the sixteenth century. Description on the verso of cover has paging, binding, and translation information.

[1598]

ORTELIUS, ABRAHAM, 1527-1598.

ARGONAUTICA.

Antwerp, Abraham Ortelius [, 1598].

Map, 13⅜″ high plus margins, colored.

On verso printed in Latin is a description of the map and the folio xxxvii. Contains a map of the Mediterranean Sea at the time of the Crusades, and the cartouche depicts the Golden Fleece protected by a dragon and two great bulls. *Atlantes* Ort 32, *Theatre De l'Univers* of 1598, has as number 38P, a new map, for the *Parergon*.

1598

WYTFLIET, CORNELIUS, d. 1597.

DESCRIPTIONIS PTOLEMAICÆ AUGMENTUM . . . SECUNDA EDITIONE.

Louvain, Gerardus Rivius, 1598.

Folio, 12″ high, bound in contemporary full vellum.

Koeman and Tooley point out that Wytfliet did the first printed atlas relating exclusively to America, and it contains nineteen double-page maps described in *Atlantes* Wyt 1A. This edition is Wyt 2 but with different Roman numeration at date. Phillips wrote of the first edition at 1140, "as important in the history of the early cartography of the new world as Ptolemy's maps are in the study of the old," and at 3645, "this second edition the same as the first, but apparently printed from new plates, though the only difference is that Page 113 in the 1597 edition is numbered 117 in this edition. The maps are not arranged in the same order." Sabin has as 105697.

1602

ORTELIUS, ABRAHAM, 1527-1598.

THEATRO D'EL ORBE DE LA TIERRA.

Antwerp, Christopher Plantin for Jan Baptista Vrients, 1602.

Folio, 17½″ high, bound in quarter leather, gold-tooled on spine.

This first Spanish edition by Vrients has an engraved and colored allegorical title page on the verso of which are the engraved arms of Philip III, and on the verso of the seventh next leaf is an engraved and colored portrait of Ortelius. The 117 colored map sheets are as described in *Atlantes* Ort 34. Phillips 3406 assigns dates to many of the maps, only the first nine of which relate to America.

See PLATE 17

[1602]

ORTELIUS, ABRAHAM, 1527-1598.

MARIS PACIFICI.

[Amsterdam, 1602.]

Map, 13½″ high plus margins.

Presented to the Philadelphia Maritime Museum in May 1984.

[1602-1619]

BLAEU, WILLEM, 1571-1638.

[PAIR OF GLOBES, CELESTIAL AND TERRESTRIAL.]

[Amsterdam, 1602-1619.]

Globes, 9¼″ diameter, on stands.

Yonge describes this pair at page 13, and Stevenson has information on Blaeu globes in Volume Two. Not seen.

Presented to the John Carter Brown Library in November 1979.

See PLATE 18

1603

BAYER, JOHANN, 1572-1625.

. . . URANOMETRIA.

Augsburg, Christopher Mangus, 1603.

Folio, 14″ high, bound in modern full vellum.

This first edition of the fundamental star-atlas is rare. Contains fifty-one plates of the constellations. Bayer was the first astronomer to use Greek letters to signify the magnitude of stars. *See* PLATE 18

1603

BLAEU, WILLEM, 1571-1638.

ILLUSTRISSO PRINCIPI AC DOMINO D. MAURITIO . . . COELUM GRATUS M.O.D.D.C.Q. GUILIELMUS JANSSONIUS BLAEU [at dedicatory cartouche].

SPHAERA STELLIFERA . . . DEPROMTA ANNO 1600 [at cartouche in upper hemisphere].

HABETIS HIC . . . DEPICTAS A. 1603 [at cartouche in lower hemisphere].

[Amsterdam, Willem Blaeu,] 1603.

Celestial globe, 13″ diameter, on contemporary Dutch circular base with four turned pillars.

Stevenson, II, 25, describes a variant with "Guilielmus Jansonius Alcmarianus" at dedicatory cartouche, and dates to 1603 as in lower cartouche described at page 26.

[1605]

LINSCHOTEN, JAN HUYGEN VAN, 1563-1610.

ITINERARIO, VOYAGE OFTE SCHIPVAERT.

Amsterdam, Cornelis Claesz [, 1605].

Folio, 12″ high, bound in modern half leather, gold-titled.

The title page has an engraving showing views of four Dutch towns, and there is an engraved portrait of Linschoten as frontispiece. The first folding double-page map of the world portrays California as part of the mainland. Many of the thirty-six double-page engravings portray natives in costumes and flora and fauna. The last of the maps shows America from Tierra del Fuego to Florida. Sabin 41358 calls for ten maps and plans in this edition. Tooley believes the maps are based on Bartolomeo Lasso.

1606

BLAEU, WILLEM, 1571-1638.

SPHAERA STELLIFERA ACCURATÉ EXHIBENS DISPOSITIONEM. . . . AUCT. GUIL. IANSSONIO [at cartouche in upper hemisphere].

DOCTISSIMO CLARISSIMOQUE VIRO D. ADRIANO METIO. . . . GUIL. IANSSONIUS 1606 [at cartouche in lower hemisphere].

[Amsterdam, Willem Blaeu,] 1606.

Celestial sphere, 5½″ diameter, on circular base with four turned pillars.

Yonge describes this as one of a pair of Blaeu globes at page 13, and Stevenson, II, 19-35, describes the Blaeu globes generally and discusses use of various names at page 23.

[1606]

MERCATOR, GERARD, 1512-1594.

VIRGINAE ITEM ET FLORIDAE.

[Amsterdam, Jodocus Hondius, 1606.]

Map, 13½″ high plus margins, colored.

On verso is French description, the folios 697 and 700, the signature mark Ooooooo, and the catchword. *Atlantes,* II, 306, has this as map number 141 in Me 15 of 1606 with different signature mark in a Latin edition, also as map number 155 in Me 198, also Latin, but not in a French edition.

[1606]

HONDIUS, JODOCUS, 1563-1612.

TARTARIA.

[Amsterdam, Jodocus Hondius, 1606.]

Map, 13⅜″ high plus margins, colored.

On verso printed in French is a description of the map, the folios 665 and 668, the signature mark, and the catchword. "America Pars" is present. *Atlantes* Me 15 has as number (133), a new map, in the *Gerardi Mercatoris Atlas* of 1606.

[1607]

CAMDEN, WILLIAM, 1551-1623.

ESSEXIA COMITATUS. . . . WILLIAM KIP SCULPSIT.

[London, George Bishop and John Norton, 1607.]

Map, 11¼″ high plus margins, colored.

Tooley's dictionary has Kip doing maps for *Britannia* of 1607, the small folio, but this map has in pencil on verso "1637." Skelton, "County Atlases," 5, has as following page 315 but this has no backing text.

1609

BRY, THEODORE DE, 1528-1598.

BREVIS NARRATIO EORUM QUÆ IN FLORIDA AMERICÆ . . . AUCTORE JACOBO LE MOYNE, CUI COGNOMEN DE MORGUES.

Frankfort on the Main, Johann Wechel for Theodore de Bry, 1609.

Folio, 12¾″ high, bound in modern half leather.

This is the second edition of 1609 and contains the eight maps, two plans, and thirty-two pictures of Florida also appearing as Part Two of de Bry's *Admiranda* of 1590-1602. For a discussion of de Bry's work see *Discovering the New World* where many of the maps and illustrations are reproduced. The larger-scale map of Virginia in Part One is the first printed map of the first English colony in America. Sabin 8784 has an extended discussion of de Bry.

1609

LANGENES, BARENT.

HAND-BOECK; OF CORT BEGRIJP DER. CAERTEN.

Amsterdam, Cornelis Claesz, 1609.

Octavo, 4⅜″ high oblong, bound in contemporary full vellum.

Atlantes, I, 60-62, has a discussion of this atlas and it is listed there as A.4. There is further discussion at II, 252-253, and at Lan 8. The maps are listed at Lan 1 and the following relate to America:

- (1) Typus Orbis
- (3) De Cloot der Aerden
- (4) Europa
- (5) Asien
- (6) Africa [i.e., South America]
- (7) De Niewe Werelt
- (60) Noorweghen
- (126) China
- (156) Tercera
- (157) Insularum Cubae [printed upside down]
- (158) Cuba Insula
- (159) Aity
- (160) America aen het Zuyden
- (161) Brasilia
- (162) Chili
- (163) Cerro de Potosi
- (164) Peru
- (165) Mexicana
- (166) Terra Nova
- (167) Fretum Magellanicum

Sabin reports at 38881 but he did not see a copy. Phillips 424 lists this Dutch edition of 1609 with 172 maps.

[1610]

CAMDEN, WILLIAM, 1551-1623.

MIDDLESEX OLIMA TRINOBANTIBUS HABITATA.

[London, William Camden, 1610.]

Map, 10¾″ high plus margins, early hand coloring.

This map is from Camden's *Britannia,* first published in 1607 with text on the verso of each map. Most of the maps were taken from Saxton's earlier works, but this is one of the few derived from Norden.

1610

SPEED, JOHN, 1552-1629.

DARBIESHIRE DESCRIBED 1610. . . . JODOCUS HONDIUS CÆLAVIT.

London, John Speed for John Sudbury and George Humble, 1610.

Map, 15″ high plus margins, colored.

On verso printed in English is a description of the map and of the county, a list of hundreds and of towns, and the folio. Speed's county maps of England and Wales were begun about 1603 and published as *Theatre of the Empire of Great Britain* in 1611 as the first of many editions. Skelton's bibliography of British county atlases in *Map Collectors' Series,* Number 9, page 30, dates Speed's atlas 1611 [1612], the earliest published atlas of Britain. This map is at page 41 of number 7.

1610

SPEED, JOHN, 1552-1629.

ESSEX DIVIDED INTO HUNDREDS. . . . DESCRIBED BY JOHN NORDEN.

London, John Speed for George Humble, 1610.

Map, 15⅛" high plus margins, colored.

On verso printed in English is a description of the map and of the county, a list of hundreds and of towns, and the folio. Skelton, "County Atlases," 7, has at page 39.

1610

SPEED, JOHN, 1552-1629.

THE COUNTY OF MONMOUTH.

London, John Speed for John Sudbury and George Humble, 1610.

Map, 15⅛" high plus margins, colored.

On verso printed in English is a description of the map and of the county, a list of hundreds and of towns, and the folio. Skelton, "County Atlases," 7, has at page 43.

1610

SPEED, JOHN, 1552-1629.

HUNTINGDON BOTH SHIRE AND SHIRE TOWN. . . . JODOCUS HONDIUS CÆLAVIT . . . 1610.

London, John Speed for George Humble, 1610.

Map, 15" high plus margins, colored.

On verso printed in English is a description of the map and of the county, a list of hundreds and of towns, and the folio. Skelton, "County Atlases," 7, has at page 40.

1610

SPEED, JOHN, 1552-1629.

THE PROVINCE OF MOUNSTER. . . . JODOCUS HONDIUS CÆLAVIT.

London, John Speed for John Sudbury and George Humble, 1610.

Map, 15¼" high plus margins, colored.

On verso printed in English is a description of the province of Munster, a list of the divisions and of the towns, and the folios. Skelton, "County Atlases," 7, has at page 44.

1610

SPEED, JOHN, 1552-1629.

THE WEST RIDINGE OF YORKESHYRE WITH THE . . . CITIE YORK DESCRIBED. 1610.

London, John Speed for John Sudbury and George Humble, 1610.

Map, 15" high plus margins, colored.

On verso printed in English is a description of the map and of the county, a list of hundreds and of towns, and the folio. Skelton, "County Atlases," 7, has at page 41.

1611

RITTER, FRANCIS.

SONNENSPIEGELS ANDERER THEIL. DAS IST: BESCHREIBUNG WIE MAN DURCH HÜLFF SIEBEN SCHÖNER KUPFFERSTÜCK.

Nuremberg, Christoff Lochner, 1611.

Quarto, 7¼″ high, bound in modern paper covers.

Contains the seven copperplate engravings called for in title, all devoted to horoscopy including an interesting map of the world as the sixth plate.

[1611]

SPEED, JOHN, 1552-1629.

THE BISHOPRICK AND CITIE OF DURHAM.

[London, John Speed for George Humble, 1611.]

Map, 14⅞″ high plus margins, colored.

On verso printed in English is a description of the map and of the diocese, a list of towns, and the folio. Skelton, "County Atlases," 7, has at page 42.

[1611]

SPEED, JOHN, 1552-1629.

THE COUNTIE WESTMORLAND AND KENDALE.

London, John Speed for George Humble [, 1611].

Map, 15″ high plus margins, colored.

On verso printed in English is a description of the map and of the county, a list of hundreds and of towns, and the folio. Skelton, "County Atlases," 7, has at page 42.

[1611]

SPEED, JOHN, 1552-1629.

HARTFORD SHIRE DESCRIBED THE SITTUATIONS OF HARTFORD. . . . JODOCUS HONDIUS CÆLAVIT.

London, John Speed for John Sudbury and George Humble [, 1611].

Map, 14⅞″ high plus margins, colored.

On verso printed in English is a description of the map and of the county, a list of hundreds and of towns, and the folio. Skelton, "County Atlases," 7, has at page 39.

1612§

BLAEU, WILLEM, 1571-1638.

THE LIGHT OF NAVIGATION.

Amsterdam, Willem Blaeu, 1612.

Octavo, oblong, 10⅜″ high, bound in modern cloth, stamped.

Facsimile published by Theatrum Orbis Terrarum, Amsterdam, 1964, as Volume VI of the First Series. The forty-one engraved charts do not relate to America. There is a discussion of the 1622 English edition at Phillips 5177 and of the 1620 French edition at 2829 and this edition is M. Bl 11 in *Atlantes*, IV.

1612 §

CHAMPLAIN, SAMUEL DE, 1567-1635.

CARTE GEOGRAPHIQUE DE LA NOUVELLE FRANSE FAICTTE PAR. . . .

[Paris,] 1612.

Map, 16⅞″ high plus margins, colored.

An old facsimile reprinted from *Les Voyages* of Paris, 1613, Sabin 11835. In Morison's biography of Champlain he states that this "is the best map of Canada, L'Acadie and Norumbega hitherto published."

[1612]

[DRAYTON, MICHAEL, 1563-1631.]

MIDLESEX HARTFORDSHYRE.

London, Mathew Lownes, I. Browne, I. Helme, and I. Busbie [, 1612].

Map, 9¾″ high plus margins and the folio 245, colored.

Skelton's bibliography of British county atlases in *Map Collectors' Series*, no. 14, Part 2, page 45, describes Drayton's *Poly-olbion* in which this is bound before page 245.

[1612]

ORTELIUS, ABRAHAM, 1527-1598.

AZORES INSULÆ. . . . DELINEAVIT LUDOVICUS TEISERA LUSITANUS . . . MDLXXXIIII.

[Antwerp, 1612.]

Map, 13″ high at plate mark plus margins, colored.

Presented to the Philadelphia Maritime Museum in May 1984.

1614 §

SMITH, JOHN, 1580-1631.

NEW ENGLAND. THE MOST REMARQUEABLE PARTS NAMED. . . . SIMON PASEUS SCULPSIT ROBERT CLARKE EXENDIT.

London, George Low, 1614.

Map, 11⅝″ high plus margins.

Positive and negative facsimiles. Sabin 82823 discusses states in Section Four of his note.

[1616?] §

CHAMPLAIN, SAMUEL DE, 1567-1635.

[LA NOUVELLE FRANCE] FAICT PAR. . . .

[Paris, 1616?]

Map, 13⅝″ high with margins, uncolored.

Facsimile published by the Champlain Society in 1956 with an explanatory note by Lawrence C. Wroth.

1616

CLUVER, PHILIP, 1580-1622.

. . . GERMANIÆ ANTIQUÆ LIBRI TRES.

Leyden, Ludwig Elzevier, 1616.

Folio, 12½″ high, bound in contemporary vellum.

Contains eleven maps, the first two of which have Greenland shown as "Cronia."

[1616]§

TATTON, GABRIEL.

NOVA ET RECE TERRARUM ET REGNORUM CALIFORNIAE, NOVAE HISPANIAE MEXICANAE, ET PERUVIAE.

[London? 1616.]

Map, 16¼″ high plus title and publisher's notice in English and margins, colored.

Facsimile published by American Heritage. On verso is a description of the map, engraved by Benjamin Wright. Tooley's entry for Tatton also mentions 1600 issue as does Streeter catalogue entry 133. Marshall, *Clements,* II, 428, enters as M. Tatton.

1617§

KEERE, PIETER VAN DEN, 1571-1646?

. . . GERMANIA INFERIOR.

Amsterdam, Petrus Montanus, 1617.

Folio, 17¾″ high, bound in modern cloth, gold-stamped.

Facsimile published by Theatrum Orbis Terrarum, Amsterdam, 1966, as Volume III of the Third Series. None of the twenty-four maps relates to America.

1617

RALEIGH, SIR WALTER, 1552-1618.

THE HISTORY OF THE WORLD.

London, William Stansby for Walter Burre, 1614.

Folio, 13⅛″ high, with contemporary blind-tooled leather boards and modern gold-tooled leather spine with gold-stamped label and date 1617.

None of the eight folding maps concerns America. The colophon is dated 1617.

1618

BERTIUS, PETRUS, 1565-1629.

. . . TABULARUM GEOGRAPHICARUM CONTRACTARUM LIBRI SEPTEM.

Amsterdam, Jodocus Hondius, 1618.

Octavo, 5″ high, oblong, bound in contemporary full vellum.

Atlantes Lan 11A lists 230 maps of which the following relate to America:

(1) Typus Orbis Terrarum
(4) Typus Orbis Terrarum Jodocus Hondius
(5) Regiones Hyperboriae
(7) Groenland

(11) Descriptio Terrae Subaustralis
(13) Magellanici
(14) Europa
(179) Asia
(184) Tartaria
(206) America
(207) Virginia
(208) Tercera
(209) Iucatana
(210) Cuba
(211) Hispaniola
(212) Nova Hispania
(213) Mexico
(214) America Meridionalis
(215) Peru
(216) Cerro de Potosi
(217) Chili
(218) Brasilia
(220) Typus Orbis Terrarum

This list of maps appears also at Le Gear 5924, by page number.

1619

BLAEU, WILLEM, 1571-1638.

LE FLAMBEAU DE LA NAVIGATION.

Amsterdam, Willem Blaeu, 1619.

Quarto, 10½″ high, oblong, bound in vellum with ties wanting.

Contains forty-one uncolored maps. *Atlantes* M. Bl 13 has the sonnet on the verso of the lesson in hydrography but here it is on the verso of the title page. The maps show the European Atlantic coast only.

1620

BOULENGER, JEAN, d. 1636.

TRAICTÉ DE LA SPHERE DU MONDE, DIVISÉ EN QUATRE LIVRES, AUSQUELS EST ADIOUSTÉ LE CINQUIESME DE L'USAGE D'ICELLE.

Paris, Jean Moreau for Melchior Tavernier, 1620.

Octavo, 6¼″ high, bound in modern half leather blind- and gold-tooled.

This very rare treatise appears neither in the British Library nor the Bibliothèque Nationale catalogues, and Mansell's *National Union Catalog Pre-1956 Imprints* locates only one copy, that at the University of Michigan.

See PLATE 19

1624

SMITH, JOHN, 1580-1631.

THE GENERALL HISTORIE OF VIRGINIA, NEW-ENGLAND, AND THE SUMMER ISLES.

London, John Dawson and John Haviland for Michael Sparkes, 1624.

Quarto, 10¾″ high, closely trimmed uncolored maps.

The engraved title page and the four maps are present in facsimile, but the engraved portraits of Princess Frances, Duchess of Richmond and Lenox, and of Pocahontas, inserted in some editions as extra-illustrations, are not present here. The text is one of the earliest impressions of the first issue with the spelling "thir" in the last line on page 90 and the marginal note is wrongly placed on page 93, but "digression" is correctly spelled on page 119. See Sabin 82823 and 82824 for descriptions of the different states.

1624 §

SMITH, JOHN, 1580-1631.

THE GENERALL HISTORIE OF VIRGINIA, NEW-ENGLAND, AND
THE SUMMER ISLES.

London, John Dawson and John Haviland for Michael Sparkes,
1624.

Folio, 13″ high, bound in modern full vellum, uncolored maps.

Facsimile published by World Publishing Company of Cleveland
and New York in 1966. This contains the four maps and the engraved
title page, and two portraits of Princess Frances, Duchess of Richmond and Lenox, are present as extra-illustrations. The text is a later
impression of the first issue with the correct spelling of "their" in the
last line on page 90 and the marginal note correctly placed on page
93. See Sabin 82823 and 82824 for descriptions of the different states.

1627 § & 1676 §

SPEED, JOHN, 1552-1629.

A PROSPECT OF THE MOST FAMOUS PARTS OF THE WORLD.

London, John Dawson for George Humble, 1627 [and 1676].

Folio, 18″ high, bound in modern cloth, gold stamped.

Facsimile published by Theatrum Orbis Terrarum, Amsterdam,
1966, as Volume VI of the Third Series of Mundus Novus. On the
1627 edition see Phillips 5928 for a list of the twenty-two maps and
the Tooley comment that this is "the first printed general atlas by an
Englishman." Relating to America are maps 1, 2, 4, 5, 20, and 21 of

the 1627 edition and the four maps added to the 1676 edition, Phillips 5949, Part Five, numbers [22], [23], [24], and [25].

[1629?]

CLUVER, PHILIP, 1580-1622.

PHILIPPI CLUVERII INTRODUCTIONIS IN UNIVERSAM GEOGRA-
PHIAM . . . LIBRI VI.

Amsterdam, Jodocus Hondius [, 1629?].

Octavo, 4¼″ high, bound in contemporary full vellum.

Contains plates none of which relates to America. See Tooley under
Cluver for date. Phillips describes the 1641 edition at 4256 and Sabin
13805 describes the editions. Bound at the end as an appendix is
PETRUS BERTIUS, BREVIARIUM TOTIUS ORBIS TERRARUM.

[1630] §

BLAEU, WILLEM, 1571-1638.

AMERICAE NOVA TABULA.

[Amsterdam, Willem Blaeu, 1630.]

Map, 11¾″ high plus margins, colored in outline in map but full
in cartouche and panels.

Facsimile of map *Atlantes* Bl 1 lists as number 5 in the 1630 *Appendix*. There is also a facsimile of a crude engraving after Blaeu, 11″
high plus margins, colored.

31

BLAEU, WILLEM, 1571-1638.

FRISIA OCCIDENTALIS ADRIANO METIO ET GERARDO FREITAG AUCTORIBUS.

Amsterdam, Willem Blaeu [, 1630].

Map, 15″ high plus margins, colored.

On verso printed in Latin is a description of the map, the folio 47, the signature mark Zz, and the catchword. *Atlantes* Bl 1 has as number (21), a new map, in the *Appendix* of 1630.

BLAEU, WILLEM, 1571-1638.

PADERBORNENSIS EPISCOPATUS DESCRIPTIO NOVA JOANNE GIGANTE LUDENSE.

Amsterdam, Willem Blaeu [, 1630].

Map, 14¾″ high plus margins, colored.

On verso printed in Latin is a description of the map, the folio 36, the signature mark Mm, and the catchword. *Atlantes* Bl 1 has as number (30) in the *Appendix* of 1630, where it is a new map.

BLAEU, WILLEM, 1571-1638.

ULTRAIECTUM DOMINIUM.

[Amsterdam, Willem Blaeu, 1630.]

Map, 15″ high plus margins, colored.

On verso printed in Latin is a description of the map, the folio 48, the signature mark Aaa, and the catchwords. *Atlantes* Bl 1 has as number (22) in the *Appendix* of 1630, where it is a new map.

JANSSON, JAN, 1588-1664.

TERRA FIRMA ET. NOVUM REGNUM GRANATENSE ET. POPAYAN.

Amsterdam, Jan Jansson [, 1630].

Map, 14¾″ high plus margins, colored.

Atlantes Me 31A has as number (73), in the *Appendix* of 1630 where it is a new map. On verso printed in French is a description of the map, the signature mark iiiii, and the catchword. The map shows the area from the equator to the thirteenth parallel north.

[LAET, JOANNES DE, 1583-1649.]

NOVA ANGLIA, NOVUM BELGIUM, ET VIRGINIA.

[Leyden, Isaac Elzevier, 1630?]

Map, 11⅛″ high plus margins, colored.

Tooley's entry for Laet dates the Dutch edition of 1630, the maps by Hessel Gerritsz. Sabin 38554 discusses *Nieuwe Wereldt* of 1625.

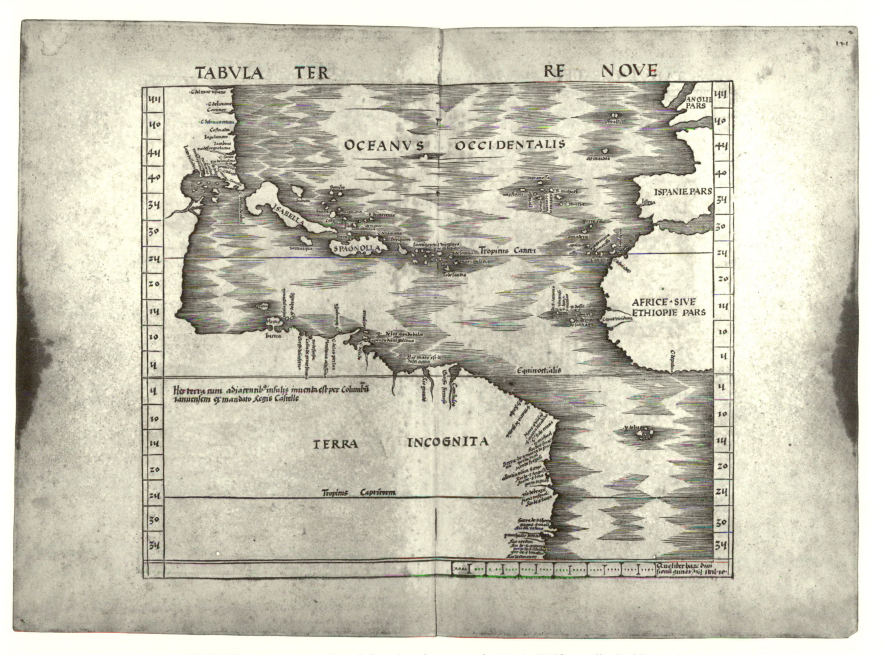

1513 PTOLEMY. GEOGRAPHIA. One of about four dozen maps by Martin Waldseemüller in this most important of Ptolemy's editions, this is known as the Admiral's Map, based on facts given by Columbus.

PLATE I

1520 SOLINUS. JOANNIS. The first cordiform world map is by Peter Apian, the second map on which the word America appears and the first to appear in a book.

PLATE 2

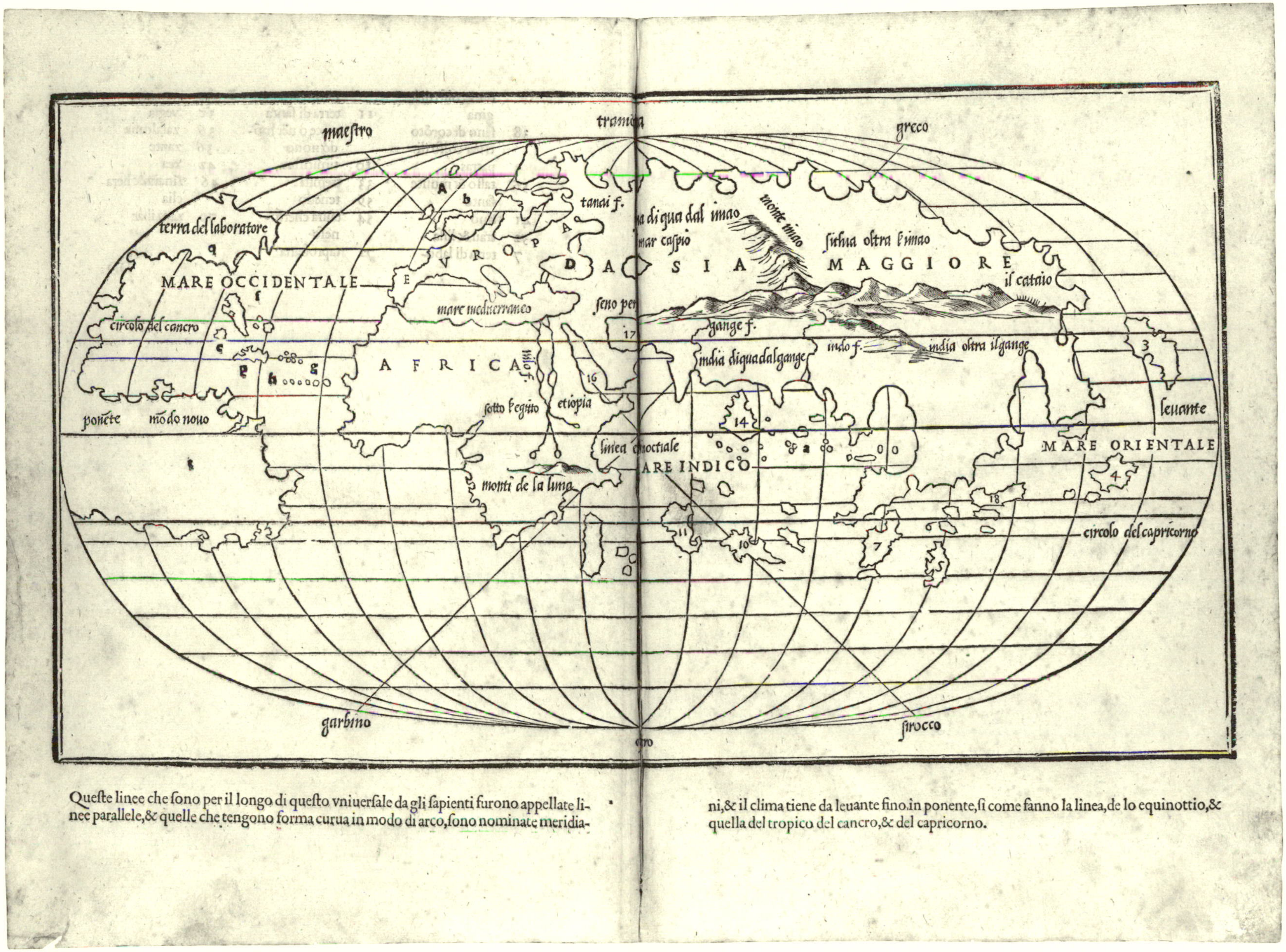

maestro
greco
terra del laboratore
MARE OCCIDENTALE
circolo del cancro
pońete
mōdo nouo
EVROPA
tanai f.
mar caspio
mare mediterraneo
AFRICA
sotto l'egitto
etiopia
ASIA MAGGIORE
sithia oltra l'imao
il cataio
gange f.
india diqua dal gange
indo f.
india oltra il gange
leuante
MARE ORIENTALE
MARE INDICO
monti de la luna
circolo del capricorno
garbino
sirocco
Queste linee che sono per il longo di questo vniuersale da gli sapienti furono appellate linee parallele,& quelle che tengono forma curua in modo di arco,sono nominate meridiani,& il clima tiene da leuante fino in ponente,si come fanno la linea,de lo equinottio,& quella del tropico del cancro,& del capricorno.

1537 BORDONE. ISOLARIO. This map is keyed for the islands of the world, the subject of the atlas, with c for Jamaica, f for Cuba, and others through q for Labrador.

1542   MÜNSTER. TYPUS. World map printed from the same block as in the 1540 edition, the first
edition of Münster's modern world.

PLATE 4

1545   MÜNSTER. NOVAE INSULAE. The first printed map of this hemisphere to show the two
continents connected by an isthmus.

PLATE 5

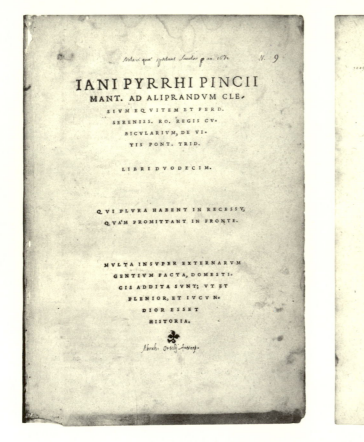

1546 PINCIUS. DE VITIS. Abraham Ortelius owned this book and his signature is on the title page.
His marginalia hint at his plan for reorganization for a new edition.

PLATE 6

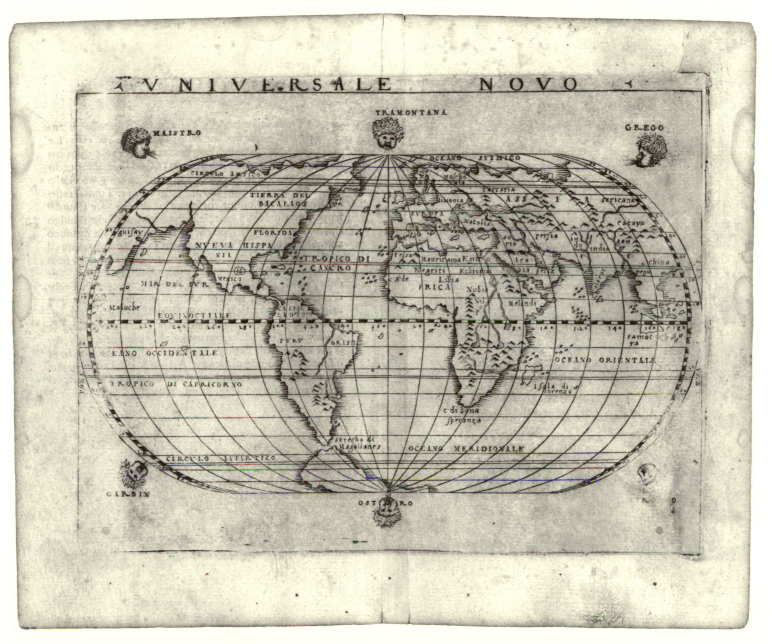

1548 PTOLEMY. LA GEOGRAFIA. Map of the world is one of sixty plates by Gastaldi in this first edition.

PLATE 7

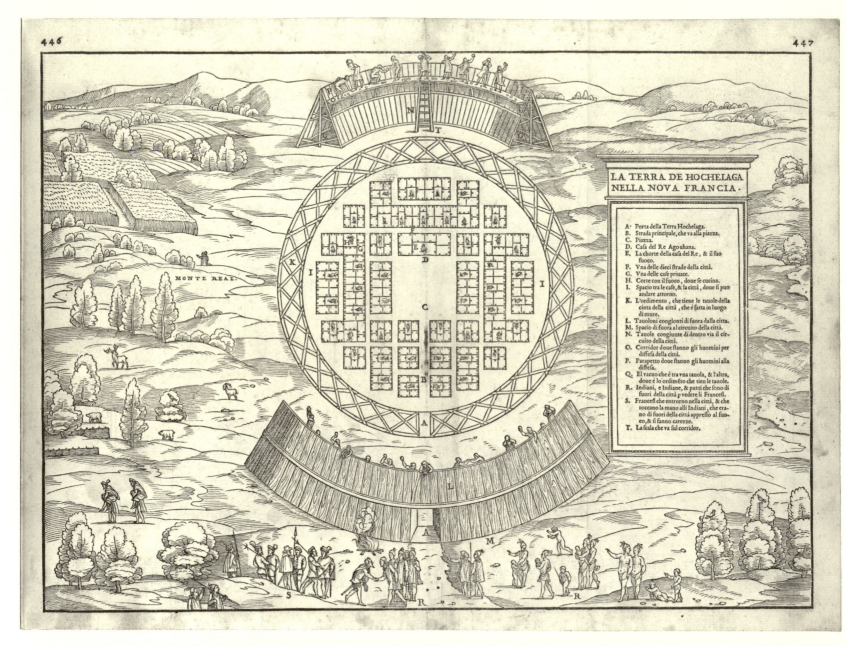

LA TERRA DE HOCHELAGA
NELLA NOVA FRANCIA.

MONTE REAL.

A· Porta della Terra Hochelaga.
B. Strada principale, che va alla piazza.
C. Piazza.
D. Casa del Re Agouhana.
E. La chorte della casa del Re, & il suo fuoco.
F. Vna delle dieci strade della città.
G. Vna delle case priuate.
H. Corte con il fuoco, doue se cucina.
I. Spacio tra le case, & la città, doue si puo andare attorno.
K. L'ordimento, che tiene le tauole della cinta della città, che è fatta in luogo di mure.
L. Tauoloni congionti di fuora dalla citta.
M. Spacio di fuora al circuito della città.
N. Tauole congiunte di dentro via il circuito della città.
O. Corridor doue stanno gli huomini per diffesa della città.
P. Parapetto doue stanno gli huomini alla diffesa.
Q. El vacuo che è tra vna tauola, & l'altra, doue è lo ordiméto che tien le tauole.
R. Indiani, e Indiane, & putti che sono di fuori della città p vedere li Francesi.
S. Francesi che entrorno nella città, & che toccano la mano alli Indiani, che erano di fuori della città appresso al fuoco, & si fanno carezze.
T. La scala che va sul corridor.

1556 RAMUSIO. DELLA NAVIGATIONI. Map of Montreal shows Jacques Cartier being greeted by Hurons in front of their walled town of Hochelaga.

PLATE 8

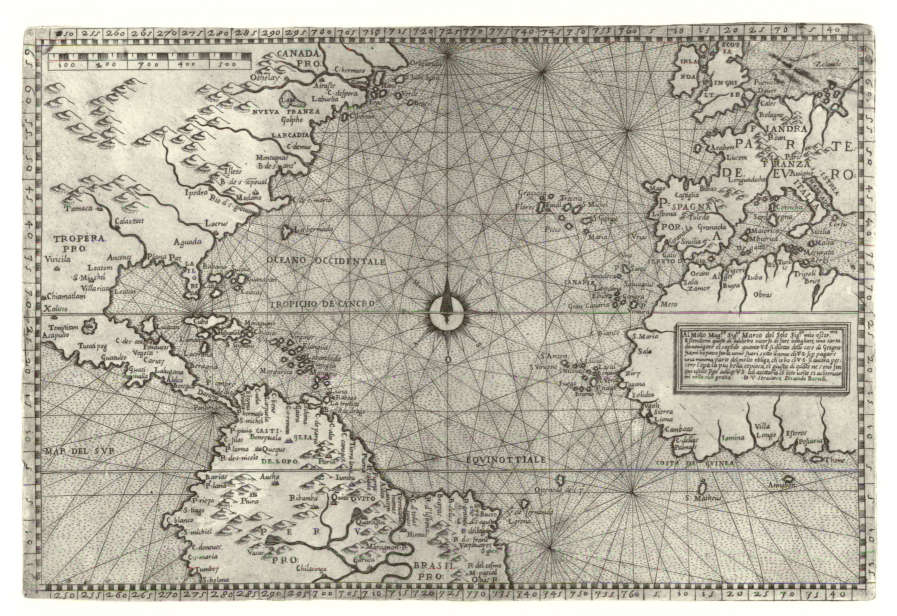

1565 BERTELLI. A very early depiction of a large lake near the present Great Lakes distinguishes this map.

PLATE 9

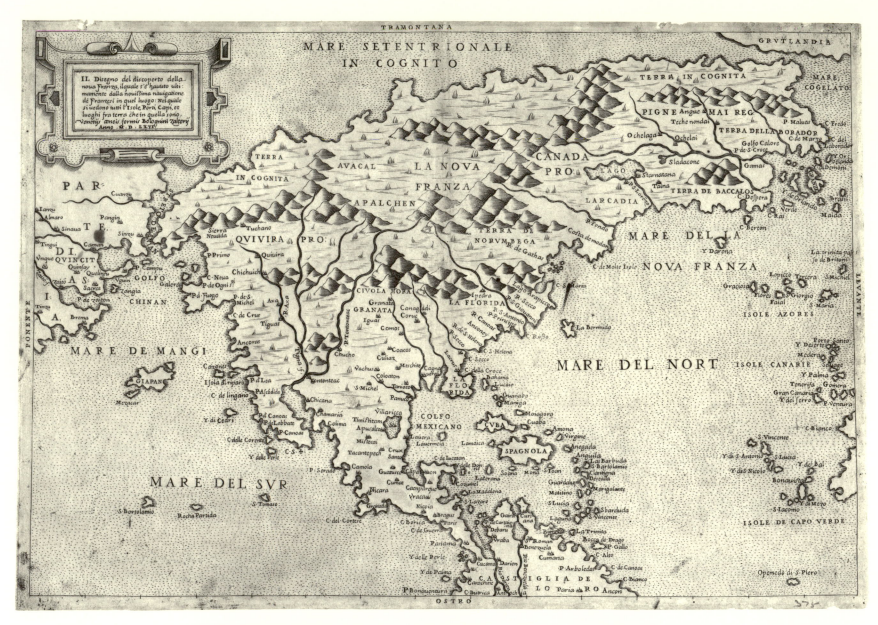

1566 ZALTIERI. IL DISEGNO. The first map to show the triangular shape of North America and the strait separating it from Asia.

PLATE 10

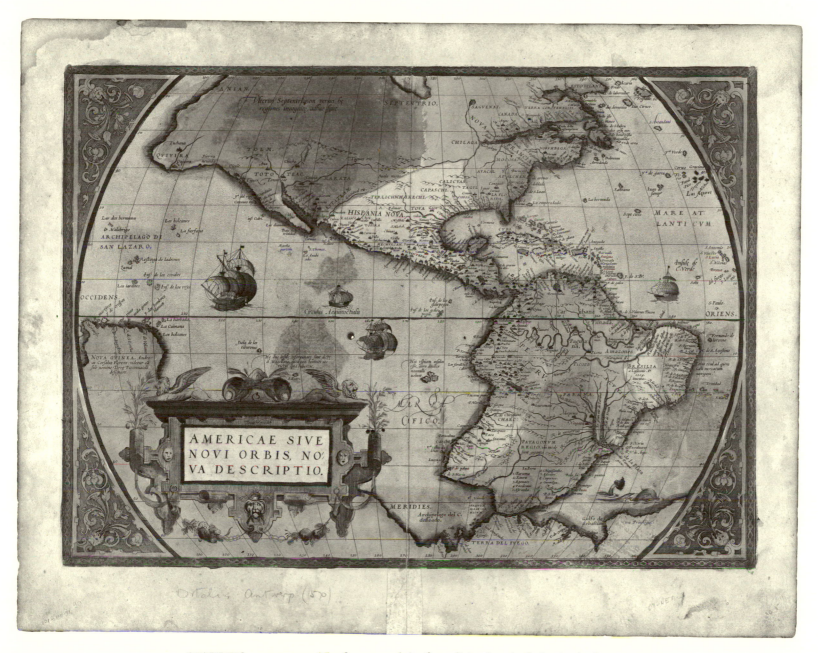

1570 ORTELIUS. AMERICAE. The first state of the first edition has the bulge in the lower western coast of South America, the ghost off the coast of Brazil, and other indications.

PLATE II

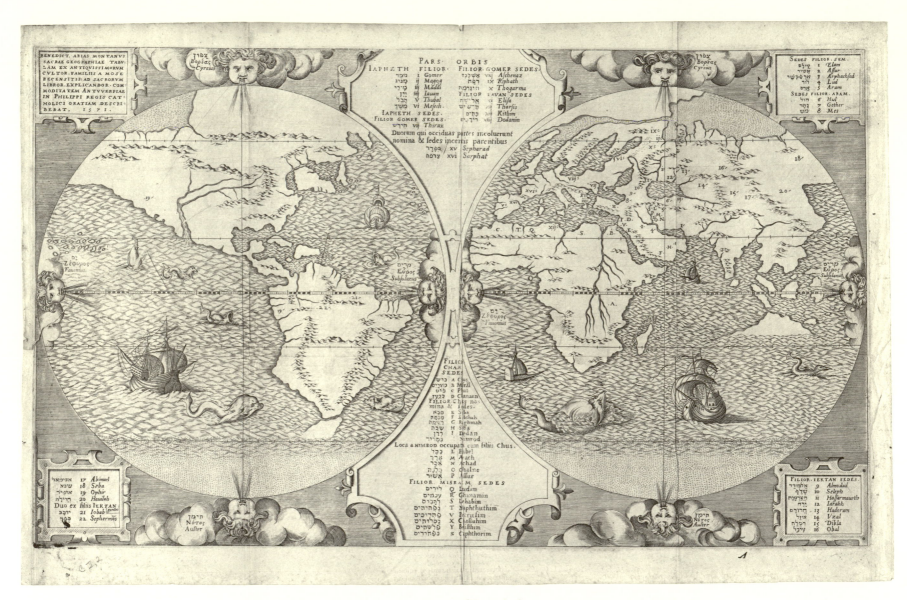

1571 ARIAS. SACRAE. From the multi-volume *Biblia Polyglotta* with text printed in Greek, Latin, Hebrew, and Syriac, this world map discusses the twelve tribes of Israel.

PLATE 12

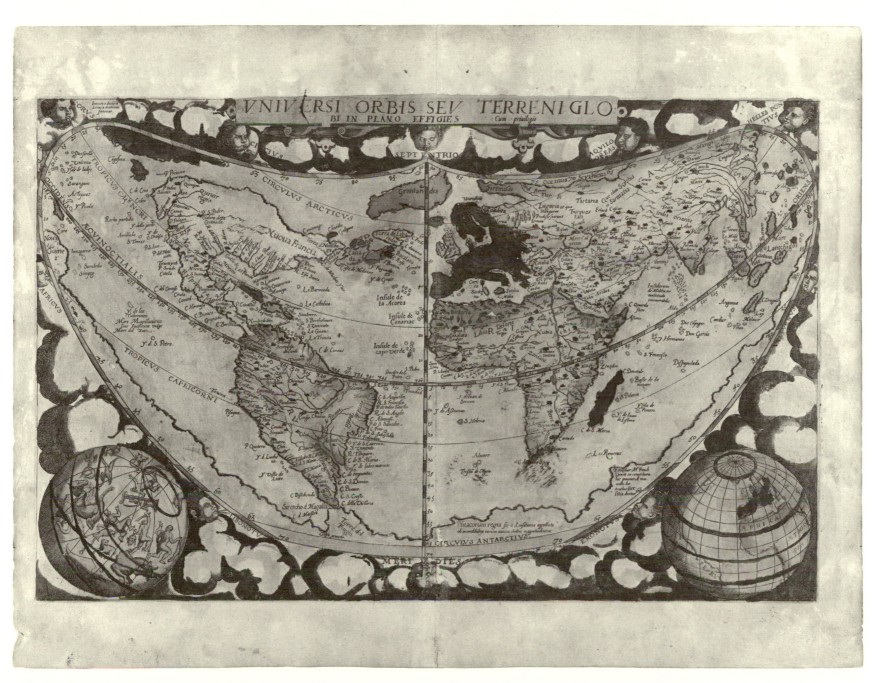

1578   JODE. SPECULUM. One of sixty-four maps in this first edition of the most rare of all atlases, this is the only copy with color.

PLATE 13

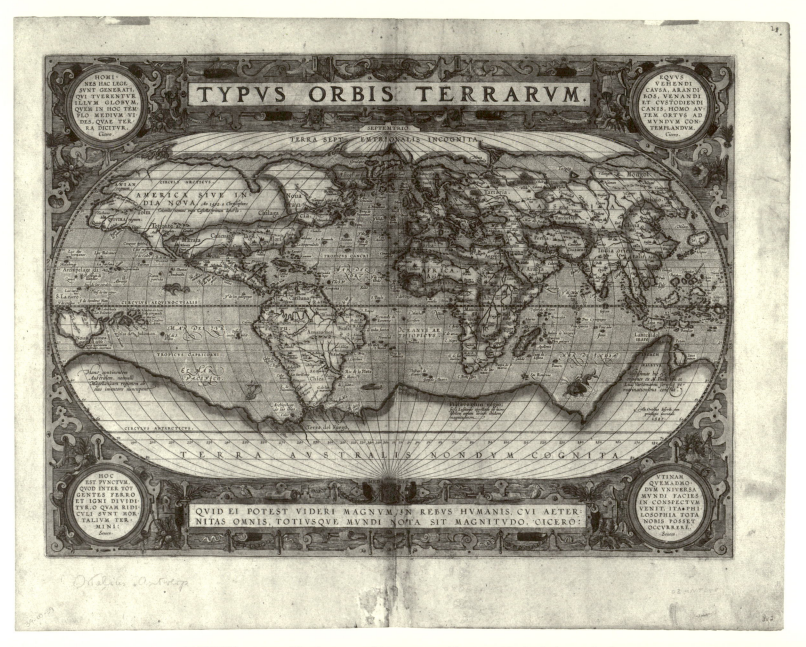

1587 ORTELIUS. TYPUS. The first state of his great world map, with classical texts in the corner medallions, and the southwestern hump in South America has been corrected.

PLATE 14

GLOBE DV MONDE.
CONTENANT VN
bref traité du Ciel & de la Terre. 3

aprennit

francois morel

Agrement

A LENGRES.
Par Iehaï des Preyz Imprimeur & Libraire tenant sa boutique au dessus de la rue des Pilliers.

1592.

---

pays, comme le Fer, la Toille, les Cuirs, le Verre, & autres semblables choses, & pour côtréchâge nous auôs l'or, les épisseryes, & fruicts tref-excellans, drogues, le sucre que vous aymés tant, & autres sortes de marchandises tref-vtiles & necessaires en ces pays. La carte suyuante vous monstre comme le nocher vogant sur mer est contraint de trasser plusieurs chemins suyuant les vens qui le poussent.

MARGVERITE.
Ie vois en la carte cy dessus plusieurs routes & voyes pour tirer ça & là, & me semble que la pluspart de ces lignes sont superflues.
CHARLES.
Si le Pilot trouuoit vn rumb de vent par lequel il fut conduit droit suyuant la route qu'il tient, il n'auroit
affaire

1592 GIRAULT. GLOBE. The previously unrecorded first issue of the first editon of a rare Langres imprint, the title page does not have the author's name.

PLATE 15

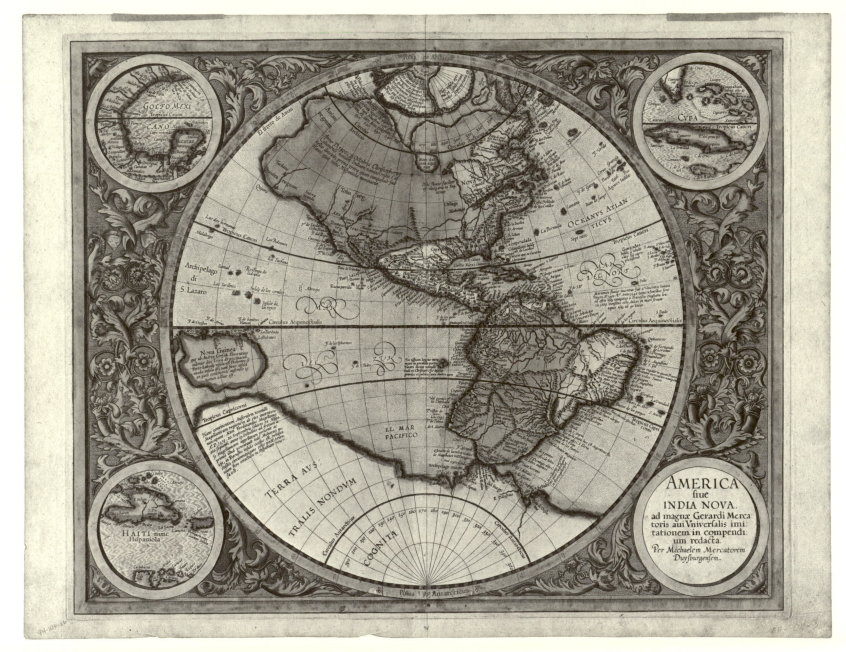

1595 **MERCATOR. AMERICA.** The southwestern hump of South America corrected by Ortelius in 1587 is here, and on the verso is a fascinating use of printer's flowers.

PLATE 16

1632

HONDIUS, HENRICUS, 1597-1651.

A GENERAL PLOTT AND DESCRIPTION OF THE FENNES.

Amsterdam, Henricus Hondius, 1632.

Map, 17¼″ high plus margins, colored.

On verso printed in English is a description of the Fens, the folios 65 and 66, and the catchword. *Atlantes* Me 152 has as number (23), [280J], "taken from older editions." It appears as a new map in *L'Appendice de l'Atlas* of 1633.

1632§

JANSSON, JAN, 1588-1664.

NOVA TOTIUS TERRARUM ORBIS GEOGRAPHICA.

Amsterdam, Jan Jansson, 1632.

Map, 13½″ high plus margins, colored in outline in maps but full in cartouches and panels.

Facsimile published by D.A.C. Inc. of New York. *Atlantes,* Index, does not include this date for world maps but see Bl 1, number (1) and Me 31A, number (1) for variants with similar title.

1633

LAET, JOANNES DE, 1583-1649.

NOVUS ORBIS SEU DESCRIPTIONIS INDIÆ OCCIDENTALIS LIBRI XVIII.

Leyden, Isaac Elzevier, 1633.

Folio, 13¼″ high, bound in full vellum, gold-printed title on spine.

Contains fourteen maps by Hessel Gerritsz all relating to America. Sabin 38557 quotes Meuselius, "Opus egregium, maximeque rarum et infrequens."

1633

MERCATOR, GERARD, 1512-1594, and
HONDIUS, JODOCUS, 1563-1612.

... ATLAS OU REPRESENTATION DU MONDE ... EN DEUX TOMES. EDITION NOUVELLE.

Amsterdam, Henricus Hondius, 1633.

Folios, 18¼″ high, bound in early eighteenth-century full leather, gold-tooled, with gilt edges, arms of Louis XIV.

Contains the colored engraved title page. The frontispiece has portraits of the authors as does the double-page map of the world. Among the 239 colored maps is the very important Virginia-Florida map at pages 698-699 which was the prototype of this region until the 1670s. California is an island wherever shown. Phillips 445 has list of twenty-six maps relating to America to which should be added maps at pages 642-643, and 678-679 should be removed for it shows only Philippines. *Atlantes* has as Me 36A with list of contents amended at Me 36B. Contents called for on leaf D2 are here on loose C2.

1634§

GUERARD, JEAN.

CARTE UNIVERSELLE HYDROGRAPHIQUE.

[Dieppe?] 1634.

Map, 30½″ high plus margins and imprint, colored.

Facsimile published by Art et Culture from a manuscript. Tooley notes in his dictionary that the cartographer lived in Dieppe.

1635

BLAEU, WILLEM, 1571-1638, and
BLAEU, JOAN, 1596-1673.

THEATRUM ORBIS TERRARUM, SIVE ATLAS NOVUS.

Amsterdam, Willem and Joan Blaeu, 1635.

Folio, 19¾″ high, bound in contemporary full vellum, gold-tooled, with gilt edges.

Two frontispieces and 207 maps appear in this first Latin edition. *Atlantes* Bl 13 and Bl 14 list all maps, the following of which relate to America: 1, 2, 3, 5, and 195 through 207.

[1635?]

BLAEU, WILLEM, 1571-1638.

FIONIA VULGO FUNEN.

[Amsterdam, Willem Blaeu, 1635?]

Map, 15″ high plus margins, colored.

On verso printed in Latin is a description of the map, the folio 11, the signature mark K, the catchword, and the title *Europa Sept. Atlantes* Bl 56 has as number (22), in the *Atlas Major* of 1662, Phillips 4263, but the map first appeared in Bl 15, the *Appendix* of "between 1635 and 1638."

[1635]

BLAEU, WILLEM, 1571-1638.

MANSFELDIA COMITATUS AUCTORE TILEMANNO STELLA SIG.

[Amsterdam,] Willem Blaeu [, 1635].

Map, 16⅛″ high plus margins, colored.

On verso printed in Latin is a description of the map, the folio 45, and the signature mark Xx. *Atlantes* Bl 5 has as number (42), a new map, in the *Novus Atlas* of 1635.

1635§

BLAEU, WILLEM, 1571-1638.

NOVA BELGICA ET ANGLIA NOVA.

[Amsterdam, Willem Blaeu, 1635.]

Maps, 15″ high plus margins, colored.

Three facsimiles, one of which has the date 1660 under Blaeu's name. Phillips, *Maps,* has at page 466, from 1667, and a citation to that edition at page 1088. *Atlantes* Bl 6 has as number (204), a new map, in the *Atlantis* of 1635.

1635

FOX, LUKE, 1586-1635.

NORTH-WEST FOX, OR, FOX FROM THE NORTH-WEST PASSAGE. . . . DEMONSTRATED IN A POLAR CARD.

London, B. Alsop and Thomas Fawcet, 1635.

Quarto, 7⅜″ high, bound in modern half leather, gold-stamped.

Contains in facsimile the chart of the polar region originally bound facing page 16. Sabin lists at 25410 where he notes that the map "is often deficient, or supplied by a facsimile."

[1636]

BLAEU, WILLEM, 1571-1638.

TABULA CASTELLI AD SANDFLITAM.

[Antwerp, Jan Jansson, 1636.]

Map, 15″ high plus margins, colored.

On verso printed in Latin is a description of the map, the folio II, and the signature mark K. *Atlantes* Me 44 describes the *Appendix* of 1636 where this is number (41), in every way similar to the description except that this ends "Excudit Guiljemus Blaeuw."

[1636]

JANSSON, JAN, 1588-1664.

AMERICA SEPTENTRIONALIS.

Amsterdam, Jan Jansson [, 1636].

Map, 18″ high plus margins, colored.

Although Jansson took many maps from Blaeu for his *Atlas,* this map

of North America is not dependent upon that source. See *Atlantes* Me 50A, where this is number (82), a new map, and Me 31A for a discussion of the Mercator-Hondius-Jansson atlases.

See PLATE 20

[1636]

JANSSON, JAN, 1588-1664.

NOVA HISPANIA, ET NOVA GALICIA.

[Amsterdam, 1636.]

Map, 13¾″ high plus margins, colored.

Atlantes has as number (105) of Me 41A, the *Atlas* of 1636, where this is a new map. This map shows Mexico from below the eighteenth to above the twenty-third north parallels.

1637

MERCATOR, GERARD, 1512-1594, and
HONDIUS, JODOCUS, 1563-1612.

HISTORIA MUNDI: OR MERCATOR'S ATLAS.

London, T. Cotes for Michael Sparke, 1637 [dated on engraved title page, but also present is the title page of the 1635 edition].

Quarto, 11¼″ high, bound in modern quarter leather, gold-tooled, with gilt edges, by W. Pratt.

This is the "Second Edition," so noted on engraved title page. One hundred and ninety-one maps are here, not the 183 called for in Phillips 451 where he lists those seventeen relating to America including, as usual, the Philippines at page 877. Also present here are the rare Ralph Hall map of Virginia at page 904 and the folding John Smith map of New England at page 930. Sabin lists at 47885 and notes the rare maps.

1639

CHILMEAD, JOHN.

A LEARNED TREATISE OF GLOBES, BOTH COELESTIALL AND TER-
RESTRIALL: WITH THEIR SEVERALL USES. WRITTEN FIRST IN
LATINE, BY MR. ROBERT HUES ... AND NOW LASTLY MADE ENG-
LISH, FOR THE BENEFIT OF THE UNLEARNED.

London, "Assigne of T.P. for P. Stephens and C. Meredith," 1639.

Octavo, 6½″ high, bound in contemporary full leather, blind-
tooled.

Contains woodcuts in text. S.T.C. 13908 identifies T.P. as Purfoote.

[1639?]

JANSSON, JAN, 1588-1664.

NOVA ANGLIA NOVUM BELGIUM ET VIRGINIA.

Amsterdam, Jan Jansson [, 1639?].

Map, 15¼″ high plus margins, colored.

On verso printed in French is a description of the map, the signature
mark ddddd, and the catchword. *Atlantes* Me 41A has as number
(104), a new map, in *Gerardi Mercatoris Atlas* of 1636. French
editions appeared in 1639, 1649, and 1652.

[1639]

JANSSON, JAN, 1588-1664.

VIRGINIAE PARTIS AUSTRALIS ET FLORIDAE.

[Amsterdam, 1640.]

Map, 15¼″ high plus margins, colored.

On verso is French description, the signature mark ggggg, and the
catchword. *Atlantes* Me 93B has as number (100), a new map, in *Le
Nouveau Theatre Du Monde* dated 1639.

[1639]§

VISSCHER, NICOLAS, 1618-1679.

ORBIS TERRARUM NOVA ET ACCURATISSIMA TABULA.

[Amsterdam, 1639.]

Map, 18″ high plus margins, colored in outline in maps but full in
cartouches.

Facsimile published by Penn Print. *Atlantes,* III, 179, lists as number
[83] of the Visscher maps and dates at 1639 in the *Index,* V, 282.

1639§

VISSCHER, NICOLAS, 1618-1679.

ORBIS TERRARUM TYPUS DE INTEGRO MULTIS. . . . PIETER GOOS
SCULPSIT.

Amsterdam, Nicolas Visscher, 1639.

Map, 14⅞″ high, trimmed close, colored in outline in maps but
full in cartouches.

Facsimile map which *Atlantes,* III, 179, lists as number [84] of the
Visscher maps.

[1640]

BLAEU, WILLEM, 1571-1638.

VIRGINIAE PARTIS AUSTRALIS ET FLORIDAE.

[Amsterdam, Joan and Cornelis Blaeu, 1640.]

Map, 15¼″ high plus margins, colored.

On verso is Latin description, the folio 10, the signature mark I, and the catchword. *Atlantes* Bl 15 has this as number 24, [299], a new map in the *Appendice* dated 1640 as well as in Latin text edition Bl 20 dated 1640.

[1645]

[BLAEU, WILLEM, 1571-1638.]

OXONIUM COMITATUS VULGO OXFORDSHIRE.

[Amsterdam, Willem Blaeu, 1645.]

Map, 15″ high plus margins, colored.

On verso printed in German is the description of the map and an engraving of Stonehenge and the folios 201 and 203, the signature mark Ppp, and the catchword. *Atlantes* Bl 42A describes the French edition of the *Theatrum* of 1645 where there is number (16), a new map, with Stonehenge on verso. Bl 47B is the German edition of 1646 with this map as number (16) with correct verso. Skelton, "County Atlases," 32, also describes a state with Blaeu's name.

[1646?]

DUDLEY, ROBERT, 1574-1649.

CARTA PARTIOLARE DEL'MARE OCCEANO DAL'ISOLE D'ASORES.

[Florence, 1646?]

Map, 18¾″ high at plate mark plus margins.

Presented to the Philadelphia Maritime Museum in May 1984.

1646

SPEED, JOHN, 1552-1629.

A PROSPECT OF THE MOST FAMOUS PARTS OF THE WORLD.

London, M. F. for William Humble, 1646.

Octavo, 3¾″ high, oblong, bound in contemporary vellum.

This first printed general atlas by an Englishman contains eighty-three maps in two parts. Phillips 3425 calls for twenty maps in the first part, of which those numbered 1, World, and 45 [?], America, are listed as related to America. Maps numbered 2, Asia; 4, Europe; and 5, America, should be added. The second part is Phillips 4000 with no maps of America. Sabin 89228 discusses this edition.

1648

BACON, FRANCIS, 1561-1626.

. . . SYLVA SYLVARUM, SIVE HIST. NATURALIS, ET NOVUS ATLAS.

Leyden, Francis Hackius, 1648.

Twelvemo, 4½″ high, bound in contemporary full vellum.

Contains no maps.

[1650]

[JANSSON, JAN, 1588-1664.]

MAR DEL ZUR HISPANIS MARE PACIFICUM.

[Amsterdam, Jan Jansson, 1650.]

Map, 17¼″ high plus margins, colored.

On verso printed in Dutch is a description of the map, the folios 85 and 86, the signature mark Ee, and the catchword. *Atlantes* Me 164, has as number (10), a new map, in *Atlantis Majoris* of 1650.

[1650]

JANSSON, JAN, 1588-1664.

TABULA ANEMOGRAPHICA SEU PYXIS NAUTICA.

Amsterdam, Jan Jansson [, 1650].

Engraving, 17⅛″ high plus margins, colored.

Atlantes Me 164 has this study of winds as an illustrated compass rose at number (1), a new map in *Atlantis Majoris* of 1650, and a manuscript note on the verso suggests Harrisse, page 286.

See PLATE 21

[1650?]

VISSCHER, NICOLAS, 1618-1679.

NOVI BELGII NOVÆQUE ANGLIÆ.

[Amsterdam,] Nicolas Visscher [, 1650?].

Map, 18¼″ high plus margins, uncolored.

See *Map Collectors' Circle,* Number 24, for the study, "New Light on the Jansson-Visscher Maps," at number 5, which describes this second state. Marshall, *Clements,* II, 492, notes as number 61 in *Atlas Minor* and as number 90 in *Atlas Contractus,* neither dated. *Atlantes,* Index, dates 1650.

See PLATE 22

[1650?]

WALTON, ROBERT, fl. 1647-1687.

A NEW, PLAINE, AND EXACT MAP OF AMERICA DESCRIBED BY N. I. VISSCHER, AND DON INTO ENGLISH . . . BLAEU.

London, Robert Walton [, 1650?].

Map, 16½″ high plus margins, uncolored.

Tooley's entry mentions Walton's maps of continents, and Cresswell describes as "a fine crisp copy of one of the most decorative English maps of North America. Use of the *carte de figure* format and mannerist decoration illustrates the high esteem held by British cartographers for Dutch mapmakers."

See PLATE 23

1651

SPEED, JOHN, 1552-1629.

A NEW AND ACCURAT MAP OF THE WORLD.

London, Thomas Bassett and Richard Chiswell, 1651.

Map, 15½″ high plus margins, colored.

From *Theatre of the Empire of Great Britain,* London, 1676, part of the text of which is on the verso.

[1652?]

JANSSON, JAN, 1588-1664.

TABULA MAGELLANICA QUA TIERRÆ DEL FUEGO.

Amsterdam, Jan Jansson [, 1652?].

Map, 16″ high plus margins, colored.

On verso printed in French is a description of the map, the signature mark S, and the catchword. There are four cartouches. Phillips, *Maps,* page 381, lists as in *Nuevo Atlas* of 1653. *Atlantes* Me 84 has as number (93), of the *Nieuwen Atlas* of [1652], where it is a new map.

[1654]

BLAEU, JOAN, 1596-1673.

PRAEFECTURA RENFROANA.

[Amsterdam, Joan Blaeu, 1654.]

Map, 15½″ high plus margins, colored.

On verso printed in Latin is a description and the signature mark Ff showing it to be from *Theatrum Orbis Terrarum* of 1654, *Atlantes* Bl 49, where it is number (27). This map first appeared in an atlas with Dutch text in this same year, Bl 48.

1655

LINDE, LUCA DI.

LUCAE DE LINDA DESCRIPTIO ORBIS.

Leyden, Peter Leffen, 1655.

Octavo, 6⅞″ high, bound in contemporary full leather, blind- and gold-tooled.

Contains no maps, but the twelfth book is a description of America.

1656

SANSON, NICOLAS, 1600-1667.

LE CANADA, OU NOUVELLE FRANCE. . . . I. SOMER SCULPSIT.

Paris, Pierre Mariette, 1656.

Map, 15¾″ high plus margins, colored in outline.

Phillips 486 has as number [23] in *Cartes* of 1675 while Marshall, *Clements,* II, 336, has as plate 86 of *Cartes* of 1658 and plate 104 of the 1664 edition. *See* PLATE 24

[1659?]

[CLUVER, PHILIP, 1580-1622.]

INDIÆ ORIENTALIS ET INSULARUM ADJACENTIUM.

[Leyden, 1659?]

Map, 8½″ high plus margins, colored.

[1660?]

VEEN, OCTAVIO VAN, 1560?-1629?

AMORIS DIVINI EMBLEMATA . . . OTHO VAENIUS.

Antwerp, "Ex Officina Plantiniana Balthasaris Moreti," 1660.

Quarto, 8½″ high, bound in nineteenth-century half leather, gold-stamped.

Contains on title page an allegorical engraving of a globe pierced by arrows as an example of Roman Catholic cosmography.

[1660?]

BLAEU, WILLEM, 1571-1638.

PALATINATUS BAVARIAE.

Amsterdam, Willem Blaeu [, 1660?].

Map, 15″ high plus margins, colored.

On verso printed in Latin is a description of the map, the folio 53, the signature mark Fff, and the catchwords. *Atlantes,* Index, has no Blaeu entry for Palatinatus as Oberpfalz.

[1660]

WIT, FREDERICK DE, 1630-1706.

NOVA TOTIUS AMERICÆ DESCRIPTIO.

[Amsterdam, 1660.]

Map, 17¼″ high plus margins, colored in outline in map but full in cartouche and panels.

Atlantes, III, 212, lists as number [10] and dates 1660. Phillips, *Maps,* page 105, dates 1660.

1662

MEURS, JACOB VAN, 1620-1680.

NAAUKERURIGE BESCHRIJVINGE VAN VRANKRYK, VIJFDE DEEL ... DOOR DR. J. B.

[Amsterdam, Jacob van Meurs, 1662.]

Twelvemo, 5¼″ high, bound in contemporary full leather, gold-tooled.

Contains sixty-one folding maps, town plans, views, and the like, all relating to France. Tooley dates 1666 in his dictionary.

[1662]

BLAEU, WILLEM, 1571-1638.

AMERICA, QUAE EST GEOGRAPHIAE BLAVIANAE PARS QUINTA: LIBER UNUS. VOLUMEN UNDECIMUM.

[Amsterdam, Joan Blaeu, 1662.]

Atlantes Bl 56 has as separate volume with list of maps. Not seen.

Presented to the Philadelphia Maritime Museum in May 1982.

[1662]

SANSON, NICOLAS, 1600-1667.

L'AMERIQUE EN PLUSIERS CARTES . . . ET EN DIVERS TRAITTEZ.

[Paris, Nicolas Sanson, 1662.]

Quarto, 9″ high, bound in contemporary full vellum.

Contains fifteen double-page maps engraved by Antony de Winter, all of which relate to America. They are listed at Phillips 1152. This copy has the bookplate of Talleyrand. Bound with BION, L'USAGE DES GLOBES, Amsterdam, 1700.

1662-1665

BLAEU, JOAN, 1596-1673.

ATLAS MAJOR, SIVE COSMOGRAPHIA [in eleven volumes].

Amsterdam, Joan Blaeu, 1662-1665.

Folios, 22″ high, bound in contemporary full vellum, gold-tooled.

This sumptuous set was in the library of George Simon, Earl of Harcourt, and is of extraordinary quality. This *Atlas* has generally been described in superlatives as by Phillips at 3430 and by Stevenson who called it a work of "unsurpassed excellence" and "the foremost atlas produced by the great Dutch atlas makers of the seventeenth century." The maps in the volumes conform to the detailed description for the Latin text in *Atlantes* Bl 56, which calls for 593 maps, except as follows: Volume One is the 1665 reprint, as is Phillips 3430, in which the text has been reset. The recto of the first leaf of signature b is dated MDCLXV and the order of the maps differs in this regard: maps are in order to (31), then signature Cc not present with folios 73 to 76 including maps (32) and (33). In Volume Three, map 49 is bound following map 50 and map 51 is missing along with signature Gggg containing folios 181 and 182. *Atlantes* on page 211 omits all folios between map 54 at Kkkk and map 55 at Ssss. The following table may help to clarify:

Map Number	Following Folio	In Signature
52	183	Hhhh
53	184	Hhhh
54	184	Hhhh
55	185	Iiii
56	189	Llll
57	191	Mmmm
58	195	Oooo
59	199	Qqqq
60	201	Rrrr
61	203	Ssss
62	205	Tttt

all maps present to last:

96	307	Vuuuuu

and index agrees with this order, not with *Atlantes*.

In Volume Four maps are bound in this order: 48, 51, 50, 49, 52. Volume Five has leaf ★ which has on recto same text as a2, the following leaf, but with less leading for same type, and catchword LECTO- is set in next smaller type. Verso of ★ has same text but with one more line and different catchword and next leaf is not present; the third map is on the verso of 73 Britannica V, not U. In Volume Seven the place of map 18, Episcopatus Albiensis, not in Index, is taken by Dioecesis Ebroicensis, in Index in order but called for in *Atlantes* as map 46. The binding order is reversed also for maps 58 and 59. In Volume Nine, maps called for in *Atlantes* are misbound in this order: 1, 2, 6, 7, 4, 5, 8, 9, 10, with number 3 missing. Another misbound series is maps 20, 22, 21, and 23.

See PLATE 25

[1665?]

BLAEU, JOAN, 1596-1673.

INSULA GADITANA, VULGO ISLA DE CADIZ.

[Amsterdam, Joan Blaeu, 1665?]

Map, 14⅞″ high plus margins, colored.

On verso printed in Dutch is a description, the folio 16, the signature mark P, and the catchword. This is map 27 in Volume Eight of the Dutch Edition of Blaeu's *Major Atlas,* see *Atlantes*, I, 243, "16 Spanjen. P." Bl 56 has as number (28) in "Liber XVII," a new map. Phillips 3430 dates [1662-1665] and 4263 dates [1662-1672].

[1666]§

GOOS, PIETER, 1616?-1675.

ORBIS TERRARUM NOVA ET ACCURATISSIMA TABULA.

Amsterdam, Pieter Goos [, 1666].

Map, 16⅝″ high plus margins, colored in outline in maps but full in cartouches.

Facsimile published by American Heritage with commentary on verso. Three copies. *Atlantes,* IV, 196, lists as number (1) of Goos 1B, dated 1666.

1667

GOOS, PIETER, 1616?-1675.

L'ATLAS DE LA MER, OU MONDE AQUATIQUE.

Amsterdam, Pieter Goos, 1667.

Folio, 21¼″ high, bound in full early vellum.

Contains forty-one colored maps called for on verso of B2 and at *Atlantes,* IV, Goos 2B, with list at Goos 1B of which numbers the following relate to America: 1, 2, 27, 30, 31, 32, 33, 34, 35, 36, 37, 38, 39, 40, and 41. Phillips does not list this edition. Tooley's study of California as an island in *Map Collectors' Circle,* Number Eight, has at number 22 this comment: "Perhaps the most attractive and certainly the most definite representation of California as an island. California is the centre and 'raison d'etre' of the map." This atlas also contains the very rare map of Manhattan and surrounding area which extends to the Dutch settlements on the Delaware River.

See PLATE 26

1668

BLAEU, WILLEM, 1571-1638.

GUILIELMI BLAEU INSTITUTIO ASTRONOMICA DE USU GLOBO-RUM.

Amsterdam, Joan Blaeu, 1668.

Octavo, 7½″ high, bound in contemporary full vellum.

Contains woodcuts in text, none of which relates to America.

1668

JACOBSZ, THEUNIS.

THE LIGHTING COLOMNE OR SEA-MIRROUR.

Rotterdam, Gerard van der Vluyn, 1668.

Folio, 18″ high, bound in modern full leather with blind-tooling on boards and nineteenth-century gold-tooled leather label on spine.

Contains sixty-five maps with only the map of Greenland at page 70 relating to America. *Atlantes,* IV, has as Jac 41, an Amsterdam 1668 edition, a very scarce book, especially with the English text.

1670

BLOME, RICHARD, fl. 1660-1705.

A GEOGRAPHICAL DESCRIPTION OF THE FOUR PARTS OF THE WORLD TAKEN FROM . . . SANSON.

London, T.N. for Richard Blome, Nathaniel Brooks, Edward Brewster, and Thomas Bassett, 1670.

Folio, 13¾″ high, bound in contemporary full leather, gold-tooled.

The Fourth Part of this volume is devoted to America, and it contains folding colored double-page maps of North America and of South America. The map of the world following the Preface shows California as an island.

[1670?] §

HONDIUS, HENRICUS, 1597-1651.

NOVA TOTIUS TERRARUM ORBIS GEOGRAPHICA AC HYDROGRAPHICA TABULA.

Paris, Francis Jollain [, 1670?].

Map, 13½″ high plus margins, colored.

Facsimile published by D.A.C. Inc. of New York.

1670

MOXON, JOSEPH, 1627-1700.

A TUTOR TO ASTRONOMIE AND GEOGRAPHIE. OR AN EASIE AND SPEEDY WAY TO KNOW THE USE OF BOTH THE GLOBES. . . . IN SIX BOOKS. . . . SECOND EDITION.

London, Joseph Moxon, 1670.

Quarto, 7⅝″ high, bound in contemporary full leather, blind- and gold-tooled.

Woodcuts and engravings in text, none of which relates to America.

This study is the best work on globes published in England in the seventeenth century and is the perfect conclusion to pre-Newtonian astronomy.

1671

GREGORY, JOHN, fl. 1649-1671.

THE DESCRIPTION AND USE OF THE TERRESTRIAL GLOBE.

London, A. Clark for T. Williams, 1671.

Quarto, 7½″ high, bound in modern Cockerell marbled paper wrapper.

1671

MONTANUS, ARNOLD.

AMERICA. . . . DE NIEUWE EN ONBEKENDE WEERELD.

Amsterdam, Jacob van Meurs, 1671.

Quarto, 12¼″ high, bound in contemporary full leather, gold-tooled.

Contains fifty-four maps and plates, earlier and better impressions than the German and English translations, indexed on verso of last leaf. Stokes, *Iconography,* lists at 262. Sabin 50086 notes that this best edition is "sought for chiefly for its plates, especially for the engraved view of New Amsterdam which is without any doubt the handsomest and at the same time the most agreeable view of Dutch New York." The frontispiece map is replaced by one from the Ogilby edition.

[OGILBY, JOHN, 1600-1676.]

AMERICA NOVITER DELINEATA.

[London, 1671.]

Map, 11″ high plus margins, uncolored.

Style and information is derived from the earlier map of the Western Hemisphere by Hondius. Dated 1670 by Tooley in the dictionary but Phillips, *Maps,* page 105, dates 1671 for publication of America. Engraved by Matthaus Merian.

[OGILBY, JOHN, 1600-1676.]

CHILI.

[London, John Ogilby, 1671.]

Map, 11¼″ high plus margins, colored.

From John Ogilby's *America* which used the plates from Arnoldus Montanus' *Amerika,* first published in the same year.

OGILBY, JOHN, 1600-1676.

TABULA MAGELLANICA, QUA TIERRÆ DEL FUEGO.

London, 1671.

Map, 11⅜″ high plus margins, colored.

Contains four elegant cartouches, ships alone and in battle, Indians, birds, and animals. Phillips, *Maps,* page 105, and the biography of Ogilby by Katherine Van Eerde date the publication of *America* as 1671.

[OGILBY, JOHN, 1600-1676.]

NOVA BELGII QUOD NUNC NOVI JORCK VOCATUR, NOVÆ QUE ANGLIÆ & PARTIS VIRGINIÆ.

[London and Amsterdam, 1671.]

Map, 11⅜″ high plus narrow margins, uncolored.

Phillips, *Maps,* page 562, mentions publication of this map in Ogilby's *America* of 1671, and Van Eerde discusses his map making at page 178. The *Map Collectors' Circle,* Number 24, has a study of this map's history and its states at number 21, and terms it Ogilby-Montanus.

OGILBY, JOHN, 1600-1676.

URBS DOMINGO IN HISPANIOLA.

[London, John Ogilby, 1671.]

Map, 11½″ high plus margins, colored.

Bird's-eye view of Santo Domingo city on the island of Hispaniola.

[MONTANUS, ARNOLDUS, 1625?-1683.]

NOVUM AMSTERODAMUM.

[Amsterdam, Olfert Dapper, 1673.]

View, 5″ high on folio page, colored.

This view is the fourth printed view of present-day New York City. It originally appeared twice in 1671 in Montanus's *Amerika,* published in Amsterdam, and in *America* published in London by John Ogilby. This is from the second continental printing. Stokes, *Iconography,* I, 142-143, discusses.

1674

SANSON, NICOLAS, 1600-1667.

MAPPE-MONDE GEO-HYDROGRAPHIQUE, OU DESCRIPTION GENE-RALE DU GLOBE.

Paris, Hubert Jaillot, 1674.

Map, 21¼″ high plus margins, colored in outline in maps but full in cartouches.

Engraved by Louis Cordier and dedicated to the Dauphin by Jaillot, who is described in his relationship to the Sanson family by Tooley at page 41 in *Maps and Mapmakers.*   *See* PLATE 27

1674

WOOD, ANTHONY À, 1632-1695.

HISTORIA ET ANTIQUITATES UNIVERSITATIS OXONIENSIS [two volumes in one].

Oxford, "E Theatro Sheldoniano," 1674.

Folio, 16⅝″ high, bound in contemporary full leather, gold-tooled.

On verso of cover is bookplate of Algernon Capell, Earl of Essex, 1701. There is a folding double-page map of Oxford bound at page 364.

[1675]

WIT, FREDERICK DE, 1630-1706.

TERRA NOVA, AC MARIS TRACTUS CIRCA NOVAM FRANCIAM . . . BRASILIAM [upper cartouche] TERRA NEUF, EN DE CUSTEN VAN NIEU VRANCKRYCK . . . VENEZUELA.

Amsterdam, Frederick de Wit [, 1675].

Map, 19⅛″ high plus margins, colored.

Atlantes, IV, M. Wit 1, has as number (25) of the *Atlas* of 1675. Compare with [1745] RENARD, TERRA NEUF, except that this has Latin cartouche and other imprint.   *See* PLATE 29

[1675?-1685?]

WIT, FREDERICK DE, 1630-1706.

ATLAS [two volumes in one].

Amsterdam, Frederick de Wit [, 1675?-1685?].

Folio, 21″ high, bound in modern full leather, gold-tooled on spine and morocco panel front board.

Volume One contains twenty-seven maps called for in the index on the verso of the first engraved title page, the first two of which relate to America. *Atlantes* Wit 3 dates [1680?] with the index reading Hungaria, Transilvania, Servia, etc. at 21. Volume Two contains twenty-seven sea-charts called for in the index on the verso of the first engraved title page. Phillips 485 dates it [1675?] and lists maps 1, 20, 21, 22, 23, 24, 25, 26, and 27 as relating to America. *Atlantes* M. Wit 2 dates after 1680. Bound in at the end is a Paris map of Japan and Korea by Crepy dated 1767. All maps are colored in outline. Israel noted that this "is the only known example combining land and sea atlases in one volume."   *See* PLATE 28

[1676]

SPEED, JOHN, 1552-1629.

AMERICA WITH THOSE KNOWN PARTS. . . . DISCRIBED AND IN-
LARGED BY . . . ANO. 1626.

London, Thomas Bassett and Richard Chiswell [, 1676].

Map, 15½″ high plus margins, colored in outline in map but full
in cartouches and panels.

On verso is a description of America. Engraved by Abraham Goos of
Amsterdam who is discussed in *Atlantes*, II, 120. Phillips, *Maps*, page
104, notes that this map was first published by George Humble in
Speed's *Prospect* in 1631, discussed in Sabin 89228.

[1676]

SPEED, JOHN, 1552-1629.

A MAP OF NEW ENGLAND AND NEW YORK. . . . F. LAMB SCULP.

London, Thomas Bassett and Richard Chiswell [, 1676].

Map, 15″ high plus margins, colored.

On verso printed in English is a description of the map, the folios 45
and 46, and the signature mark Z. This is based on the Jansson prototype of a quarter-century earlier as discussed in *Map Collectors' Circle*,
Number 24, where it is number 23.

[1676]

SPEED, JOHN, 1552-1629.

A NEW DESCRIPTION OF CAROLINA.

London, Thomas Bassett and Richard Chiswell [, 1676].

Map, 14¾″ high plus margins and lake top, colored.

On verso printed in English is a description of Carolina and Florida,
the folios 49 and 50, and the signature mark Bb. Phillips 488 has this
as number 75 in Speed's *Theatre*, and Cumming, *Southeast*, has as
number 77. Marshall, *Clements*, II, 397, notes it being based on the
Ogilby map of 1672, from Cape Charles in north to St. Augustine in
south.

[1676]

SPEED, JOHN, 1552-1629.

A NEWE MAPE OF TARTARY. . . . DIRCK GRIJP SCULP.

London, Thomas Bassett and Richard Chiswell [, 1676].

Map, 15½″ high plus margins, colored.

On verso printed in English is a description of the map and the folios
39 and 40. A part of America is shown. Phillips 488 describes the
1676 edition of the *Prospect* of which this is number [20] as also in
5949. The printing history of the editions is discussed in the facsimile
of the 1627 edition. Sabin 89228 describes this.

[1676]

SPEED, JOHN, 1552-1629.

NORTHAMTONSHIRE. . . . JODOCUS HONDIUS CÆLAVIT . . . 1610.

London, John Speed for Thomas Bassett and for Richard Chiswell
[, 1676].

Map, 15⅛″ high plus margins, colored.

On verso printed in English is a description of the map and of the
county, a list of hundreds and of towns, and the folio. See note at
Tooley on Bassett, and Skelton, "County Atlases," 92.

[1676]

SPEED, JOHN, 1552-1629.

PENBROKSHYRE. . . . JODOCUS HONDIUS CÆLAVIT.

London, John Speed for Thomas Bassett and Richard Chiswell [, 1676].

Map, 15⅛″ high plus margins, colored.

On verso printed in English is a description, the signature mark Hhh, and the folios 101 and 102 of Book Two, Chapter Three. This map is listed as Part Two, [2], in Le Gear 5949 which describes *The Theatre of the Empire.* Speed is discussed by Tooley at pages 68 through 70 in his *Maps and Mapmakers.*

1677

DU VAL, PIERRE, 1618-1683.

LE CANADA FAICT PAR LE SR DE CHAMPLAIN.

Paris, Pierre Du Val, 1677.

Map, 13¾″ high plus margins, colored, bound on tab in burlap-covered boards in slipcase.

Phillips 501 has as number [15] of 1688 edition, dated 1677, as in cartouche. This is the Streeter copy, I, 99. For a discussion of the various states, see Verner's *North Part of America.*   *See* PLATE 30

1677§

FOSTER, JOHN, 1648-1681.

A MAP OF NEW-ENGLAND.

Boston, John Foster, 1677.

Map, 11⅝″ high plus margins.

Facsimile published by W. Elliot Woodward of Roxbury in 1865 to accompany the reissue of William Hubbard's *History of the Indian Wars.* Wheat & Brun 144 describes the map and the controversy, and it is reproduced in Shipton-Mooney 231.

1677§

FOSTER, JOHN, 1648-1681.

A MAP OF NEW-ENGLAND.

Boston, John Foster, 1677.

Map, 11⅝″ high plus margins.

Facsimile published by the Massachusetts Historical Society in 1888 to accompany the remarks of Samuel Abbott Green. Wheat & Brun 144 describes and Shipton-Mooney 231 reproduces.

1677

HEYLIN, PETER, 1599-1662.

COSMOGRAPHY IN FOUR BOOKS. . . . THE 5TH EDITION.

London, A. Clark for Philip Chetwind, Anna Seile, Thomas Bassett, J. Wright, Richard Chiswell, and T. Sawbridge, 1677.

Folio, 13½″ high, bound in modern full leather, gold- and blind-tooled with gilt edges, by Townsend.

Contains four folding maps, that of America being bound at page 128, dated 1663.

1677

IZACKE, RICHARD, 1624?-1698.

ANTIQUITIES OF THE CITY OF EXETER.

London, E. Tyler and R. Holt for Richard and George Marriott, 1677.

Octavo, 7¼" high, bound in contemporary full leather, blind-tooled.

Contains a map of the City of Exeter. Mansell locates four copies: at UCLA, Yale, Newberry, and Pratt in Baltimore.

1677 §

SELLER, JOHN, fl. 1664-1697, and
FISHER, WILLIAM, fl. 1669-1691.

A MAPP OF NEW JERSEY IN AMERICA.

London, John Seller and William Fisher, 1677.

Map, 22¼" high plus margins trimmed close at top, colored.

Facsimile published in collotype by Meriden Gravure Company in 1958.

[1679]

SELLER, JOHN, fl. 1664-1697.

ATLAS MINIMUS OR A BOOK OF GEOGRAPHY.

London, John Seller [, 1679].

Forty-eightmo, 3⅞" high, bound in modern full leather, gold-stamped.

Dated by Tooley in his dictionary under Seller, following Phillips 490 citation of an advertisement. Contains the fifty-three maps called for in Phillips 490 where the following numbers relate to America: [1], [42], [43], [44], [45], [46], [47], [48], [49], [50], [51], [52], and [53], to which should be added the frontispiece and [17], Asia. Sabin 79025 joins Phillips in not including the frontispiece in the number. Donald Cresswell writes that "the maps are superb and of the effulgent baroque quality that would soon be taken up by John Senex in England. Lovely and masterful work by Seller that is unlike the primitive work found in the *English Pilot* that is usually associated with him."

[1680]

KEULEN, JOHANNES VAN, 1654-1715.

PASCAARTE VANDE ZEE CUSTEN VAN GUINEA, EN BRASILIA.

Amsterdam, Johannes van Keulen [, 1680].

Map, 20¼" high plus margins, colored.

Atlantes, IV, 382, has as number [26] of the Van Keulen charts, and it appears in Keu 2 as number 27 of the French edition of the *Zee-Atlas,* dated 1680. This map shows the South Atlantic and the coast of Africa from Cape Verde to the Cape of Good Hope and of America from above the Amazon to below the Plate rivers.

[1680]§

WIT, FREDERICK DE, 1630-1706.

NOVA ORBIS TABULA, IN LUCEM EDITA.

[Amsterdam, Frederick de Wit, 1680.]

Map, 18⅛″ high plus margins, colored in outline at maps but full in cartouches.

Facsimile of map which *Atlantes,* III, 212, lists as number [3] of the de Wit maps and dates as 1680 in the Index, V, 282.

[1682?]

VISSCHER, NICOLAS, 1649-1702.

NOVISSIMA ET ACCURATISSIMA TOTIUS AMERICAE DESCRIPTIO.

[Amsterdam, 1682?]

Map, 17⅛″ high plus margins, colored.

Atlantes, III, 179, lists as number [92*], with the privilege which was given in 1682, according to Vis 11. Phillips, *Maps,* page 105, dates 1660?, and two elaborate cartouches are present.

1682

VRIES, SIMON DE.

CURIEUSE AENMERCKINGEN . . . OOST EN WEST-INDISCHE. . . . EERSTE STUCK.

Utrecht, Johann Ribbius, 1682.

Octavo, 8½″ high, bound in contemporary full vellum.

Engraved allegorical title page followed by rubricated type title page. Plates, some folding, portray crafts and industries, flora and fauna, and a folding map of Ceylon and the Maldives at page 68 and of Brazil at page 338.

[1683?]

KEULEN, JOHANNES VAN, 1654-1715.

PAS KAART VAN WEST INDIEN.

Amsterdam, Johannes van Keulen [, 1683?].

Map, 20¼″ high plus margins closely trimmed, colored in outline in chart but full in cartouche.

Atlantes, IV, 394, has as number [116]* of the charts and it appears as number (1) of the *Zee-Fakkel* of 1684, Keu 109A. Contains the coasts of America from fourth south to fifty-sixth north parallels, from the mouth of the Amazon through the gulf of Mexico.

1684

DU VAL, PIERRE, 1618-1683.

L'AMERIQUE AUTREMENT LE NOUVEAU MONDE.

Paris, "Madlle Du Val Fille de l'Auteur," 1684.

Map, 14½″ high plus margins, colored.

Phillips, *Maps,* page 105, lists as having been first published in 1655.

[1686]

[MALLET, ALAIN MANESSON, 1630-1706.]

CANADA OU NOUVELLE FRANCE.

[Paris, D. Thierry, 1686.]

Map, 5½″ high plus "die Landtschafft Canada oder dass Neue Franckreich. Fig: 9" in margins, colored.

Tooley's entry dates at 1686 the German edition of the five-volume *Description de l'Univers* of 1683 of Paris. Phillips 3447 has as Volume Five, page 273.

[1686]

[MALLET, ALAIN MANESSON, 1630-1706.]

ISLE DE TERRE NEWE.

[Paris, D. Thierry, 1686.]

Map, 5¾″ high plus "die Insel der Neuen Erde. Fig: 12" in margins, colored.

Tooley's entry dates at 1686 the German edition of the five-volume *Description de l'Univers* of 1683 of Paris. Phillips 3447 has as Volume Five, page 283.

1688§

BEREY, CLAUDE AUGUSTE.

CARTE GENERALE CONTENANTE LES MONDES DES COELESTE TERRESTRE ET CIVILE. . . . GRAVÉ PAR JEAN CRESPY. . . . ECRITE PAR CLAUDE AUGUSTE BEREY.

[Paris,] 1688.

Map, 22¼″ high plus margins, colored.

Facsimile published in France.

1688

BLOME, RICHARD, fl. 1660-1705.

L'AMERIQUE ANGLOISE, OU DESCRIPTION.

Amsterdam, Abraham Wolfgang, 1688.

Twelvemo, 5¾″ high, bound in modern half-leather, gold-stamped.

This first French edition contains seven folding maps by Robert Morden: (1), Jamaique; (2), Barbades; (3), Pensylvanie; (4), Barmudes; (5), Caroline; (6), Nouvelle Angleterre; and (7), [Cape Charles to Baffin Bay].

1689

DONCKER, HENDRIK, 1625-1699.

DE NIEUWE GROOTE VERMEERDERDE ZEE-ATLAS OFTE WATER-WERELT.

Amsterdam, Hendrick Doncker, 1689 [printed, but altered by pen to 1688].

Folio, 21¾″ high, bound in contemporary full vellum, gold-tooled.

Contains forty-eight sea charts. The text belongs to another edition and the register at page 18 does not agree with the maps published here.

They are colored in outline and all nude figures "clothed" with heavy color. This edition is described, in all of its complexity, in *Atlantes,* IV, Don 23, with the following related to America using numbers in order of binding followed by Koeman's *Atlantes* number in brackets: 1, [53*]; 2, [81]; 3, [82]; 4, [83]; 39, [101]; 40, Mar del Zur Hispanis Mare Pacificum, [78]; 41, [77*]; 42, [75*]; 43, [102]; 44, [103]; 45, [73*]; 46, [74*]; 47, [104] containing the first view of Philadelphia published outside of London, a copy of the Holme plan; and 48, [49]. This edition is not listed in Phillips nor Le Gear at numbers 168, 472, or 5688.

1689

MORTIER, PIERRE, 1661-1711.

MANIERE DE FORTIFIER DE MR. DE VAUBAN. . . . LE TOUT MIS EN ORDRE PAR MR. LE CHEVALIER DE CAMBRAY.

Amsterdam, Pierre Mortier, 1689.

Octavo, 8″ high, bound in contemporary full leather, gold-tooled.

Contains plans of fortifications on many folding plates.

[1689?]

VISSCHER, NICOLAS, 1649-1702.

ATLAS MINOR.

Amsterdam, Nicolas Visscher [, 1689?].

Folio, 21″ high, bound in blind-tooled vellum wanting ties.

Engraved colored frontispiece is dated 1689? at *Atlantes,* Vis 12, and the twenty-five colored double-page maps called for in index are here

plus unindexed colored folding map of The Kingdom of England and Wales. *Atlantes,* III, 150-155, discusses the atlases published by the Visscher family, none of which, from Vis 11 through Vis 28, describes exactly this atlas with the index of twenty-five maps, nor does Phillips 552. Those maps relating to America are numbers 1, 2, 23, 24, and 25.

1690

MOLL, HERMAN, d. 1732.

A MAP OF THE WEST INDIES . . . SEVERAL TRACTS MADE BY THE GALEONS AND FLOTA.

London, Herman Moll, 1690.

Map, 23¼″ high plus margins, colored in outline.

Contains view of Mexico City and plans of harbors. Phillips, *Maps,* page 1054, notes publication in *World Described.*

Presented to the Philadelphia Maritime Museum in May 1984.

[1690]

RAM, JOHANNES DE, 1648-1693.

LONDONI ANGLIÆ.

Amsterdam, Johannes de Ram [, 1690].

Map, 19½″ high plus margins, colored.

Atlantes, Aa 9, Volume Ten, number 7, has the first four words of the title. Phillips 3485 dates *La Galerie* [1729]. Nebenzahl assigns the date 1690 in a catalogue entry. Inset has portraits of William and Mary and a view of the river and the city beyond.

1692

SANSON, NICOLAS, 1600-1667.

L'AMERIQUE SEPTENTRIONALE.

[Paris, Hubert Jaillot,] 1692.

Map, 21¼″ high plus title and margins, colored in outline in map and full in cartouche.

Dedicated to the Dauphin by Jaillot who is described in his relationship to the Sanson family by Tooley at page 41 in *Maps and Mapmakers*. There is a discussion of the 1692 *Atlas Nouveau* of Sanson at Phillips 514 where this map is numbered 5.   *See* PLATE 31

1693

MORDEN, ROBERT, d. 1703.

GEOGRAPHY RECTIFIED: OR, A DESCRIPTION OF THE WORLD. . . . THIRD EDITION, ENLARGED.

London, Robert Morden and Thomas Cockerill, 1693.

Octavo, 7¾″ high, bound in contemporary full leather, blind-tooled.

Here are seventy-eight colored maps, the last seventeen of which are of parts of the Western Hemisphere, and the map of the world is at page 12. Phillips has at 4268 with a list of maps of America at 498.

[1695?]§

ALLARD, CAREL, 1648-1709.

ORBIS HABITABILIS OPPIDA ET VESTITUS.

Amsterdam, Carel Allard [, 1695?].

Folio, 12⅞″ high, bound in modern cloth, stamped.

Facsimile published by Theatrum Orbis Terrarum, Amsterdam, 1966, as Volume IV of the First Series on Urbanization. One hundred engraved plates depicting towns and costumes with the following numbers related to America: 77, Hudson's Bay; 78, 79, New Amsterdam; 80, Mexico; 81, Acapulco; 82, San Francisco de Campeche; 83, 84, Havana; 85, San Domingo; 86, 87, Porto Rico; 88, Barbados; 89, Nombre de Dios; 90, Panama; 91, 92, Cartagena; 93, 94, Pernambuco; 95, St. Augustine; 96, Surinam; 97, San Salvador; 98, 99, Potosi; and 100, Lima.

1695

CAMDEN, WILLIAM, 1551-1623.

CAMDEN'S BRITANNIA, NEWLY TRANSLATED INTO ENGLISH. . . . PUBLISHED BY EDMUND GIBSON.

London, Freeman Collins for Abel Swale and Awnsham and John Churchill, 1695.

Folio, 17½″ high, bound in contemporary full leather, blind- and gold-tooled.

This first edition contains an engraved portrait of Camden as frontispiece, and the fifty maps are by Robert Morden.

[1695]

KEULEN, JOHANNES VAN, 1654-1715.

PASKAERT WAER IN DE GRADEN.

Amsterdam, Johannes van Keulen [, 1695].

Map, 20⅜″ high plus margins, colored.

Phillips 3453 has as number [101] in *Die Groote Niewe Vermeer-derde Zee-Atlas* of 1695, entered in *Atlantes,* IV, as Keu 20B. Cres-well notes as "a wonderful European's view of the Atlantic Ocean oriented to the west."

See PLATE 32

[1695]

KEULEN, JOHANNES VAN, 1654-1715.

WASSENDE GRAADE KAART VAN ALLE BEKENDE ZEEKUSTEN. . . .
P. PICKART FEC.

Amsterdam, Johannes van Keulen [, 1695].

Map, 20¼″ high plus margins, uncolored.

This chart of the world incorporates all then known by the Dutch, when they were the leaders of the sea trade. *Atlantes,* Keu 33A, notes that the first fifteen-year privilege was granted in 1680 and was re-newed in 1695. Keu 20B notes this chart's first appearance in the sea-atlas of 1695 as number (5), and also as number (1) in Keu 38A. Phillips 509 has as number [3] in Nicolas Visscher, *Atlas Minor* of [1692?].

1695

[MOLL, HERMAN, d. 1732.]

THESAURUS GEOGRAPHICUS. A NEW BODY OF GEOGRAPHY.

London, Abel Swale and Timothy Child, 1695.

Quarto, 12½″ high, bound in modern half-leather, gold-stamped.

Phillips 536 describes another Moll work and mentions this *Thesau-rus* as containing two maps relating to America, America at page 473 and British Plantations at page 480. America also appears in the planisphere following page 44 of the Introduction.

[1695]

MORDEN, ROBERT, d. 1703.

SUFFOLK.

London, Abel Swale and Awnsham and John Churchill [, 1695].

Map, 14½″ high plus margins, colored.

Tooley on Swale notes the collaboration with Churchills for Morden's *Britannia* of 1695. Skelton, "County Atlases," 116, has as the twenty-first map.

1695-1697

CORONELLI, VINCENZO MARIA, 1650-1718.

MARE DEL NORD.

Venice, 1695-1697.

Map, 17⅝″ high plus margins, colored.

Phillips 521 has as number [15] in the two-volume *Atlante Veneto* of 1695-1697.

1695-1697

CORONELLI, VINCENZO MARIA, 1650-1718.

MARE DEL NORD.

Venice, 1695-1697.

Map, 24″ high plus margins, colored.

Phillips 521 has as number [22] in the two-volume *Atlante Veneto* of 1695-1697.

1696

WHISTON, WILLIAM, 1667-1752.

A NEW THEORY OF THE EARTH.

London, R. Roberts for Benjamin Tooke, 1696.

Octavo, 7½″ high, bound in contemporary full leather, blind- and gold-tooled.

Contains seven folding plates plus engravings in the text.

[1696-1718]

DANCKERTS, JUSTUS, 1635-1701.

ATLAS.

Amsterdam, Justus Danckerts [, 1696-1718].

Folio, 19¾″ high, bound in full leather.

The eightieth map, that of Mantua, numbered 72 in MS on verso, describes an event of 1718. *Atlantes,* I, 88-90, discusses the atlases published by the Danckerts family, none of which, from Dan 1 through Dan 5, describes exactly this atlas of 147 maps. Those maps relating to America are numbers 2; 3; 6; 136, America; 138, Novi Belgii; 139, Louisiana by Seutter; 144, Guiana by Thelot of Frankfurt, 1669; and 145, Chili by Janssonius of Amsterdam.

1697

FER, NICOLAS DE, 1646-1720.

PETIT ET NOUVEAU ATLAS.

Paris, Nicolas de Fer, 1697.

Octavo, 9″ high, bound in contemporary full leather, gold-tooled.

The eighteen maps colored in outline are double-page, the first of which is a world map, the fourth is of Africa showing part of Brazil, and the fifth is of North America, showing California as an island. The next is of South America. Phillips 547 lists only the last two as relating to America.

1698

HENNEPIN, LOUIS DE, 1640-1701.

A NEW DISCOVERY OF A VAST COUNTRY IN AMERICA.

London, M. Bentley, J. Tonson, H. Bonwick, T. Goodwin, and S. Manship, 1698.

Sixteenmo, 7½″ high, bound in contemporary full leather.

This first English edition has two folding maps, one of North America from 60° North to 20° North, and the other of the New World from 60° North to 20° South. This is considered by Lande as "one of the most important volumes in the early history of North America," at page 423. Sabin 31371 describes it as does Vail 278 and Wing H 1450. It contains the first view of Niagara Falls in English.

1698

OGILBY, JOHN, 1600-1676.

BRITANNIA: OR, THE KINGDOM OF ENGLAND.

London, Abel Swale and Robert Morden, 1698.

Folio, 15″ high, bound in contemporary full leather, blind- and gold-tooled.

Contains one hundred double-page uncolored maps of "the Principal Roads," the first book of road maps and the first to use the mile of 5,280 feet.

1700

BION, NICOLAS, 1652-1733.

L'USAGE DES GLOBES CELESTES ET TERRESTRES . . . NOUVELLE EDITION.

Amsterdam, Francis Halma, 1700.

Quarto, 9″ high, bound in contemporary full vellum.

Contains fifteen engraved plates on the use of globes, none of which relates to America. Bound with SANSON, L'AMERIQUE [1662].

[1700?]

HOMANN, JOHANN BAPTIST, 1663-1724.

BELGII PARS SEPTENTRIONALIS.

Nuremberg, Johann Baptist Homann [, 1700?].

Map, 18⅞″ high plus margins, colored.

Shows North American coast from Maine to Virginia in inset map along with a view of the city of New Amsterdam. Not found among maps in Maritime 460 and 461 nor in Stokes.

[1700?]

HOMANN, JOHANN BAPTIST, 1663-1724.

SUPERIORIS ET INFERIORIS DUCATUS SILESIÆ.

Nuremberg [, 1700?].

Map, 19⅛″ high plus margins, colored in map but uncolored in cartouches.

Maritime 460 has as number 66 in the *Atlas Novus*.

[1700?]

HOMANN, JOHANN BAPTIST, 1663-1724.

TOTIUS MARCHIONATUS LUSATIAE.

Nuremberg, Johann Baptist Homann [, 1700?].

Map, 19″ high plus margins, colored in map but uncolored in cartouches, as is characteristic.

[1700]

[WELLS, EDWARD, 1667-1727.]

A NEW MAP OF THE MOST CONSIDERABLE PLANTATIONS OF THE ENGLISH IN AMERICA . . . SUTTON NICHOLLS SCULP.

[London, Edward Wells, 1700.]

Map, 14″ high plus margins, colored.

This appeared in his *New Sett of Maps* of [1700], where Phillips 531 has as number [41]. There are inset maps of Nova Scotia, Carolina, Jamaica, Barbados, and Bermuda.

[1700]

WELLS, EDWARD, 1667-1727.

A NEW MAP OF THE TERRAQUEOUS GLOBE.

[Oxford, 1700.]

Map, 14½″ high plus margins, colored in outline in maps but full elsewhere with sumptuous color heightened by gum arabic.

Engraved by Michael Burghers of Oxford University and dated 1700 by Tooley in his dictionary. Phillips 531, number [1], is dated 1700.

Wells set a new standard for elegant atlas making when he produced his atlas for the education of youth with each map dedicated to young William, Duke of Gloucester.

See PLATE 33

1700-1712

L'ISLE, GUILLAUME DE, 1675-1726.

[ATLAS DE GÉOGRAPHIE.]

[Paris, 1700-1712.]

Folio, 20½″ high, bound in contemporary full vellum wanting ties.

Thirty-nine maps colored in outline are in this untitled atlas. Those maps relating to America are the following ten: 1, 1700; 3, Theatrum Historicum. . . . Pars Occidentale, 1705; 4, l'Amerique Meridionale, 1700; 5, l'Amerique Septentrionale, 1700; 6, l'Asie, 1700; 7, l'Afrique, 1700; 36, du Paraguay du Chili, 1703; 37, de la Terre Firme du Perou du Bresil, 1703; 38, du Canada, 1703; and 39, du Mexique (second state), 1703. Phillips 533 lists eight of these.

1700-1760

VARIOUS.

[Five volumes of maps and sea charts by various hands.]

Folios, 21½″ high, bound in contemporary half leather, blind- and gold-tooled.

Maps relating to America are:

Band I, Map 1   Le Monde Eclipsé . . . 1748. Nuremberg, Homann Heirs, 1747,

2   Planiglobii Terrestris. Nuremberg, Homann [, 1720?],

Band V, Map 2   . . . Caraibicarum Insularum. Amsterdam, Reinier and Josua Ottens [, 1720?], Phillips 4257, VII, number 112, and Phillips 3490, number 125,

13   . . . Map of South America. London, Herman Moll [, 1720?],

14   Nova Tabula . . . Borealiorem Americæ Partem. Amsterdam, Visscher [, 1700?], Phillips 3478, numbers 125 and 126,

15   Amplissimæ Regionis Mississippi. Nuremberg, Homann [, 1720?], Cumming, *Southeast,* pages 186 and 187, describes as the base map for all eighteenth-century maps of the Mississippi Valley,

16   Virginia Marylandia et Carolina. Nuremberg, Homann [, 1720?],

17   . . . Ludovicianæ vel Gallice Louisiane. Augsburg, Seutter [, 1745?],

18   Carte Nouvelle Contenant la Partie d'Amerique la plus Septentrionale. Amsterdam, Visscher [, 1700?],

19   Nova Tabula . . . Borealiorem Americæ Partem. Amsterdam, Visscher [, 1700?],

20   Nova et Accurata Brasiliæ . . . Auctore Joanne Blaeu. Amsterdam, Schenck [, 1720?],

21   America Septentrionalis a Domino d'Anville. Nuremberg, Homann Heirs, 1756,

22   Americae Mappa Generalis. Nuremberg, Homann Heirs, 1746,

23   Totius Americae. Nuremberg, Homann [, 1720?],

25   Nova Virginiæ Tabula. Amsterdam, Schenck and Valck [, 1710?],

26   Partie Orientale de la Nouvelle France ou du Canada par Mr. Bellin. [Nuremberg,] Homann Heirs, 1755,

27   Partie Occidentale de la Nouvelle France ou du Canada par Mr. Bellin. [Nuremberg,] Homann Heirs, 1755,

28   Virginiæ Partis Australis . . . Nova Descriptio. Amsterdam, Valck and Schenck [, 1700?],

29   Pensylvania Nova Jersey et Nova York. Augsburg, Seutter [, 1740?],

30   Domina Anglorum. [Nuremberg,] Homann Heirs [, 1740?],

31   Carte de l'Isle de la Martinique. . . . Houel . . . Delisle . . . Philippe Buache. Amsterdam, Covens and Mortier, 1732,

32   Jamaica. Amsterdam, Visscher [, 1700?],

33   Représentation . . . de l'Isle Martinique. Augsburg, Seutter [, 1740?],

35   Mappa Geographica Complectens Indiæ Occidentalis. [Nuremberg,] Homann Heirs [, 1731?],

36   Typus Geographicus Chili, Paraguay. Nuremberg, Homann Heirs, 1733,

37   Tabula Americæ Specialis Geographica Regni Peru. [Nuremberg,] Homann Heirs [, 1735?],

38   Nova Isthmi Americani . . . Panama. Amsterdam, Ottens [, 1740?],

39   Terra Firma. Amsterdam, Valck and Schenck [, 1740?],

40   Yucatan. Amsterdam, Covens and Mortier [, 1750?],

41   Americæ Pars Meridionalis. Amsterdam, Valck and Schenck [, 1740?],

42-47   Amerique Septentrionale . . . Par le Docteur Mitchel. Paris, le Rouge, 1756,

48   Regni Mexicani seu Novæ Hispaniæ. Nuremberg, Homann [1720?].

1702

FER, NICOLAS DE, 1646-1720.

CARTES ET DESCRIPTIONS.

Paris, Nicolas de Fer, 1702.

Quarto, 12″ high, bound in modern quarter leather, gold-tooled.

Engraved colored double-page title page is followed by nineteen double-page maps, colored in outline, of which eight relate to America: Mappe-Monde at leaves 11 and 12, L'Europe at 13 and 14, California at 35 and 36, Nouvelle Espagne at 37 and 38, Les Isles at 39 and 40, La Terre Firme at 41 and 42, Le Chili at 43 and 44, and Le Detroit de Magellan at 45 and 46, nearly all dated 1702.

1702

MATHER, COTTON, 1663-1728.

MAGNALIA CHRISTI AMERICANA.

London, Thomas Parkhurst, 1702.

Quarto, 12½" high, bound in rebacked contemporary full leather, blind-tooled.

This first edition contains the map of New England opposite page 1. Sabin 46392 describes the map as "often wanting."

See PLATE 34

1702-1710

SCHERER, HEINRICH, 1628-1704.

GEOGRAPHIA NATURALIS [in seven parts in three volumes].

Munich, Mary Magdalen Rauchen and, for Part Seven, Mathias Riedl, for Johann Caspar Bencard, 1702-1710.

Quartos, 10¾" high, bound in contemporary full vellum, blind-tooled.

Contains one hundred and ninety-two maps. For descriptions of the seven parts and for maps relating to America see Phillips 3460 for Part One, 3459 for Part Two, 3457 and 538a for Part Three, 3461 for Part Four, 3458 for Part Five, 3462 for Part Six, and 3471 for Part Seven. Also described in Sabin 77606 is an eight-volume edition of 1703.

1703

ALINGHAM, WILLIAM.

A SHORT ACCOUNT OF THE NATURE AND USE OF MAPS.

London, R. Janeway for Benjamin Barker, 1703.

Octavo, 6⅜" high, bound in contemporary full leather, gold-tooled.

Mansell, 8, 654, lists this but supplies no dates for author.

1703

CELLARIUS, CHRISTOPHORUS, 1638-1707.

NOTITIA ORBIS ANTIQUI.

Cambridge, John Owens, 1703.

Quarto, 10" high, bound in contemporary full leather, gold-tooled.

None of the twenty-one maps relates to America.

1703

LAHONTAN, LOUIS ARMAND, BARON DE, 1666-1715.

MEMOIRES DE L'AMERIQUE SEPTENTRIONALE. . . . TOME PREMIER [and second].

La Haye, Frères l'Honoré, 1703.

Twelvemo, 6½" high, bound in contemporary full leather, gold-tooled.

This second issue of the first edition contains twenty-six plates. Sabin describes it as a spurious edition at 38638 but Paltsits corrects him. The maps are at the following pages: 9, Canada; 14, Quebec; 116, Lake Huron; 136, Mississippi; 242, Plaisance Bay; and, in the second volume, Canada at page 5. In his dictionary Tooley identifies François l'Honoré of Paris as the publisher.

1703-1773

VARIOUS.

ATLAS MINOR SIVE TOTIUS ORBIS TERRARUM [engraved title page, volume of maps by various hands].

Folio, 21″ high, bound in contemporary full leather, blind-tooled.

Contains one hundred and twenty-three maps of which this map relates to America: 1, Totius Americae Septentrionalis et Meridionalis . . . Norimberge, Homann.

[1705?]

EIMMART, GEORG CHRISTOPHER, 1638-1705.

LOCA STELLARUM, COELESTI HUIC GLOBO.

[Nuremberg, Georg Christopher Eimmart, 1705?]

Globe, 12″ diameter, on circular wood base.

A celestial globe described by Yonge at page 27.

1705

FER, NICOLAS DE, 1646-1720.

PLAN DES VILLES . . . DE CARTAGENE. . . . INSELIN SCULPSIT.

[Paris,] Nicolas de Fer, 1705.

Map, 9¾″ high plus margins, uncolored.

Marshall, *Clements,* I, 349, notes publication in *Atlas Curieux,* Paris, 1705-1717, as number 130 in Volume Two, and elsewhere. Kapp 39 discusses the 1700 map and mentions this edition.

[1705?]

ROOK, G.

A MAP OF THE CITY AND BAY OF GIBRALTAR.

[London? 1705?]

Map, 8¾″ high plus margins, uncolored.

Contains maps, views, and a plan dedicated "to the Prince of Hessen Darmstadt by Col: Ol: D'Harcourt."

[1705-1739]

CHATELAIN, HENRY ABRAHAM, 1684-1743.

PREMIERE CARTE . . . HISTOIRE DU MONDE . . . LA SPHERE, LE GLOBE CELESTE.

Amsterdam, Henry Abraham Chatelain [, 1705-1739].

Map, 13¼″ high plus title and margins, uncolored.

Contains eight engraved illustrations of the universe, the world, and various interpretations of the same in history, from an edition of Chatelain's *Atlas Historique.*

1706

CORONELLI, VINCENZO MARIA, 1650-1718.

TEATRO DELLA GUERRA [BELGIO].

Naples, 1706.

Octavo, oblong, 8⅜″ high, bound in contemporary paper-covered limp boards.

Contains forty-eight plates including maps, views of cities, and plans of fortifications, none of which relates to America.

1706

CURSON, HENRY.

A NEW DESCRIPTION OF THE WORLD.

London, John Nutt, 1706.

Twelvemo, 4⅞" high, bound in contemporary full leather, blind-tooled.

The only map relates to America and is the frontispiece, Typus Orbis Terrarum. Mansell, 130, 4 and 5, list publications of Curson but not this edition.

[1707?]

AA, PIETER VAN DER, 1659-1733.

D'ENGELZE VOLKPLANTING IN VIRGINIE DOOR IOHAN SMITH.

Leyden, Pieter van der Aa [, 1707?].

Map, 6" high plus margins and imprint and folio "Pag. 7," colored.

Atlantes, I, 4, has this as map number (72) in *Carte des Itineraires,* Leyden, 1707, Aa 1, and as map number (108) in Aa 2 of 1714.

1708

KAI TSU SHOU KOU.

[Geography of the world by Nisuikawa Joken in five volumes bound in two.]

Kyoto, Umemura Jiemon, 1708.

Octavos, 9" high, bound in contemporary paper.

Contains maps of the world and of China, among other illustrations, and a modern seal of ownership of Watanabe.

1708

MOXON, JOSEPH, 1627-1700.

THE USE OF A MATHEMATICAL INSTRUMENT CALLED A QUADRANT. . . . SEVENTH EDITION.

London, Joseph Moxon, 1708.

Octavo, 6" high, disbound.

Contains a woodcut in text and eight-page advertisement for globes, maps, instruments, and the like following page 46, pages misimposed in printing.

[1709-1736]

MOLL, HERMAN, d. 1732.

THE WORLD DESCRIBED: OR, A NEW AND CORRECT SETT OF MAPS.

London, John Bowles [, 1709-1736].

Folio, 25½" high, bound in contemporary full leather, blind-tooled on boards and gold-tooled on spine.

Contains thirty maps, colored in outline, which are listed on the prospectus on verso of front cover. Phillips 554 lists those relating to America as numbers 1, 2, 7, 8, 9, 10, 11, and 12, and dates the entry 1709-1720. Map 6 should be added, for it shows part of Brazil. Phillips 3469 describes the states of map number 8, of which this is the third state with the Cherokees note. Map number 1 is dedicated to King George II who came to the throne in 1727.

[1710?]

HOMANN, Johann Baptist, 1667-1724.

PORTUGALLIÆ ET ALGARBIÆ . . . LITTORA BRASILIÆ . . . AMERI-CÆ.

Nuremberg, Johann Baptist Homann [, 1710?].

Map, 19¾″ high plus margins, colored.

Maritime 460 has as number 30 in *Atlas Novus.*

[1710?]

KEULEN, Gerard van, 1678-1727.

[SEA CHARTS.]

Amsterdam, Gerard van Keulen [, 1710?].

Folio, 24¾″ high, bound in contemporary full vellum.

In his entry for van Keulen, Tooley writes that some copies of atlases were made up to customers' "special requirements," similar to the trip tickets issued by modern auto clubs. This is one of those, taken from the 185 charts in the 1708-1709 edition of the great *Zee-Atlas,* Keu 28, in *Atlantes,* IV. The six charts are colored and are titled:

1. The New Sea Chart of the South Part of the North Sea,
2. The New Sea Map Chanell Betwext Engsland et France,
3. The New Sea Map of the Spannish Zee Betwext Chanell and the I. Cuba,
4. Nieuwe . . . Geheel-Westindien,
5. Pascaerte vande Caribes,
6. Nieuwe . . . Curacao.

[1710]

SENEX, John, d. 1740.

NORTH AMERICA CORRECTED FROM THE OBSERVATIONS.

[London,] John Senex [, 1710].

Map, 37½″ high plus margins, colored.

Marshall, *Clements,* II, 365, notes Wheat 21 as a reference.

[1710?]

SENEX, John, d. 1740.

SOUTH AMERICA CORRECTED FROM THE OBSERVATIONS.

[London,] John Senex [, 1710?].

Map, 37¾″ high at neat lines plus lines and margins, colored.

Dedicated to Edmund Halley.

Presented to the Philadelphia Maritime Museum in May 1984.

[1710?]

VALCK, Gerard, 1650?-1726.

NOVUS PLANIGLOBII TERRESTRIS PER UTRUMQUE POLUM CONSPECTUS.

Amsterdam: Gerard Valck [, 1710?].

Map, 16″ high plus closely trimmed margins, colored.

Atlantes Val 2 is followed by a list of maps of the Valcks of which this is number [1].

VISSCHER, NICOLAS, 1587-1652.

BRABANTIÆ BATAVÆ PARS OCCIDENTALIS. . . . NUNC APUD PE-
TRUM SCHENK JUNIOR.

Amsterdam, Peter Schenck [, 1710?].

Map, 19¼″ high plus margins, colored.

Atlantes C & M 10 has as number (88) in the *Nieuwe Atlas* dated
(1707-1741).

[1714]

AA, PIETER VAN DER, 1659-1733.

AMERICA IN PRAECIPUAS IPSIUS PARTES. . . . L'AMERIQUE SELON
LES NOUVELLES OBSERVATIONS.

Leiden, Pieter van der Aa [, 1714].

Map, 18½″ high plus title and margins, colored in outline in map
but full in cartouche which depicts cooking and eating of human
limbs.

Atlantes Aa 2 lists as number (92) and dates (1714).

See PLATE 35

[1714]§

JOUTEL, HENRY, 1640-1735.

A NEW MAP OF THE COUNTRY OF LOUISIANA.

[London, 1714.]

Map, 14¼″ high plus margins, colored.

Facsimile of map cited in Phillips, *Maps,* page 563, which notes a
1684 edition by Jean Baptiste Louis Franquelin, and page 566, which
notes this map being published in *The Journal of the Last Voyage . . .*

M. de la Salle in London in 1714. Phillips notes that the inset panel
shows a view of Niagara Falls.

[1715?]

KEULEN, JOHANNES VAN, 1654-1715.

PAS-KAART VANDE ZEE KUSTEN INDE BOGHT VAN NIEW ENGE-
LAND.

Amsterdam, Johannes van Keulen [, 1715?].

Atlantes, IV, 385, has as number [136] among the charts.

Presented to Maine State Museum.

1715

MOLL, HERMAN, d. 1732.

A NEW AND EXACT MAP OF THE DOMINIONS OF THE KING . . .
NORTH AMERICA.

London, Herman Moll, 1715.

Map, 39¾″ high plus margins, colored in outline in map but full
in cartouche and in engraved scene of beaver at Niagara.

This is the first issue of the map as described by Henry N. Stevens in
the headnote to Phillips 3469, there described as very rare in this
state. Also listed as state A in Cumming, *Southeast,* 158.

[1715?]

MOLL, HERMAN, d. 1732.

TO THE RIGHT HONOURABLE JOHN LORD SOMMERS. . . . THIS
MAP OF NORTH AMERICA.

London, Herman Moll and Thomas Bowles and by Philip Overton [, 1715?].

Map, 22½″ high plus margins, colored.

Marshall, *Clements,* II, 97, notes publication in *World Described* as number 7, and also notes ten inset maps of harbors. In addition there is a depiction of cod-fishing and drying under the elegant cartouche.

Presented to Maine State Museum.

1716

CHURCH, BENJAMIN, 1639-1718.

ENTERTAINING PASSAGES RELATING TO KING PHILIP'S WAR.

Boston, Bartholomew Green, 1716.

Quarto, 7⅝″ high, bound in modern full leather, gold-tooled.

Shipton-Mooney 1800 assigns authorship to Church over T.C. on title page on basis of "LOC card," and reproduces in Early American Imprints.

1716

HOMANN, JOHANN BAPTIST, 1663-1724.

GROSSER ATLAS.

Nuremberg, Johann Ernst Adelbulner for "Auctioris," 1716.

Folio, 20½″ high, bound in contemporary quarter vellum.

Contains 126 colored maps and plates listed in the Register. LeGear lists as 5966 with 118 maps dated 1702 through 1748 which she compared with Johann Georg Mager, *Geographischer Buchersaal,* I, 666-703. Phillips 586 calls for 148 maps for the 1737 edition with dates from 1710 through 1775. Maps relating to America are title page; 12, Planiglobii; 16, America; and 17, Regni Mexicani, which shows North America from 46° north to 7° north and from Trinidad to Lower California. Donald Cresswell writes that "this early edition of this atlas contains maps of uncommon beauty. The Homann family issued many editions of its atlases for the next eight decades. The cartouches and other ornaments were etched on the copper plates while the maps were line engraved. The etched lines of the ornaments faded due to the wear of subsequent editions, but this copy has beautiful strong lines throughout each map and exquisite color to match. A beautiful example of Homann's work."

[1716]

HOMANN, JOHANN BAPTIST, 1663-1724.

SPHÆRARUM ARTIFICIALIUM TYPICA REPRAESENTATIO.

Nuremberg, Johann Baptist Homann [, 1716].

Plate, 19″ high plus margins, showing celestial, terrestrial, and armillary globes, colored.

LeGear 5966 describes Homann's *Grosser Atlas* of 1716, and this plate is number [2]. It does not appear in her listings for his *Neuer Atlas* of 1705-1773, 5959, nor of 1707, 5960.   *See* PLATE 36

1717

FER, NICOLAS DE, 1646-1720.

INTRODUCTION A LA GEOGRAPHIE. . . . SECONDE EDITION.

Paris, Guillaume Danet, 1717.

Twelvemo, 7½″ high, bound in contemporary full leather, gold-tooled.

Engraved title page and folding frontispiece world maps portray California as an island, as does the folding map of the Western Hemisphere at page 148. There are three other folding maps, of Europe, Asia, and Africa.

1717 §

SOUTHACK, CYPRIAN, 1662-1745.

[A NEW CHART OF THE ENGLISH EMPIRE IN NORTH AMERICA.]

Boston, Francis Dewing, 1717.

Map, 27½″ high, in four sheets, plus margins, uncolored.

Facsimile published by the John Carter Brown Library, second printing, 1961. This is the first engraved map printed in the present-day United States. Wheat & Brun 44-46 discuss states.

1718

WELLS, EDWARD, 1667-1727.

A NEW SETT OF MAPS BOTH OF ANTIENT AND PRESENT GEOGRAPHY.

London, William Churchill, 1718.

Folio, 17″ high, oblong, bound in contemporary half leather.

Contains forty-one maps called for in Phillips 3479. Those relating to America are numbers 1; 2; 39, North America; 40, South America; and 41, as listed in the Catalogue. This atlas has an unusual format with ancient and modern maps side by side.

[1719]

CHATELAIN, HENRY ABRAHAM, 1684-1743.

CARTE DE LA NOUVELLE FRANCE . . . POUR L'ETABLISSEMENT DE LA COMPAGNIE. . . .

[Amsterdam, 1719.]

Map, 19½″ high plus margins, colored.

Atlantes Cha 7 has as number (7) of the *Atlas Historique* of [1719].

[1719?]

MOLL, HERMAN, d. 1732.

A NEW AND CORRECT MAP OF THE WORLD.

London, John Bowles, Thomas Bowles, Philip Overton, and John King [, 1719?].

Map, 22¼″ high plus margins, colored in outline in map and full in cartouche.

Marshall, *Clements,* II, 95, notes publication in *World Described* of 1719 as number 1.

[1720]

KOEHLER, JOHAN DAVID, 1684-1755.

DESCRIPTIO ORBIS ANTIQUI.

Nuremberg, Christoph Weigel [, 1720].

Folio, 15¼″ high, bound in contemporary full leather, blind-tooled.

Contains the forty-four maps called for in title, colored, none of which relates to America except number 43. Tooley's dictionary dates 1720 while Phillips 30 and 31 date [1720?].

1602 ORTELIUS. THEATRO. Engraved and colored title page is of the rare first Spanish edition of his *Theatrum* which also has this portrait of Ortelius.

PLATE 17

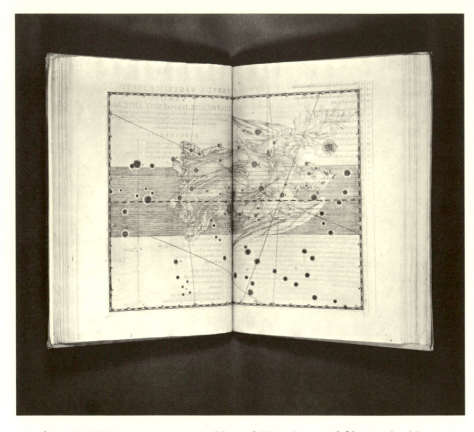

1603 BAYER. URANOMETRIA. Plate of Virgo is one of fifty-one in this rare star-atlas by the first astronomer to indicate the magnitude of stars by use of the Greek alphabet.

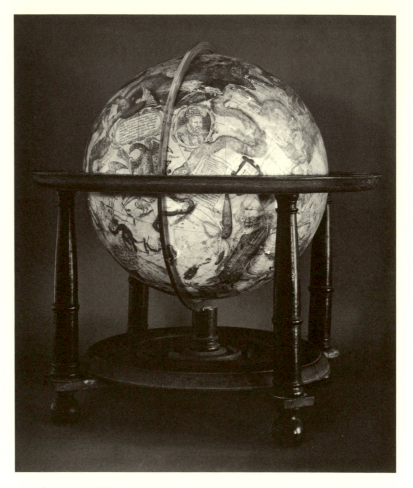

1603 BLAEU. CELESTIAL GLOBE. The globe on a Dutch base has a portrait of Tycho Brahe, teacher of Blaeu.

PLATE 18

TRAICTE'
DE LA SPHERE

DV MONDE, DIVISE'
EN QVATRE LIVRES, AVS-
quels est adiousté le cinquiesme
de l'vsage d'icelle.

Par le sieur Boulenger, lecteur du Roy.

A PARIS   M. DC.XX.
Et ce Vendent   les Spheres Chez
MELCHIOR TAVERNIER Graueur et Imprimeur
du ROY. en ses Tailles   Doulces Demeurant
sur le pont Marchant,   Auec Priuilege du Roy.
Et Chez Iean   Moreau rue S.t Iaques

A PARIS. Chez Iean Moreau, rue S. Iacques
à l'enseigne de la Croix Blanche. 1620.
Auec Priuilege du Roy.

---

yauoit quelque vtilité au téps passé d'en-
tendre cecy, pource que auant que l'art
fut determiné selon le mouuement du
Soleil, les Poëtes historiens, autheurs de
l'agriculture, definissoient les saisons de
l'annee, les mutations de l'air, par le leuer
& coucher des estoiles, comme il se voit
dãs Virgile, Ouide, Columelle, & autres.

DES ECLIPSES.

LEs Phænomenes qui plus inci-
tent à l'admiration, sont les eclipses
qui sont du Soleil & de la Lune.

DE L'ECLIPSE DV
soleil.

L'Eclipse du Soleil, est vn auer-
sion des rayons du Soleil de
dessus nous, par l'interposition de
la Lune entre le Soleil, & nostre
veuë.

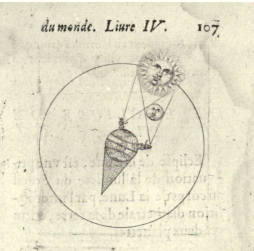

Car la Lune estant vn corps opaque,
se mettant entre le Soleil & nous, nous
priue de la lumiere du Soleil, ce qui ne
se fait iamais qu'en la nouuelle Lune, qui
est quand le Soleil, la Lune, & nos yeux
sont en vne mesme ligne droitte. Secon-
dement faut noter que les eclipses du
Soleil sont particulieres. C'est à dire que
le Soleil en mesme temps n'est pas ob-
scurcy par tout. Tiercement que les
eclipses du Soleil commencent au cou-

H ij

1620   BOULENGER. SPHERE. Title page shows an armillary sphere as part of an advertisement, and the pages
describe and illustrate a solar eclipse. Only one other copy of this treatise is known in America.

PLATE 19

1636 **JANSSON.** AMERICA. One of the most interesting maps of North America of this period, in some respects better than Blaeu's work, it shows California as an island.

PLATE 20

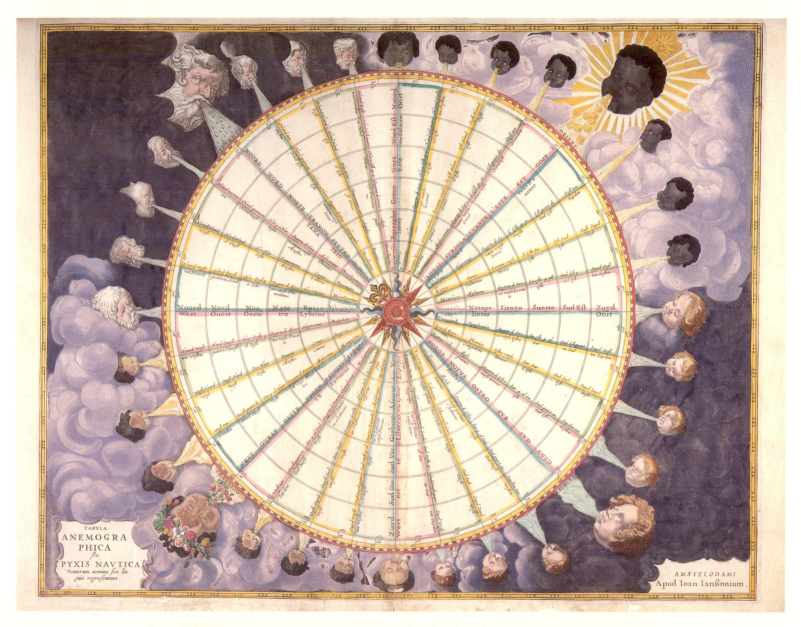

1650 JANSSON. TABULA. Rare compass rose and study of winds is an interesting engraving with contemporary color. It shows Africans in the east and Asiatics in the west.

PLATE 21

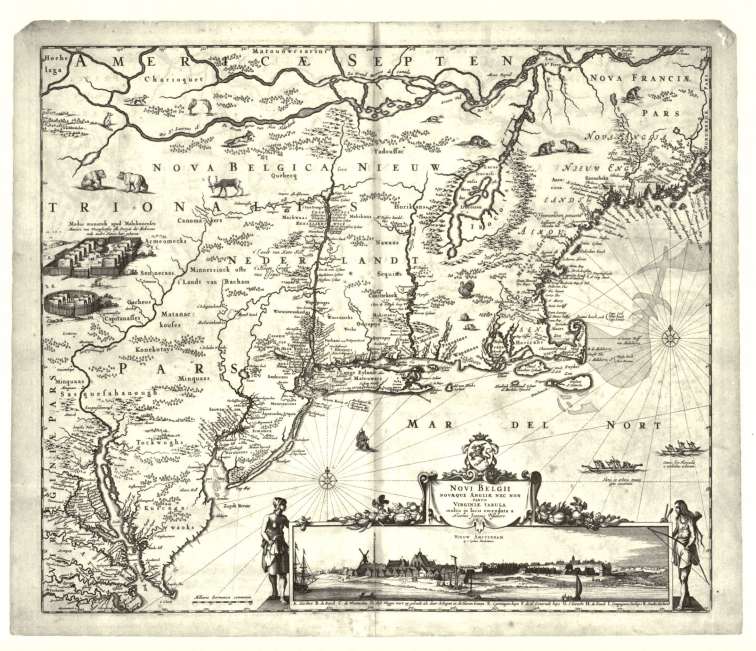

1650 VISSCHER. NOVI BELGII. Map of North America from the Chesapeake to the Penobscot is a very strong impression, among the first off the plate. Native American animals as beaver, bear, deer, and turkey are here along with Indian villages and New Amsterdam.

PLATE 22

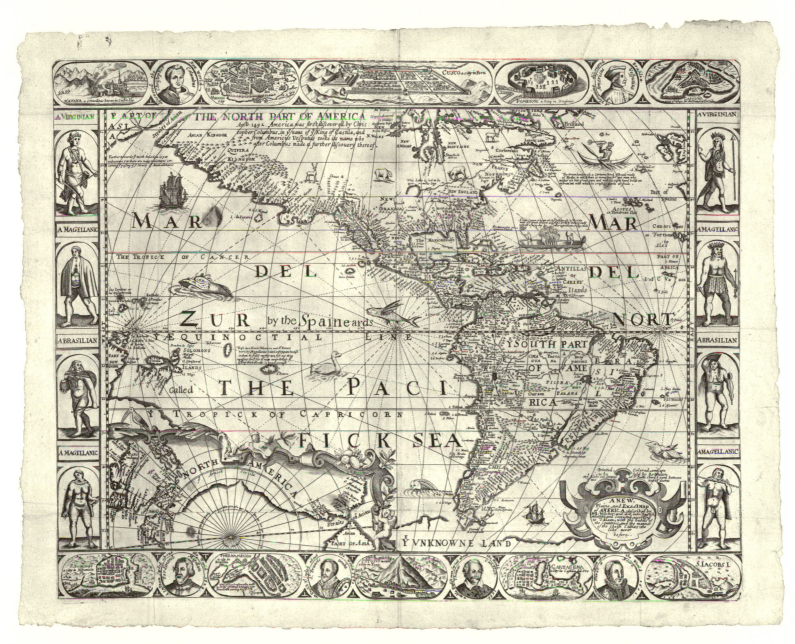

1650 WALTON. AMERICA. One of the most decorative English maps of America uses the *carte de figure* format. Here are town
views and portraits of explorers and of natives, including an Eskimo in a kayak and Florida Indians in a dugout canoe.

PLATE 23

1656   SANSON. CANADA. An important Great Lakes map with contemporary outline color and
generous margins, the possibility of a northwest passage is left open.

PLATE 24

1662   BLAEU. ATLAS. This eleven-volume set of six hundred maps is the foremost Dutch atlas of that century, and this copy is sumptuous in its gold-tooled vellum binding. The map of maritime Canada and New England is typical in its extraordinary brightness and exquisite coloring.

PLATE 25

1667 GOOS. ATLAS. All of the major Goos maps of America are in superlative original color in this forty-one-map atlas. The engraved title page has the instruments of map-makers and a battle at sea.

PLATE 26

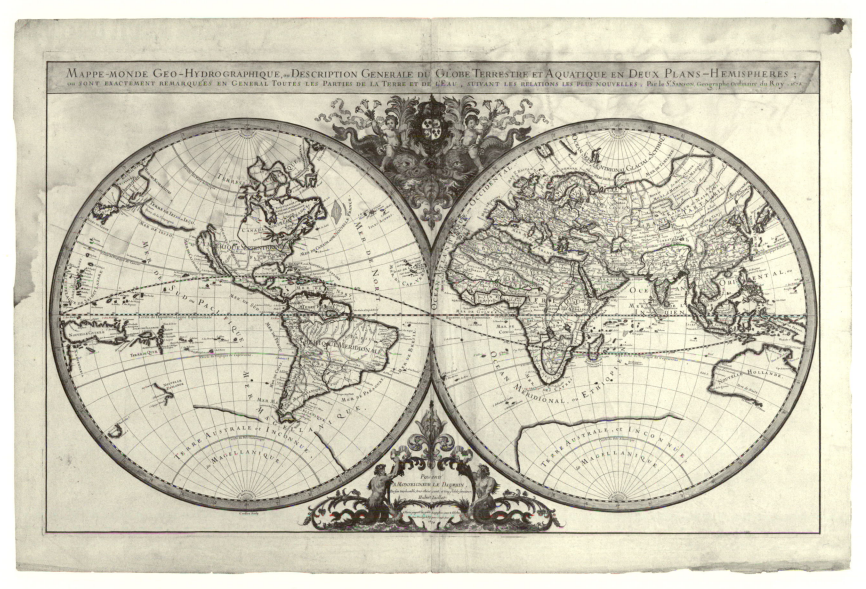

1674 SANSON. MAPPE-MONDE. The first state of the eight versions of this popular large map initially published separately by Jaillot, the hemispheres are on an enlarged scale and the decoration is limited to two central cartouches.

PLATE 27

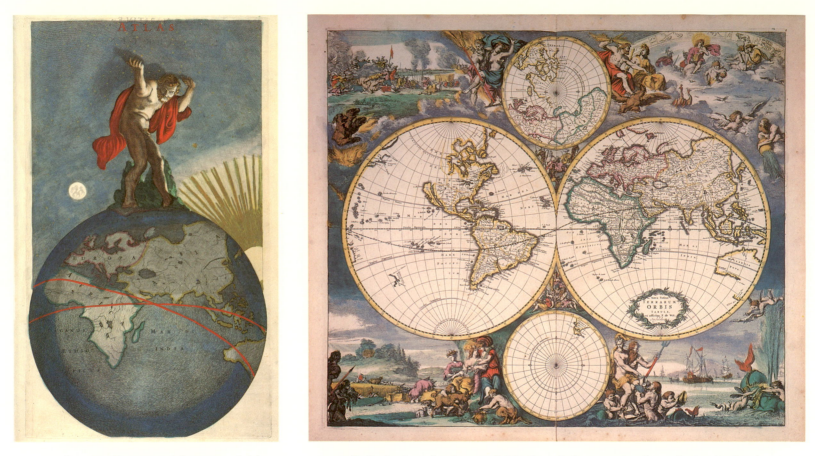

1675   WIT. ATLAS. The engraved title page appears at the beginning of each part of this, the only known example combining land and sea atlases in one volume. The world map is from the maritime atlas and shows the four elements of earth, fire, air, and water.

PLATE 28

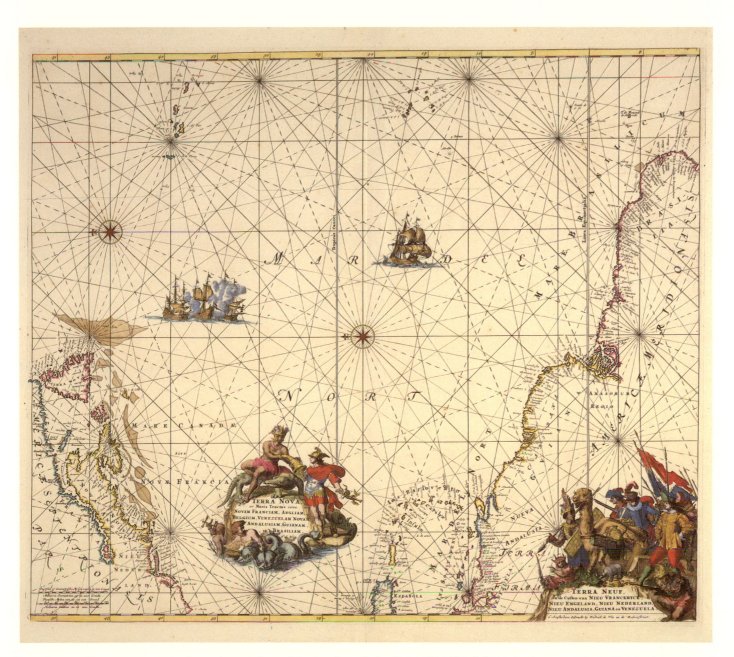

1675 **WIT.** TERRA NOVA. Attractive sea chart of the area from Labrador to Brazil and from the Azores to Cape Charles has cartouches with Latin and Dutch texts. Its essential features were being copied even after three-quarters of a century had passed.

PLATE 29

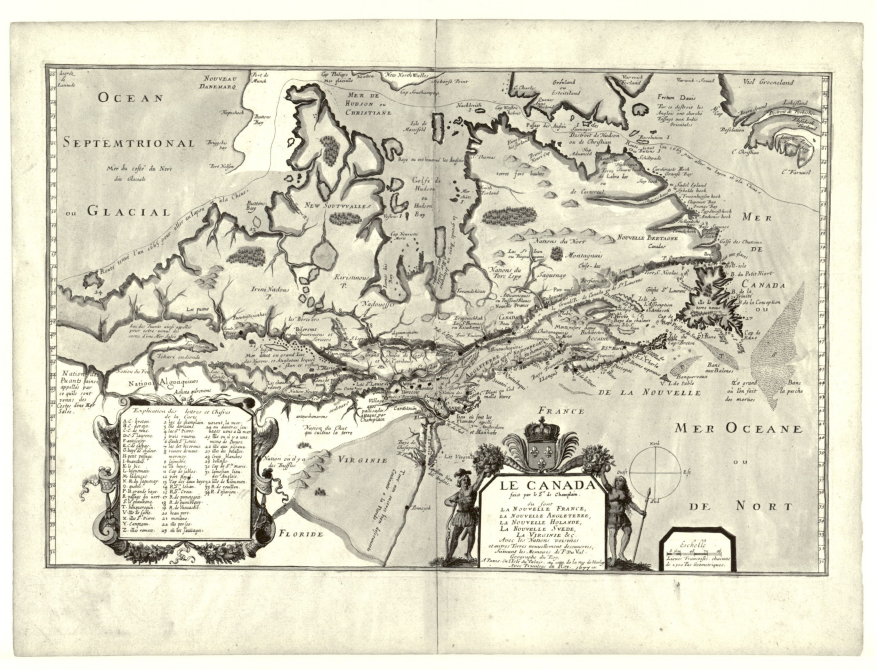

1677 DU VAL. CANADA. The fifth state of this unusual map of Canada reflects no signficant change in the land delineation for sixty years, and it kept alive the hope for perhaps two northwest passages long into a period when all cartographers and most of their public knew better.

PLATE 30

1692 SANSON. AMERIQUE. This map of North America was the predominant one for the latter half of the seventeenth century. The cartouches depict Indians, birds, and strange animals, and the map shows the settlements of the Europeans.

PLATE 31

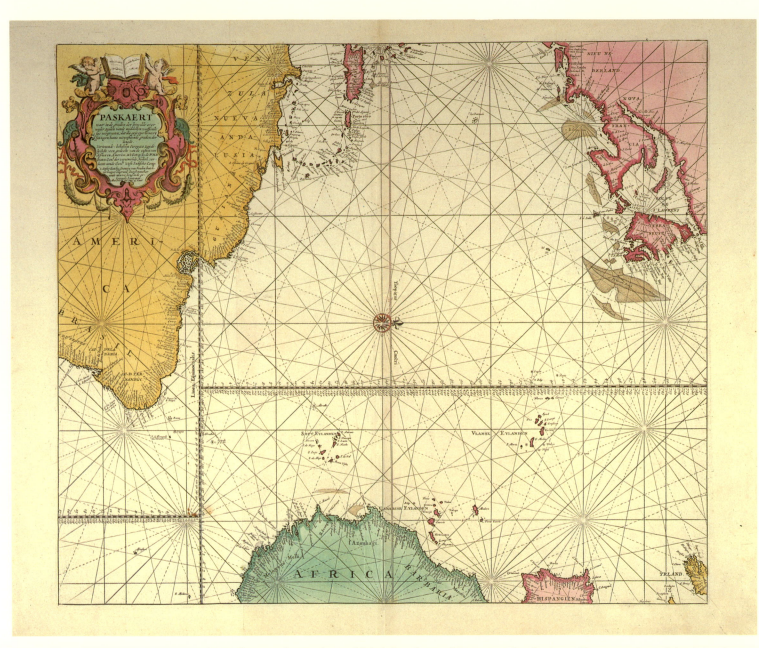

1695 KEULEN. PASKAERT. A superb copy of a sea-chart with bright colors and large margins, it gives a European view of the Atlantic Ocean oriented to the west and with a series of strong rhumb lines emanating from a circle of compass roses.

PLATE 32

1720

NEAL, DANIEL.

A NEW MAP OF NEW ENGLAND.

London, James Clark, R. Ford, and R. Cruttendon, 1720.

Map, 9″ high plus margins, closely trimmed, colored.

Phillips, *Maps,* page 468, has as the frontispiece for Neal's *History of New England* of London that year. Contains inset maps of Eastern Canada and of Boston Harbor. Sabin 52140 contains critical comments on the book.

[1720?]

SCHERER, HEINRICH, 1628-1704.

NAVIGATIONES PRÆCIPUÆ EUROPÆORUM AD EXTERAS NATIONES.

[Munich, 1720?]

Map, 8¾″ high plus margins, colored in outline in map but full elsewhere.

Major routes of sea travel are shown and in each corner is a ship with stern engraved with arms of nations. Phillips 538a, number [1], has corners representing the four continents.

1720

SENEX, JOHN, d. 1740.

A NEW MAP OF LONDON . . . REVISED BY JNO. SENEX. . . . S. PARKER DELIN. ET SCULPT.

London, John Senex, 1720.

Map, 19¾″ high plus margins, closely trimmed especially at top, colored.

[1721]

SENEX, JOHN, d. 1740.

A DRAFT OF THE GOLDEN & ADJACENT ISLANDS WITH PART OF THE ISTHMUS OF DARIEN [title of upper map].

A NEW MAP OF THE ISTHMUS OF DARIEN IN AMERICA, THE BAY OF PANAMA [title of lower map].

[London, Daniel Browne, 1721.]

Map, 23½″ high plus margins, both maps colored in outline but cartouches uncolored.

Phillips, *Maps,* page 657, has this as appearing in *New General Atlas* of 1721, facing page 254. Lower map shows Central America from below the seventh to above the fourteenth parallels north.

1721

SENEX, JOHN, d. 1740.

A NEW GENERAL ATLAS.

London, Daniel Browne, Thomas Taylor, John Darby, John Senex, William Taylor, Joseph Smith, Andrew Johnston, William Bray, and Edward Symon, 1721.

Folio, 21½″ high, bound in contemporary full leather, gold-tooled.

Contains thirty-three maps called for in binder's direction at Preface, colored in outline. Those relating to America are numbers 1; 2; 24, Asia where northwest America appears; 28; 29; 30; 31; 32; and 33. Phillips 563 points out that the map of Louisiana is dedicated to William Law. Sabin has at 79124 where the maps are described as "immense."

SENEX, JOHN, d. 1740.

A NEW MAP OF AMERICA FROM THE LATEST OBSERVATIONS REVIS'D BY. . . .

[London, 1721.]

Map, 19″ high plus margins, colored in outline in map but full in cartouche in which Indians are depicted in battle and cooking and consuming the losers.

Phillips 563 lists as number [29] in the *New General Atlas* of 1721.

See PLATE 37

[1721]

SENEX, JOHN, d. 1740.

A NEW MAP OF FRANCE AGREEABLE TO THE OBSERVATIONS.

[London,] John Senex [, 1721].

Map, 17¼″ high plus margins, colored.

Phillips 563 describes the *New General Atlas* of 1721 with thirty-four maps, nearly all with the word New in the title. Tooley discusses Senex in his *Maps and Mapmakers* at page 55.

[1721]

SENEX, JOHN, d. 1740.

[A NEW MAP OF THE ENGLISH EMPIRE IN THE OCEAN OF AMERICA, OR] WEST INDIES . . . I. HARRIS SCULP.

[London, Daniel Browne, 1721.]

Map, 19⅞″ high overall, trimmed with loss of text on three sides including most of title.

Phillips, *Maps,* page 1054, has full title of this map which appeared in *New General Atlas* of 1721, opposite page 186.

[1721?]

SENEX, JOHN, d. 1740.

A NEW MAP OF THE WORLD.

[London, 1721?]

Map, 16½″ high plus margins, colored in outline in maps but full in cartouche and decorative elements.

Phillips 563 describes a 1721 atlas of Senex with "[1] A new map of the world."

1722

L'ISLE, GUILLAUME DE, 1675-1726.

CARTE DE L'ISLE DE SAINT DOMINGUE.

Amsterdam, Johannes Covens and Cornelis Mortier, 1722.

Map, 18¼″ high plus title, "Insulæ S. Dominicæ Tabula Accuratissima," and margins, colored in outline in map but full in cartouche.

Atlantes C & M 4 has as number 49 in *Atlas Nouveau* of 1730.

1722

L'ISLE, GUILLAUME DE, 1675-1726.

CARTE DU MEXIQUE ET DE LA FLORIDE.

Amsterdam, Johannes Covens and Cornelis Mortier, 1722.

Map, 18¼″ high plus title, "Tabula Geographica Mexicæ et Floridæ &c," and margins, colored with "I. Stemmers Senior Sculp." below title cartouche.

Atlantes C & M 3 has as number 7, in a variant title, in the first of the De L'Isle atlases, the 1730 *Atlas Nouveau*. This map shows North America to the forty-fifth parallel, from Newfoundland Banks to California.

1723

MOLL, HERMAN, d. 1732.

THE COMPLEAT GEOGRAPHER. . . . FOURTH EDITION [two parts in one volume].

London, John Knapton, R. Knaplock, J. Wyat, John and B. Sprint, John Darby, D. Midwinter, E. Bell, A. Bettesworth, William Taylor, William and J. Innys, R. Robinson, J. Osborne, Francis Fayram, John Pemberton, J. Hooke, Charles Rivington, F. Clay, Edward Symon, J. Batley, J. Nix, and T. Combes, 1723.

Quarto, 13¼″ high, bound in contemporary full leather, blind- and gold-tooled.

Contains forty-five maps. Phillips 566 lists thirteen maps relating to America, at pages i and liii in Part One and 3, 106, 189, 194, 195, 214, 237, 244, 258, 265, and 272 in Part Two, including map of the Philippines at 106 which this catalogue does not include as relating to America. Sabin 49905 lists this among other editions.

1723

VEGA, GARCILASSO DE LA.

LA FLORIDA DEL INCA.

Madrid, Officina Real for Nicolas Rodriguez Franco, 1723.

Quarto, 11½″ high, bound in modern half leather, blind- and gold-tooled.

Sabin 98745 lists this among other editions.

1725

WELLS, EDWARD, 1667-1727.

THE YOUNG GENTLEMAN'S ASTRONOMY. . . . THIRD EDITION.

London, James and John Knapton, 1725.

Octavo, 7½″ high, bound in contemporary full leather, blind- and gold-tooled.

Contains twenty engraved plates, some folding.

[1727-1780]

ANVILLE, JEAN BAPTISTE BOURGUIGNON D', 1697-1782.

[ATLAS GENERAL.]

[Paris, 1727-1780.]

Folio, 22″ high, bound in contemporary half-leather, gold-tooled.

A collection of forty-two maps, some colored in outline, without a title page but with manuscript list which differs from that listed by Phillips at 571:

MS List	Phillips
2	[1]
not present	1
3-4	2
5-6	3
7-8	4
14-15	5

MS List	Phillips
16-17	6
18-19	7
28	8
29	9
35	10
36	11
41-42	12
43	13
9-10	14
11-12	15
13	16
not present	17
21	18
24	19
25	20
26-27	21
20	22
23	23
33	24
34	25
not present	26
not present	27
30-31	28
not present	29
not present	30
32	31
37-38	32
39	33
44	34
not present	35-51
22, Phonicie	not present

Of those fifty-one maps listed by Phillips and present here, the following Phillips numbers relate to America: 1, 2, 10, 11, 12, 13, 32, 33, and 34.

1728

CUTLER, NATHANIEL.

A GENERAL COASTING PILOT [title page of volume two of Senex Atlas of 1728].

London, James and John Knapton, William and John Innys [, etc.], 1728.

See SENEX, ATLAS 1728 and Phillips 3298.

[1728?]

HOMANN, JOHANN BAPTIST, 1663-1724.

TOTIUS AMERICAE SEPTENTRIONALIS ET MERIDIONALIS NOVISSIMA REPRÆSENTATIO.

Nuremberg [, Johann Baptist Homann, 1728?].

Map, 19¼″ high plus margins, closely trimmed, colored in map but cartouches uncolored.

Phillips 3474 has as number [20] in the *Neuer Atlas* of 1712 [-1730] and at 539 as number 13 in the *Atlas Novus* of [1702-1750]. Also see Homann listings at 556, 577, and 586. Wear to the cartouches suggests a later printing of this map.

1728

SENEX, JOHN, d. 1740.

ATLAS MARITIMUS & COMMERCIALIS; OR, A GENERAL VIEW OF THE WORLD [in two parts in one volume].

London, James and John Knapton, William and John Innys, John Darby, Arthur Bettesworth, John Osborn and Thomas Longman, John Senex, Edward Symon, Andrew Johnston, and "the Executors of William Taylor deceas'd," 1728.

Folio, 22″ high, bound in modern half leather, blind- and gold-tooled on spine.

The fifty-four sea-charts are bound at the end of the volume following Cutler's *Coasting Pilot* of 1728. The charts relating to America are listed in Phillips 3298 as numbers 2, 21, 40, 41, 42, 43, 44, 45, 46, 47, 48, 49, 50, 51, and 52, to which should be added chart number 1.

[1729?]

MOLL, HERMAN, d. 1732.

NEW ENGLAND, NEW YORK, NEW JERSEY AND PENSILVANIA.

London, Herman Moll [, 1729?].

Map, 8″ high plus margins and folios, colored in outline.

Marshall, *Clements,* II, 94, dates [1730] but 96 dates to *Atlas Geographus* of 1717. It is the earliest postal map of the present-day United States.

See PLATE 38

[1729?]

MOLL, HERMAN, d. 1732.

A PLAN OF PORT ROYAL HARBOUR IN CAROLINA.

[London,] Herman Moll [, 1729?].

Map, 7¾″ high plus margins, colored.

Phillips 574 notes publication in the *Atlas Minor* of 1729 as number [48]. Marshall, *Clements,* II, 97, notes publication in [1736] edition as number 52.

[1729?]

MOLL, HERMAN, d. 1732.

THE SCOTS SETTLEMENT IN AMERICA CALLE'D NEW CALEDONIA. A.D. 1699.

[London,] Herman Moll [, 1729?].

Map, 9¾″ high plus margins and binder's linen thread, colored in outline.

Phillips 574 notes publication in the *Atlas Minor* of 1729 as number [53]. Marshall, *Clements,* II, 97, notes publication in [1736] edition as number 60.

[1730?]

AA, PIETER VAN DER, 1659-1733.

L'ITALIE SUIVANT LES NOUVELLES OBSERVATIONS.

Leyden, Pieter van der Aa [, 1730?].

Map, 8¾″ high plus margins, uncolored.

On verso written in pencil is "Voyage le chevalier de Chastellux en Amerique Paris 1796." *La Galerie* of [1729] is described at Phillips 3485 where Italy is found at Volume Twenty-seven and also in *Atlantes* Aa 9.

[1730?]

HOMANN, Johann Baptist, 1663-1724.

REGNI MEXICANI SEU NOVÆ HISPANIÆ, LUDOVICIANÆ, N. ANGLIÆ. . . .

Nuremberg [, 1730?].

Map, 18⅞″ high plus margins, colored.

Phillips 586 has as number [147] in the *Grosser Atlas* of 1737. It is based on De l'Isle's 1718 map of Louisiana.

[1730?]

HOMANN, Johann Baptist, 1663-1724.

PLANIGLOBII TERRESTRIS CUM UTROQ HEMISPHÆRO CÆLESTI.

Nuremberg, Johann Baptist Homann [, 1730?].

Map, 18¾″ high plus margins, colored.

Phillips 539 describes the *Atlas Novus* which has number 1, Planiglobii Terrestris.   *See* PLATE 40

[1730?]

L'ISLE, Guillaume de, 1675-1726.

L'AMERIQUE SEPTENTRIONALE [cartouche].

AMERICA SEPTENTRIONALIS [top margin].

Amsterdam, Johannes Covens and Cornelis Mortier [, 1730?].

Map, 17¾″ high plus title and margins, colored.

Phillips, *Maps*, page 569, dates [1733?] from the *Atlas Nouveau* published [1741?] by Johannes Covens and Cornelis Mortier, as number 29 in Volume Two. *Atlantes* C & M 3 has as number 3 and dates 1730.

[1730]

L'ISLE, Guillaume de, 1675-1726.

AMERICA MERIDIONALIS IN SUAS PRAECIPUAS PARTES [upper title].

L'AMERIQUE MERIDIONALE DRESSÉE SUR LES OBSERVATIONS [cartouche title].

Amsterdam, Johannes Covens and Cornelis Mortier [, 1730].

Map, 18″ high plus title and margins, colored in outline in map but uncolored in cartouche.

Atlantes C & M 3 has as number 4 in the *Atlas Nouveau* of 1730.

[1730]

L'ISLE, Guillaume de, 1675-1726.

TABULA GEOGRAPHICA PARAGAIÆ, CHILIS, FRETI A MAGELLA-NICI [upper title].

CARTE DU PARAGUAY, DU CHILI, DU DETROIT DE MAGELLAN [cartouche title].

Amsterdam, Johannes Covens and Cornelis Mortier [, 1730].

Map, 19⅛″ high plus title and margins, colored in outline in map but uncolored in cartouche.

Phillips 3442 lists this edition of *Atlas Nouveau* under Covens & Mortier and dates [1683-1761]. This is number 95 in Volume Nine there. In *Atlantes* C & M 3, the 1730 *Atlas Nouveau*, it appears as number 10 in a variant short title without articles. In C & M 4, number 52, the definite article is used, and C & M 7, number 116 has no articles. C & M 8, dated (after 1757) has full titles where this is number 121.

L'ISLE, GUILLAUME DE, 1675-1726.

TABULA GEOGRAPHICA PERUAE, BRASILIAE & AMAZONUM RE-
GIONIS [upper title].

CARTE DE LA TERRE FERME DU PEROU, DU BRESIL ET DU PAYS
DES AMAZONES [cartouche title].

Amsterdam, Johannes Covens and Cornelis Mortier [, 1730].

Map, 18¾″ high plus title and margins, colored in outline in map
but uncolored in cartouche.

Phillips 3448 lists this edition of *Atlas Nouveau* under Covens &
Mortier and dates [1683-1761]. This is number 81 in Volume Nine
there. In *Atlantes* C & M 3, the 1730 *Atlas Nouveau*, it appears as
number 9 in a variant short title using the definite articles not the
possessives, as at C & M 4 at number 51. C & M 7, number 115, has
without articles, and C & M 8, dated (after 1757), has full titles
where this is number 120.

[1730?]

L'ISLE, GUILLAUME DE, 1675-1726.

CARTE DU CANADA OU DE LA NOUVELLE FRANCE ET DES DE-
COUVERTES.

Amsterdam, Johannes Covens and Cornelis Mortier [, 1730?].

Map, 19¼″ high plus margins, colored in outline in map but uncolored in cartouche.

Atlantes C & M 2 has as number 5 in the *Atlas Nouveau* of 1730, "the
earliest we know of for a Covens & Mortier reissue of De l'Isle atlas."

C & M 4 has as number 46 with fuller title. Marshall, *Clements*, I,
528, dates [1696?] but at *Atlantes* Mor 1 the title differs.

[1730]

SEUTTER, GEORGE MATTHAUS, 1678-1757.

ATLAS HISTORIQUE TOME I [-II, binder's title].

Augsburg, George Matthaus Seutter [, 1730].

Slipcases, 4¼″ high, of contemporary paper with engraved covers
in two contemporary full leather gold-tooled volume boxes.

Contains twenty-four maps, 7¾″ high plus margins, colored. None
of the maps relates to America. Although the slipcase title of one is
"Nova Hispaniæ," the map is of Spain and Portugal. None of the
seven items listed for Seutter by Phillips and LeGear describes this
atlas. Cresswell describes as "a beautiful, baroque presentation of a
collection of maps, an elegant assembly."

[1730?]

SEUTTER, GEORGE MATTHAUS, 1678-1757.

NOVUS ORBIS SIVE AMERICA MERIDIONALIS ET SEPTENTRIO-
NALIS.

Augsburg, George Matthaus Seutter [, 1730?].

Map, 19½″ high plus margins, closely trimmed, colored in map
but cartouches uncolored.

Phillips 583 has as number 8 in *Grosser Atlas* of [1734?], and 593
has as number 6 in *Atlas Novus* of [1740?].

[1730]§

SEUTTER, GEORGE MATTHAUS, 1678-1757.

RECENS EDITA TOTIUS NOVI BELGII IN AMERICA SEPTENTRIO-NALI.

Augsburg, George Matthaus Seutter [, 1730].

Map, 18½" high plus margins, colored.

A facsimile lithographed on two sheets joined. See *Map Collectors' Circle,* Number 24, for the study, "New Light on the Jansson-Visscher Maps," at number 25, which describes this second state. Marshall, *Clements,* II, 368, dates [1730]. Within a handsome cartouche is a view of the city of New York.

[1731?]

CUSHEE, RICHARD, 1708-1732.

A NEW GLOBE OF THE EARTH.

[London?,] Richard Cushee [, 1731?].

Globe, 2¾" diameter, in spherical case lined with celestial map.

Yonge describes at page 22 a globe of "Cashee" dated 1731, "miniature, free ball in black-leather, hinged spherical case which is lined with a celestial map," but gives as diameter 51 cm.

1733

LEMAU DE LA JAISSE.

CARTE GENERALE DE LA MONARCHIE FRANÇOISE.

[Paris], Lemau de la Jaisse, 1733.

Folio, 19¾" high, bound in contemporary full leather, gold-stamped.

Contains many plans of fortifications, walled towns, and harbors, none of which relates to America.

1733

POPPLE, HENRY, d. 1743.

A MAP OF THE BRITISH EMPIRE IN AMERICA.

London, S. Harding and William Henry Toms, 1733.

Folio, 21" high, bound in contemporary quarter leather.

Contains twenty plates not colored with rare contents leaf and the one-sheet map. Sabin 64140 describes as having "views of Niagara Falls, New York, Quebec, etc." Stevens termed it the "finest and largest map of North America engraved up to this time."

See PLATE 39

1733

POPPLE, HENRY, d. 1743.

A MAP OF THE BRITISH EMPIRE IN AMERICA.

[London,] S. Harding and William Henry Toms, 1733.

Folio, 19⅞" high plus full-size map engraved in twenty sheets of approximate size, colored.

See Sabin 64140 and POPPLE 1733 above.

Presented to the Philadelphia Museum of Art.

1734

DU SAUZET, HENRI.

ATLAS DE POCHE.

Amsterdam, Henri du Sauzet, 1734.

Octavo, 8⅝″ high, bound in contemporary half vellum, gold-stamped.

The Index calls for forty maps of which these present relate to America: 5, Asia; 6, Africa; 7, North America; and 8, South America. The first three maps listed in Index are missing. The thirty-seven remaining are colored in outline. Listed in *Atlantes* as Sau 2 and in Phillips as 584a but in both cases describing two later European maps not present in this edition.

1734

HOCKER, JOHANN LUDWIG.

. . . ERD-UND HIMMELS-KUGEL.

Nuremberg, Peter Conrad Monath, 1734.

Quarto, 8″ high, bound in contemporary half vellum.

Contains engraved frontispiece and ten plates of globes of which plates I, III, and IV relate to America. Stevenson lists this in Volume Two, page 232, of his study of terrestrial and celestial globes where he gives the longer title in a variant form.

[1734?]

POPPLE, HENRY, d. 1743.

A MAP OF THE BRITISH EMPIRE IN AMERICA . . . BY . . . [cartouche title].

CARTE PARTICULIERE DE L'AMERIQUE SEPTENTRIONALE [top margin title].

Amsterdam, Johannes Covens and Cornelis Mortier [, 1734?].

Map, 19¼″ high plus title and margins, closely trimmed, colored in outline in map but uncolored in cartouche.

This is one of the copies about which Tooley writes on page 55 in *Maps*. A variant title appears at *Atlantes,* II, 82, numbers 104 through 107 of C & M 11, *Nieuwe Atlas* of (1705-1759). Another similar title is at C & M 7, number 101. This is a copy of the key map to the larger twenty-one-sheet map, and is the second edition. The first edition is here at 1733. Phillips, *Maps,* pages 569 and 570, lists.

[1734?]

SEUTTER, GEORGE MATTHAUS, 1678-1757.

DIVERSI GLOBI TERR-AQUEI STATIONE VARIANTE.

Augsburg, George Matthaus Seutter [, 1734?].

Map, 19¾″ high plus margins, colored.

Phillips 583 is dated [1734?] and has this map as number 3.

[1736?]

MOLL, HERMAN, d. 1732.

NEW FOUND LAND ST. LAURENCE BAY, THE FISHING BANKS.

London, Herman Moll [, 1736?].

Map, 7⅞″ high plus margins, uncolored.

Marshall, *Clements,* II, 96, has as number 47 in *Atlas Minor* of [1736]. Phillips 574 has as number [57] "... Laurens bay ... 1729." This was changed along with other things for Phillips 578, [1732?], number 47.

[1737?]

ENGLISH PILOT.

A CHART OF THE SEA COAST OF NEW FOUND LAND, NEW SCOT-
LAND . . . MARYLAND.

London, William Mount & Thomas Page [, 1737?].

Map, 18″ high plus margins, closely trimmed, uncolored.

Phillips 1157 has as number [5] in *The English Pilot, The Fourth
Book,* London, 1737. Sabin discusses editions at 22616 to 22619.

[1737?]

JAILLOT, ALEXIS-HUBERT, 1632-1712.

PRINCIPAUTÉ DE TRANSILVANIE DIVISÉE EN CINQ NATIONS.

Amsterdam, Reinier and Josua Ottens [, 1737?].

Map, 19⅛″ high plus margins and Latin title, "Nova Transil-
vaniae Principatus Tabula," colored.

Atlantes, III, 89, lists this map as number 206 in the Ottens catalogue
"published after 1737 and before 1750."

[1737?]

WRIGHT, THOMAS, fl. 1735-1790.

THE PASSAGE OF THE ANNULAR PENUMBRA OVER SCOTLAND
&C. IN THE CENTRAL ECLIPSE OF THE SUN ON THE 18TH DAY
OF FEBRUARY 1736/7 IN THE AFTERNOON.

London, John Senex [, 1737?].

Map, 14¾″ high plus imprint and cut to platemarks.

A dedication in the title cartouche reads, "Inscribed to the President,
Council and Fellows of the Royal Society. By Thomas Wright." An
unusual piece showing the route of an eclipse taking place above the
British Isles.

1738

LAUNAY, CARL LUDWIG.

. . . PROFAN- UND KIRCHEN-HISTORIE . . . GEOGRAPHIE. . . .
ERSTER THEIL. . . . ANDERTER THEIL [in one volume].

Augsburg, Martin Veith, 1738.

Octavo, 8¼″ high, bound in contemporary full leather, blind-
tooled.

Contains thirty maps of which these in Volume Two relate to America: Typus Orbis at 4, Sphaerarum at 16, Europae at 20, Asiae at 20,
Africae at 26, and Americae at 28.

[1739]

MOLL, HERMAN, d. 1732.

A VIEW OF THE GENERAL TRADE WINDS.

London, Thomas Salmon [, 1739].

Map, 7¼″ high plus margins and "Vol. 3. p. 129," uncolored.

From Salmon's *Modern History* of 1739. Sellers & Van Ee, II, 98,
lists Moll's other maps on trade winds.

1739

RENARD, Louis.

ATLAS DE LA NAVIGATION, ET DU COMMERCE.

Amsterdam, Reinier and Josua Ottens, 1739.

Folio, 22″ high, bound in modern half vellum with gold printing on green leather label on spine.

Contains thirty-one sea-charts following title page as described in *Atlantes,* IV, Ren 2, dated 1739, but the maps are those of Ren 3 with the exception that 5 is between 1 and 2 and 31 is missing. Those relating to America are numbers 1, 5, 2, 3, 4, 26, 27, 28, 29, 30, and 32. Phillips 592 lists the Ren 2 maps, twenty-eight in number. Sabin 69598 lists some of the American maps.

1740

BOWEN, Emanuel, 1700?-1767.

A NEW MAP OR CHART OF THE WESTERN OR ATLANTIC OCEAN.

London, Edward Cave, 1740.

Map, 14¼″ high at plate mark plus margins, colored.

Cartouche has portraits of Admirals Robert Blake and Edward Vernon.

Presented to the Philadelphia Maritime Museum in May 1984.

[1740?]

BUACHE, Philippe, 1700-1773.

CARTE D'UNE PARTIE DE L'AMERIQUE POUR LA NAVIGATION DES ISLES . . . DEPUIS LA BERMUDE JUSQU'A CAYENNE.

Paris, Philippe Buache [, 1740?].

Map, 19¼″ high plus margins, colored in outline.

Follows Popple's rendition of the Gulf of Mexico and the West Indies.

Presented to the Philadelphia Maritime Museum in May 1984.

1740

L'ISLE, Guillaume de, 1675-1726.

ATLANTE NOVISSIMO. . . . VOLUME PRIMO.

Venice, Giambatista Albrizzi, 1740.

Folio, 17¼″ high, bound in contemporary full vellum with gold-tooled leather title panel on spine.

Thirty-four maps are contained in this first volume, an Italian edition of the *Nouveau Atlas* of 1730, published posthumously. Maps number 1 and 21 relate to America, according to Phillips 594, to which should be added number 2 which shows northwestern America. See 1750 for Volume Two.

1740

LESLIE, Charles.

A NEW HISTORY OF JAMAICA. . . . SECOND EDITION.

London, J. Hodges, 1740.

Octavo, 8″ high, bound in contemporary full leather, gold-tooled.

Frontispiece is a folding map of Jamaica. Sabin 40190 discusses the Edinburgh editions.

LOTTER, TOBIAS CONRAD, 1717-1777.

AMERICA SEPTENTRIONALIS CONCINNATA . . . JUXTA ANNO-
TATIONES RECENTISSIMAS PER G. DE L'ISLE.

Augsburg, Tobias Conrad Lotter [, 1740?].

Map, 17⅞″ high with no margins, colored.

Marshall, *Clements*, I, 538, notes publication in *Atlas Factice,* 1720-
1770, at plate number 225 and in the 1732-1780 edition as number 5.

1740

POINTIS, JEAN BERNARD LOUIS DESJEAN, BARON, 1645-1707.

AN AUTHENTICK AND PARTICULAR ACCOUNT OF THE TAKING
OF CARTHAGENA . . . 1697 . . . SECOND EDITION.

London, Olive Payne, 1740.

Quarto, 7¾″ high, bound in modern half leather, gold-stamped.

Contains a Plan of the Harbour & City facing page 1 as called for in
Sabin 63705.

[1740?]

LES PRINCIPALES FORTERESSES PORTS . . . PLACENTIA. . . . ANAP-
OLIS ROYAL. . . . BOSTON. . . . NEW YORK. . . . CHARLES TOWN.
. . . ST. AUGUSTINE. . . . PROVIDENCE. . . . HAVANA. . . . ST. IAGO.
. . . PORT ANTONIO. . . . PORTO BELLO. . . . I.K.S.

[Paris? 1740?]

Map, 19⅛″ high plus margins and title, colored.

Marshall, *Clements,* II, 289, does not give author, date, or imprint.

[1740?]

SELLER, JOHN, fl. 1664-1697.

A GENERAL CHART OF THE WESTERN OCEAN.

London, William Mount and Thomas Page [, 1740?].

Map, 18¼″ high plus margins, colored.

Duplicate of map in the *English Pilot, Fourth Book* but a later impression when firm was Mount & Page, 1733 to 1748.

Presented to the Philadelphia Maritime Museum in May 1984.

[1740?]

SEUTTER, GEORGE MATTHAUS, 1678-1757.

ATLAS NOVUS.

Augsburg, George Matthaus Seutter [, 1740?].

Folio, 20½″ high, bound in contemporary limp full leather, blind-
tooled.

Phillips 593 is dated [1740?] and calls for forty-nine colored maps.
This has nineteen of which the first two listed by Phillips and number
four, Asia, relate to America.

[1740?]

SPECHT, CASPAR.

HOLLANDIÆ COMITATUS . . . PER C. SPECHT. KAART VAN'T
GRAAFSCHAP HOLLAND.

Amsterdam, Reinier and Josua Ottens [, 1740?].

Map, 20″ high plus title and margins, colored.

Atlantes, III, 87-89, lists maps in the Ottens catalogue of which this is number 138. Ott 1 is dated (1725-1750) and the catalogue "after 1737 and before 1750."

1740

TOMS, WILLIAM HENRY, fl. 1723-1758.

THIS PLAN OF . . . PORTO BELLO . . . DRAWN BY LIEUTENT. PHILIP DURELL. . . . W. H. TOMS SCULPT.

London, S. Harding and William Henry Toms, 1740.

Map, 17″ high plus margins, closely trimmed, colored.

Marshall, *Clements,* I, 302, lists Durell's maps but not including this, and II, 454, lists Toms's maps but not including this. Sabin 21419 describes Durell's Louisbourg book.

1740

TOMS, WILLIAM HENRY, fl. 1723-1758.

THIS PLAN OF THE HARBOUR . . . OF CARTAGENA . . . W. H. TOMS SCULPT 1740.

London, S. Harding and William Henry Toms, 1740.

Map, 16⅝″ high plus margins and imprint with price, colored.

Marshall, *Clements,* II, 444, describes, and Kapp in *Map Collectors' Circle,* number 77, lists this map as number 66 on page 17.

1740

VALCK, LEONARD, 1675-1755.

. . . HEMEL EN AARD-GLOBEN [two books in one].

Amsterdam, Leonard Valck, [1740].

Quarto, 7⅞″ high, bound in contemporary half leather, gold-stamped.

Contains four engraved plates, none of which relates to America. Bound with MARCI, QUADRATA MAGICA 1744.

The pair of globes here described were presented to Stenton in Germantown in 1983.

[1740?]

VISSCHER, NICOLAS, 1587-1652.

COMITATUS ZELANDIÆ NOVISSIMA DELINEATIO PER . . . NUN[C] APUD PET. SCHENCK JUN.

[Amsterdam, 1740?]

Map, 18¼″ high plus margins, colored in map but uncolored in cartouche.

Atlantes Vis 2 has an earlier map at number (36), "Nova Descriptio Anno 1636." Neither of the Schenck maps listed in *Atlantes,* Index, is "Zelandia," and Schenck's dates are 1698?-1775. *Atlantes,* III, 111-114, has catalogue of Schenck maps with number 124 as "Zelandia Comitatus."

[1740?]

VISSCHER, NICOLAS, 1587-1652.

FLANDRIÆ COMITATUS PARS BATAVA. . . . NUNC APUD PETRUM SCHENK JUNIOR.

Amsterdam [, 1740?].

Map, 19¼″ high plus margins, colored.

Atlantes C & M 10 has as number (70) in the *Nieuwe Atlas* dated (1707-1741).

[1740?]

VISSCHER, NICOLAS, 1587-1652.

NIEWE KAERTE VAN T LANDT VAN WAES ENDE HULSTER AM-BACHT. . . . NUNC APUD PET. SCHENK JUNIOR.

[Amsterdam, 1740?]

Map, 18⅜″ high plus margins, colored in map but uncolored in cartouche.

Atlantes C & M 10 has as number (72) in the *Nieuwe Atlas* dated (1707-1741).

1740

WRIGHT, THOMAS, 1711-1786.

THE USE OF THE GLOBES: OR, THE GENERAL DOCTRINE. . . . ECLIPSES.

London, John Senex, 1740.

Octavo, 8¼″ high, bound in contemporary marbled paper wrapper.

Contains thirty plates of which those related to America are numbered VI and IX. This is the first edition, first state, with the advertisement for Senex globes facing title page. Wright of Durham was an important link in astronomy between Newton and Laplace, who held an ever expanding view of the nature of the universe. He advanced the theory of the Milky Way and the rings of Saturn, and he identified the nebulae as external galaxies.

1741

CHASSEREAU, PIERRE.

A NEW AND CORRECT PLAN OF . . . CARTHAGENA.

London, Thomas Bowles and John Bowles, 1741.

Map, 16⅛″ high plus margins and imprint and "R. Parr Sculp," colored.

Kapp 62 describes the 1740 map before the fleet was engraved after information by Captain William Laws. *See* PLATE 41

[1741?]

HOMANN HEIRS.

CARTAGENA IN TERRA FIRMA AMERICAE SITA.

Nuremberg, Homann Heirs [, 1741?].

Map, 9″ high plus title in narrow margins, light touches of color.

The ill-fated attack by Admiral Vernon in 1741-1742 is not mentioned in the historical note at bottom. Kraus found this only in "Brit. Mus. Cat. (Maps) I, 1704." Kapp 78 dates 1743.

1741

LAWS, WILLIAM.

PLAN DU PORT . . . DE CARTHAGENE . . . VAN CARTAGENA.

Amsterdam, Johannes Covens & Cornelis Mortier, 1741.

Map, 17¾″ high including references in French and Dutch plus margins and titles in French and Dutch, colored.

Kapp 75 notes attack. Marshall, *Clements,* I, 512, cites *Atlas Nouveau* of Amsterdam [1741], Volume Three, and *Atlantes* C & M 8, dated (after 1757), lists as number 115.

[1741]

SEALE, RICHARD WILLIAM, fl. 1732-1785.

A MAP OF THE KINGDOM OF IRELAND . . . FOR MR. TINDAL'S CONTINUATION OF MR. RAPIN'S HISTORY.

[London, 1741.]

Map, 19″ high plus margins and "R. W. Seale delin. et sculp.," uncolored.

1742

DOPPELMAYR, JOHANN GABRIEL, 1677-1750.

ATLAS NOVUS COELESTIS.

Nuremberg, Homann Heirs, 1742.

Folio, 20″ high, bound in contemporary full limp leather.

Contains thirty engraved colored plates called for in Index.

[1742?]

LETH, HENDRIK DE, 1703-1766.

NOUVEL ATLAS GEOGRAPHIQUE & HISTORIQUE.

Amsterdam, Hendrik de Leth [, 1742?]

Octavo, 7⅝″ high, bound in contemporary full vellum.

Phillips 143 credits as author Jean Rousset de Missy and dates [1742?]. Tooley's dictionary under Rousset de Missy dates [1742]. *Atlantes* Leth 1 does not date but lists forty maps, twenty-six of which appear in this edition, colored in outline. The following numbers relate to America: 5, Terrestrial Globe; 7, Asia; 9, North America; and 10, South America.

1743

SQUIRE, JANE.

A PROPOSAL TO DETERMINE OUR LONGITUDE . . . SECOND EDITION.

London, Jane Squire, and S. Cope, 1743.

Octavo, 8″ high, bound in contemporary full leather, gold-tooled on boards and gold-stamped on modern spine.

One historian has called this "probably the most ludicrous solution to the longitude problem ever devised."

MARCI, ADOLPH FREDERIK.

... QUADRATA MAGICA.

Amsterdam, "De Janssoons van Waesberge," 1744.

Quarto, 8¼" high, bound in contemporary half leather, gold-stamped.

Contains four engraved plates not related to America. Bound with VALCK, HEMEL EN AARD-GLOBEN [1740].

[1744?]

SEALE, RICHARD WILLIAM, fl. 1732-1785.

A MAP OF NORTH AMERICA WITH THE EUROPEAN SETTLEMENTS.

[London, Nicholas Tindal, 1744?]

Map, 14¾" high plus line "R.W. Seale delin. et sculp" and margins closely trimmed at top, colored.

Published as part of Tindal's continuation of Rapin's History of England which began to be published about 1744 and continued into the 1780s. The plate was used in many editions, and Phillips, *Maps,* page 571, cites earlier ones of which this is one, judging from the strength and delicacy of the lines. Phillips 2886 has as number 31 and dates the book [1785-1789?]. Sellers & Van Ee 195 dates [1789].

HARRIS, JOHN, 1656?-1746.

NAVIGANTIUM. ... A COMPLETE COLLECTION OF VOYAGES AND TRAVELS. ... IN TWO VOLUMES. ... REVISED.

London, T. Woodward, Aaron Ward, S. Birt, Daniel Browne, Thomas Longman, Richard Hett, Charles Hitch, Henry Whitridge, Stephen Austen, J. Hodges, J. Robinson, B. Dod, T. Harris, John Hinton, and J. Rivington, 1744 [Volume One], 1748 [Volume Two].

Folio, 16" high, bound in contemporary full leather, gold-tooled.

Contains thirty-two maps by Emanuel Bowen among the sixty-two plates which are listed and numbered on the verso of the last leaf of Volume Two. Those relating to America are numbers: 1, 2, 4, 8, 29, 30, 31, 33, 34, 35, and 36. Sabin 30482 and 30483 describe editions including this one.

1745

L'ISLE, GUILLAUME DE, 1675-1726.

CARTE D'AMERIQUE, DRESSÉE POUR L'USAGE DU ROY.
Paris, Philippe Buache, 1745.

Map, 19¼" high plus margins and "Ph. Buache. ... Avec Privilege du 30 Av. 1745," colored.

Phillips, *Maps,* page 108, has a similar map dated 1739 with a Covens & Mortier imprint. This map is a fine copy of one of the derivative maps designed by De l'Isle, the leading French cartographer when that nation's mapmaking dominated in Europe.

RENARD, LOUIS.

SEPTEMTRIONALIORA AMERICÆ A GROENLANDIA [upper cartouche]. DE NOORDELYCKSTE ZEE KUSTEN . . . TOT TERRA NEUF [lower cartouche].

Amsterdam, Reinier and Josua Ottens [, 1745].

Map 19″ high plus margins, colored.

Atlantes, IV, Ren 3, has as number 32 in the *Atlas* of 1745, Sabin 69599.

RENARD, LOUIS.

TERRA NEUF, EN DE CUSTEN VAN NIEU VRANCKRYCK, NIEW ENGELAND . . . VENEZUELA.

Amsterdam, Reinier and Josua Ottens [, 1745].

Map, 19⅛″ high plus margins, colored.

Atlantes, IV, Ren 3, has as number 30 of the *Atlas* of 1745, Sabin 69599. Compare with WIT, TERRA NOVA [1675].

1746

ANVILLE, JEAN BAPTISTE BOURGUIGNON D', 1697-1782.

AMERIQUE SEPTENTRIONALE.

Paris, "chez l'Auteur," 1746.

Map, 32½″ high plus margins, colored in outline but full in cartouche.

Map is engraved by Guillaume Nicolas Delahaye, and cartouche engraved by "le Sr. Major" from a design of Hubert Francois Bourguignon Gravelot, "frere de l'Auteur." Marshall, *Clements,* I, 35, notes Wheat 33 as a reference. Tooley in *Map Collectors' Circle,* Number 68, has as map number 103 at page 15.

1746

HOMANN HEIRS.

AMERICAE MAPPA GENERALIS SECUNDUM LEGITIMAS PROJECTIONIS.

Nuremberg, Homann Heirs, 1746.

Map, 18½″ high plus margins, closely trimmed, colored in map but cartouche is uncolored and shows North and South American Indians and volcanoes.

Phillips 3498 has as number [69] in *Atlas Compendarius* of 1752 [-1755] and at 3499 as number 50 with full title. It is also entered at 604 as number 20, and elsewhere. An important map for the Pacific coast of America, reflecting recent discoveries.

1746

ROCQUE, JOHN, fl. 1734-1762.

[LONDON]

London, John Rocque, 1746.

Map, 18½″ high, trimmed with loss of image at top and sides but with imprint in bottom margin, uncolored.

In the words of Francis Edwards this was the standard map of London and the surrounding countryside in the eighteenth century. When this was bought in 1967 at the Kenneth Roberts auction it was framed and covered the map of Roberts's own land.

BOWEN, EMANUEL, 1700?-1767.

A COMPLETE SYSTEM OF GEOGRAPHY . . . IN TWO VOLUMES.

London, William Innys, Richard Ware, Aaron Ward, John and Paul Knapton, John Clarke, Thomas Longman, T. Shewell, Thomas Osborne, Henry Whitridge, Richard Hett, Charles Hitch, Stephen Austen, Edmund Comyns, Andrew Millar, James Hodges, Charles Corbett, and John and James Rivington, 1747.

Folios, 16¼″ high, bound in modern half leather, gold-tooled.

Contains sixty-nine maps among the seventy-one plates which are listed and numbered following the Preface. Those relating to America are numbers: 3, 4, and 51 through 71.

[1747]

BOWEN, EMANUEL, 1700?-1767.

A NEW & ACCURATE MAP OF LOUISIANA, WITH PART OF FLORI-DA AND CANADA.

[London,] Emanuel Bowen [, 1747].

Map, 13⅝″ high plus margins and plate number 100, colored.

Marshall, *Clements,* I, 108, notes publication in the *Complete System* of London, 1747, in Volume Two at page 620.

[1747]

BOWEN, EMANUEL, 1700?-1767.

A NEW AND ACCURATE MAP OF NEW JERSEY, PENSILVANIA, NEW YORK AND NEW ENGLAND.

[London,] Emanuel Bowen [, 1747].

Map, 13¾″ high plus margins and plate number 100, colored in outline.

Marshall, *Clements,* I, 108, places this at Volume Two, page 654, of Bowen's *Complete System* of 1747.

[1747]

BOWEN, EMANUEL, 1700?-1767.

A NEW AND ACCURATE MAP OF THE PROVINCES OF NORTH & SOUTH CAROLINA GEORGIA.

[London, William Innys, 1747.]

Map, 13⅝″ high plus margins and "No. 76," colored.

Phillips 603 has this as map number 59 in *A Complete System of Geography,* published in 1747. Marshall, *Clements,* I, 109, locates at Volume Two, page 642. From Rappahannock River in north to St. Augustine in south.

[1747]

BOWEN, EMANUEL, 1700?-1767.

PARTICULAR DRAUGHTS AND PLANS OF . . . AMERICA AND WEST INDIES. . . . BOSTON. . . . NEW YORK. . . . FORT ROYAL. . . .

[London, William Innys, 1747.]

Map, 14″ high plus margins and "No. 105," colored.

Phillips 603 has this as number 63 in the 1747 edition of *A Complete System of Geography.* Marshall, *Clements,* I, 109, notes location at Volume Two, page 684.

1747[-1754]

BICKHAM, GEORGE, 1684-1758.

SECOND VOLUME. INTITLED THE BRITISH MONARCHY: OR, A NEW CHOROGRAPHICAL DESCRIPTION.

[London], George Bickham, 1747[-1754].

Folio, 12¾" high, bound in contemporary full leather, gold-tooled.

The first volume was published in 1743 and is not in the collection. This volume has information about America at pages 169 to 185. Tooley's description is at page 71 of his *Maps,* "curious representations of the counties of England. . . . They are hardly maps but rather bird's-eye perspective views, the county being shown in relief, with attractive figures in the foreground depicting the costumes of the period," an example of which is Tooley's figure 59. Sabin 5222 lists the 1748 edition.

[1747-1780]

BELLIN, JACQUES NICOLAS, 1703-1772.

[ATLAS TO ACCOMPANY "HISTOIRE GENERALE DES VOYAGES" OF ANTOINE F. PREVOST.]

[Paris, 1747-1780.]

Octavo, 10" high, bound in contemporary quarter leather, gold-tooled.

Seventy-two folding uncolored maps of which the following relate to America:

    [31] Carte du Golphe du Mexique et des Isles . . . 1754,
    [32] Carte de l'Empire du Mexique . . . 1754,
    [33] Carte du Lac de Mexico,
    [34] Carte du Perou,
    [35] Carte du Cours du Maragnon,
    [36] Carte de l'Amerique Meridionale,
    [37] Carte de la Riviere de la Plata,
    [38] Carte du Paraguay . . . 1756,
    [39] Carte de la Guyane,
    [40] Carte du Bresil,
    [41] Suite du Bresil Depuis la Baye,
    [42] Suite du Bresil Pour Servir,
    [43] Carte de la Floride, de la Louisiane . . . 1757,
    [44] Carte de la Virginie, de la Baye,
    [45] Carte de la Nouvelle Angleterre . . . 1757,
    [46] Carte de la Caroline et Georgie . . . 1757,
    [47] Carte de la Baye de Hudson . . . 1757,
    [48] Carte de l'Acadie, Isle Royale . . . 1757,
    [49] Carte du Cours du Fleuve de St. Laurent . . . 1757,
    [50] Suite du Cours du Fleuve . . . 1757,
    [51] Carte du Golphe du St. Laurent,
    [52] Carte de l'Isle de Saint Dominque,
    [53] Carte de l'Isle de la Martinique . . . 1758,
    [54] Carte de l'Isle de la Guadeloupe . . . 1758,
    [55] Carte de l'Isle de la Grenade . . . 1758,
    [56] Carte de l'Isle de Sainte Lucie . . . 1758,
    [57] Carte de l'Isle St. Christophe,
    [58] Carte de l'Isle de la Jamaique . . . 1758,
    [59] Carte de l'Isle de la Barbade,
    [60] Carte Reduite du Detroit de Magellan . . . 1753,
    [61] Carte du Detroit de la Maire . . . 1753,
    [62] Carte Particuliere de l'Isle de Juan Fernandes,
    [63] Carte Reduit des Mers du Nord . . . 1758,
    [64] Carte du Groenland . . . 1770.

Phillips 591 describes La Harpe's abridgement of 1820 and lists most of these maps relating to America, in different order. Sabin 65402 calls for 393 maps and plates.

[1748]

BOWEN, EMANUEL, 1700?-1767.

A NEW & ACCURATE CHART OF THE WESTERN OR ATLANTIC OCEAN.

[London,] Emanuel Bowen [, 1748].

Map, 14¼″ high plus margins, uncolored.

From Harris's *Voyages,* Volume Three, page 3, with mention of Madoc's voyage from Wales to the New World in 1170.

Presented to the Philadelphia Maritime Museum in May 1984.

[1748?]

BOWEN, EMANUEL, 1700?-1767.

A NEW AND CORRECT CHART OF ALL THE KNOWN WORLD.

[London, Emanuel Bowen, 1748?]

Map, 14⅜″ high plus margins, colored in outline.

Bowen's maps are listed by Phillips in his *Maps* at page 1091.

1748

ROBBE, JACQUES, 1643-1721.

METHOD POUR APPRENDRE FACILEMENT LA GEOGRAPHIE. . . . NOUVELLE EDITION [in two volumes].

Paris, Bordelet, 1748.

Twelvemo, 6½″ high, bound in contemporary full leather, gold-tooled.

Contains twenty-three maps of which these relate to America: in the first volume, page 21, Globe, and in the second volume, page 311, South America, and page 351, North America.

1749

BROUCKNER, ISAAC, 1686-1762.

NOUVEL ATLAS DE MARINE [title from map number III].

Berlin, Isaac Brouckner, 1749.

Folio, 19″ high, bound in contemporary half leather, blind-tooled, boards of French marbled paper.

There are twelve maps colored in outline and numbered in Roman numerals. The following relate to America: I, III, IV, VII, VIII, and XII. At front are two explicatory plates with maps, the second of which is of the world. Phillips 612 lists only four of the maps relating to America.

1749§

MORRIS, CHARLES, 1711-1781.

. . . DRAUGHT OF THE NORTHERN ENGLISH COLONIES.

1749.

Map, 21½″ high plus margins.

Facsimile from the manuscript draft in the New York Public Library published by Dodd, Mead & Company in 1896 to accompany *The Journal of Captain William Pote, Jr.* Mansell, 395, 656, provides dates for Morris.

[1749?]

SCHREIBER, JOHANN GEORG, 1676-1750.

CHARTE VON DEM ENGELLAENDISCHEN U. FRANZOESISCHEN BESITZUNGEN IN NORD AMERICA.

Leipzig, Johann Georg Schreiber [, 1749?].

Map, 6⅞" high plus legend line and margins, colored.

Phillips 609 has this map as number 8 of those published in *Atlas Selectus,* dated [1749?].

1750

IRIE (HEIMA), KOBAYASHI (SHIMBEI).

TENKYO WAKUMON CHUKAI ZUKAN [illustrated astronomy in two volumes].

Yedo, 1750.

Quarto, 10¾" high, bound in contemporary paper.

Contains maps of the world and of the hemispheres.

1750

L'ISLE, GUILLAUME DE, 1675-1726.

ATLANTE NOVISSIMO. . . . VOLUME SECONDO.

Venice, Giambatista Albrizzi, 1750.

Folio, 14¾" high, bound in contemporary full vellum with gold-tooled leather title panel on spine.

Forty-four maps are contained in this volume, the last six of which relate to America, numbers 39 through 44, according to Phillips 594, to which should be added number 37 which shows part of Brazil. See 1740 for Volume One.

1750

ROBERT DE VAUGONDY, DIDIER, 1723-1786.

AMÉRIQUE SEPTENTRIONALE, DRESSÉE SUR LES RELATIONS.

[Paris,] Didier Robert de Vaugondy, 1750.

Map, 19" high plus margins, colored in outline in map but full in cartouche.

On verso is stencilled short title. Phillips 608 has as number 184 but dated 1749 and Sellers & Van Ee 8 is dated 1758, an obvious typographical error, for entries either side are dated 1750.

[1750?]

SEALE, RICHARD W., fl. 1732-1785.

TERRESTRIAL GLOBE. CELESTIAL GLOBE.

[London? 1750?]

Engraving, 6¼" high plus margins, uncolored.

Contains depictions of globes. Also present is a French copy of same size and placement with blank verso and folio 7 in upper right recto. Another engraving in the collection is of the same size with folio 8 in upper right recto with French text describing the measurement of the earth and the heavens. Also present is an engraving 7" high plus margins with "Globe Terrestre" as the only text and a depiction of a globe in a structure with a view beyond.

[1750?]

SENEX, JOHN, d. 1740.

A NEW MAP OF ASIA.

[London, 1750?]

Map, 19″ high plus margins, colored in outline in map but uncolored in cartouche.

America is shown east of Japan and named "Company's Land." Mansell locates only copy, at Cornell dated [1720?].

[1750?]

SEUTTER, GEORGE MATTHAUS, 1678-1756.

PARTIE ORIENTALE DE LA NOUVELLE FRANCE. . . . DRESSÉ PAR ALB. CHARL SEUTTER, GEOGR. TOB. CONR. LOTTER, SC.

Augsburg, George Matthaus Seutter [, 1750?].

Map, 22⅜″ high plus margins, colored.

Tooley dates 1750 and Sellers & Van Ee 278 describes the changed imprint "between 1756 and 1762." Present in three copies.

1750

VALCK, GERARD, 1650?-1726, and
VALCK, LEONARD, 1675-1755.

PAIR OF GLOBES, CELESTIAL AND TERRESTRIAL.

Amsterdam, Valcks, 1750.

Globes, 12″ diameter, on stands 21¼″ high.

Valck globes are discussed by Stevenson in his study of globes at pages 143 to 151 of Volume Two, where he states that many dated 1750 must have been made earlier. Yonge describes this pair at pages 62 and 63. Not seen.

Presented to Stenton in Germantown in 1983.

1751

ANSON, GEORGE, 1697-1762.

VOYAGE AUTOUR DU MONDE. . . . NOUVELLE EDITION.

Amsterdam and Leipzig, Arkstée and Merkus, 1751.

Quarto, 10⅛″ high, bound in contemporary half vellum.

In addition to many plates depicting headlands and other matters, this volume contains fourteen maps of which the following relate to America: facing pages xiv, Globe Terrestre Par M. N. Bellin; 58, Port St. Julien in Patagonia; 80, Southern South America; 94, Juan Fernandez; 94, Cumberland Bay on Juan Fernandez; 114, Chile; 154, Paita, Peru; 178, Quibo, Mexico; 195, Acapulco; 200, Acapulco Coast; 206, Petaplan; also 206, Chequetan; and 305, Pacific.

1751-1776

FRANCE. DEPOT DE LA MARINE.

[SEA CHARTS BY JACQUES NICOLAS BELLIN.]

[Paris,] "Depost des Cartes, Plans, et Journaux de la Marine," 1751-1776.

Folio, 23″ high, bound in canvas-covered leather.

This gathering of sea charts is bound with ROUX, CARTE DE LA MER 1764 and it contains, in order:

1. Carte Reduite de la Mer de Marmara, 1772,
2. Carte Reduite de la Mer Noire, 1772,

86

3. Carte Hydrographique de la Baye de Cadix, 1772,
4. Plan du Port de Lisbonne, 1756,
5. Carte Reduite des Costes de France de Portugal et d'Espagne, 1771,
6. Carte Reduite de la Manche [, 1772?],
7. Carte des Entrées de la Tamise, 1769,
8. Carte Reduite des Costes de Flandre et de Holland, 1763,
9. Carte Reduite des Mers du Nord, 1751,
10. Carte Reduite des Costes Occidentales d'Afrique, 1753,
11. Carte Reduite de l'Ocean Occidental, Quatrieme Edition, 1761,
12. Carte Reduite de l'Ocean Meridional, 1753,
13. Carte Reduite de l'Ocean Oriental, Seconde Edition, 1767,
14. Carte Reduite des Mers Comprises Entre l'Asie et l'Amerigue . . . corrigée en 1776, of which maps numbers 9, 11, 12, and 14 relate to America.

[1752]

BOWEN, EMANUEL, 1700?-1767.

AN ACCURATE MAP OF THE HOLY LAND DIVIDED INTO THE XII TRIBES.

[London, William Innys, 1752.]

Map, 12⅝″ high plus margins, uncolored.

Phillips 614 describes the *Complete Atlas* of which this is number 35.

[1752]

BOWEN, EMANUEL, 1700?-1767.

A NEW GENERAL MAP OF AMERICA DRAWN FROM SEVERAL ACCURATE PARTICULAR MAPS.

[London, William Innys, 1752.]

Map, 13⅞″ high plus margins and mark "No. 138," colored.

Phillips, *Maps,* page 108, dates 1752 from Bowen's *Complete Atlas* and the measurements are correct. Phillips 614 has as number 49.

[1752?]

L'ISLE, GUILLAUME DE, 1675-1726.

CARTE GÉNÉRALE DES DÉCOUVERTES DE L'AMIRAL DE FONTE.

[Paris, 1752?]

Map, 11¼″ high plus margins, uncolored.

From the *Grande Encyclopedie* of Diderot and Delambert, showing the routes of explorers.

Presented to the Philadelphia Maritime Museum in May 1984.

1753

FRANCE. DEPOT DE LA MARINE.

SUITE DE LA CARTE RÉDUITE DU GOLPHE DE ST. LAURENT . . . DETROIT DE BELLE-ISLE . . . TERRE NEUVE.

Paris, Jacques Nicolas Bellin, 1753.

Map, 34½″ high plus margins.

Sellers & Van Ee 254 gives imprint as [Paris, 1753].

[1753?]§

JOHNSTON, THOMAS, 1708-1767.

A TRUE COPPY FROM AN ANCIENT PLAN OF E. HUTCHINSON'S [of Casco Bay].

[Boston, 1753?]

Map, 11¾" high plus margins, uncolored.

A facsimile which Marshall, *Clements*, I, 480, dates [175–?] while Wheat & Brun 161 fixes date in 1753 and notes its publication history.

[1753?]

ROBERT DE VAUGONDY, GILLES, 1686-1766.

LE ROYAUME D'ECOSSE.

[Paris, Didier and Gilles Robert de Vaugondy, 1753?]

Map, 19⅛" high plus margins, colored in outline in map but uncolored in cartouche.

This is the same as the map in the *Atlas Universel* of 1757 except that the date and privilege are lacking in the cartouche.

[1753?]

ROBERT DE VAUGONDY, GILLES, 1686-1766.

ROYAUME D'IRLANDE.

[Paris, Didier and Gilles Robert de Vaugondy, 1753?]

Map, 19⅛" high plus margins, colored in outline in map but uncolored in cartouche.

On verso is the folio 19 stenciled in ink and, in pencil, "Robert's Ireland." The cartouche is signed "Groux" and the map "Guill. Delahaye." This is the same as the map in the *Atlas Universel* of 1757 except that the date and privilege are lacking in the cartouche.

1754

FERGUSON, JAMES, 1710-1776.

AN IDEA OF THE MATERIAL UNIVERSE.

London, James Ferguson, 1754.

Octavo, 9" high, bound in modern half leather, gold-stamped.

Mansell, 169, 636, locates seven copies.

1754

FRANCE. DEPOT DE LA MARINE.

CARTE RÉDUITE DU GOLPHE DE ST. LAURENT CONTENANT . . . TERRE-NEUVE . . . L'ISLE ROYALE, L'ISLE ST. JEAN . . . ANTICOSTI.

Paris, Depot, 1754.

Map, 21" high plus longitude and margins.

Marshall, *Clements*, I, 188, notes publication in Bellin's *Hydrographie*, II, number [57b] and dates [1754].

1755

BALDWIN, RICHARD, JR., d. 1770.

A MAP OF VIRGINIA, NORTH AND SOUTH CAROLINA, GEORGIA, MARYLAND, WITH PART OF NEW JERSEY, &C.

London, Richard Baldwin, Jr., 1755.

Map, 8½″ high plus margins and title and imprint, colored.

Sellers & Van Ee 1381 notes publication in *Gentleman's Magazine* in July 1755 and that it "appears to be based on the work of John Mitchell." Marshall, *Clements,* I, 51, notes publication in *London Magazine* in July 1755 at page 312.

1755

BELLIN, JACQUES NICOLAS, 1703-1772.

PARTIE OCCIDENTALE DE LA NOUVELLE FRANCE OU DU CANADA PAR MR. BELLIN.

[Nuremberg,] Homann Heirs, 1755.

Map, 17¾″ high plus margins, colored in outline.

Phillips 622 has as number 146 in Volume One of the *Atlas Geographicus* of 1759[-1781].

1755

BELLIN, JACQUES NICOLAS, 1703-1772.

PARTIE ORIENTALE DE LA NOUVELLE FRANCE OU DU CANADA.

[Nuremberg,] Homann Heirs, 1755.

Map, 17″ high plus margins, uncolored.

Phillips 622 has as number 145 in Volume One of the *Atlas Geographicus* of 1759[-1781].

1755§

EVANS, LEWIS, 1700-1756.

A GENERAL MAP OF THE MIDDLE BRITISH COLONIES IN AMERICA.

Philadelphia, Benjamin Franklin and David Hall, 1755.

Map, 19⅜″ high plus margins, colored.

Facsimile published in 1953 by Ethyl Corporation of New York. This was the first map to note the existence of petroleum near the site where the industry was founded a century later. Wheat & Brun 298 and Miller, *Franklin,* number 605, discuss and Sabin 23175 lists. Shipton-Mooney 7411 reproduces the map.

1755

EVANS, LEWIS, 1700-1756.

A GENERAL MAP OF THE MIDDLE BRITISH COLONIES.

Philadelphia, Lewis Evans, and London, Robert Dodsley, 1755.

Map, 19⅜″ high plus margins, uncolored.

Wheat & Brun 298 and 299 describe the states, while Miller, *Franklin,* number 605, and Sabin 23176 discuss. Shipton-Mooney 7411 reproduces the map. See also EVANS 1755 above for the earlier state.

Presented to the Pennsylvania Historical and Museum Commission in November 1981.

89

HUSKE, JOHN, 1721?-1773.

A NEW AND ACCURATE MAP OF NORTH AMERICA. . . . THO. KITCHIN SCULPT.

London, Robert and James Dodsley, 1755.

Map, 15¾" high plus margins and "Published for the Present State of North America . . . 1755," colored in map but uncolored in cartouche.

Sellers & Van Ee 67 notes that Huske's *Present State* of 1755 was the second edition. The map is described in Mansell, 261, 579, along with its publication history. Phillips, *Maps,* page 575, cites the same map being published in William Douglass, *Summary Historical* of 1760 but as this map has no evidence of former folds, it was probably issued separately or in a large atlas volume apart from either Huske or Douglass.

1755

JEFFERYS, THOMAS, 1710?-1771.

EXPLANATION FOR THE NEW MAP OF NOVA SCOTIA AND CAPE BRITAIN.

London, Thomas Jefferys, 1755.

Quarto, 10¼" high, bound in modern half leather, gold-tooled.

Missing and torn pages in the original are present in facsimile including title page, last leaf of text, and leaf of advertisements. The map is found at page 128 of *The Natural and Civil History of the French Dominions in North and South America,* published by Jefferys in 1760, present in this collection.

MOLL, HERMAN, d. 1732.

MODERN HISTORY: OR, THE PRESENT STATE.

Dublin, William Williamson, 1755.

Quartos, 9" high, bound in contemporary full leather, gold-stamped on spine label.

In the two parts of Volume Five are twenty maps, all of which relate to America: at pages 1; 526, 5 maps; 579; 690; 750; 778; 779; 800; 816; 822; 832; 834; 838; and 854, 3 maps. Contains the famous but scarce map of the post roads formulated by Franklin and emanating from Philadelphia.

[1755?]

RIDGE, J., engraver.

A MAP OF THE BRITISH AND FRENCH SETTLEMENTS IN NORTH AMERICA.

[Dublin? 1755?]

Map, 10⅞" high plus margins, uncolored.

Sellers & Van Ee have as number 60, dated [1755?], while Phillips, *Maps,* page 578, dates [1758]. Tooley's entry for Ridge notes P. F. X. de Charlevoix's *British Dominions in North America* as a Dublin 1766 publication, as does Mansell, 104, 170.

1756

LE ROUGE, GEORGE LOUIS, fl. 1740-1780.

CARTE DES ENVIRONS DE LISBONE.

Paris, George Louis Le Rouge, 1756.

Map, 19″ high plus margins, uncolored.

The major inset map shows "Royaume de Portugal," and the four small maps show "Estremos," "Aronches," "Villa Viciosa," and Le Rouge's chart on volcanoes. On verso is a map of Paris, see description at CREPY 1772.

1756-1759

LE ROUGE, GEORGE LOUIS, fl. 1740-1780.

ATLAS NOUVEAU PORTATIF . . . TOME 1ER. . . . 2E.

Paris, George Louis Le Rouge, Le Fils Prault, and La Veuve Robinot, 1756-1759.

Quarto, 9¾″ high, bound in contemporary full leather, gold-tooled.

Contains one hundred and eighty-seven maps, double-paged, colored in outline. Phillips 618 lists the following as relating to America: 4, 8, 9, 83, 84, 85, 86, 87, and 88, but 83 shows only the Philippines which typically are considered part of America by Phillips, here as elsewhere.

[1757?]

HINTON, JOHN, fl. 1745-1781.

A PLAN OF THE CITY AND HARBOUR OF LOUISBURG [upper cartouche].

A PLAN OF THE CITY & FORTIFICATIONS [lower cartouche].

London, *Universal Magazine* for John Hinton [, 1757?].

Maps, 10⅝″ high, with no margins in one copy, with margins in other copy, colored.

Three maps on one plate. Sellers & Van Ee 337 describes similarly titled maps but 15″ high and dated 1757.

1757

ROBERT DE VAUGONDY, GILLES, 1686-1766, and
ROBERT DE VAUGONDY, DIDIER, 1723-1786.

ATLAS UNIVERSEL.

Paris, Gilles and Didier Robert de Vaugondy and Antoine Boudet, 1757.

Folio, 20½″ high, bound in contemporary full leather, gold-tooled.

Contains 108 large folding maps colored in outline, and lacks last three called for by Phillips but has 10, 14, 24, and 79 lacking there. Phillips 4292 is dated 1757-1786 and lists, as maps relating to America, numbers 1, 1752; 13, 1783; 102, 1783; 103; 104; 105; 106, 1783; 107; 108; and 111, 1785. Different maps here are 13, 1752; 102, 1750; and 106, 1750; but 111, Etats-Unis de l'Amerique, is missing, as would be expected in this earlier edition. It is not the edition described at either 619 or 620. In his *Maps and Mapmakers,* Tooley notes that this atlas marks "the transition from speculative cartography to exact observation on the ground." Sabin 71864 calls for 103 maps and adds, "some copies contain five additional maps." See Pedley for admirable scholarship on this piece and this period.

1757[-1770]

L'ISLE, GUILLAUME DE, 1675-1726.

CARTES ET TABLES DE LA GEOGRAPHIE PHYSIQUE OU NATU-RELLE. PRÉSENTÉES AU ROI . . . 1757.

Paris, J. A. Dezauche, 1757[-1770].

Folio, 17¼″ high, bound in contemporary half leather, gold-tooled on spine.

These eleven maps of De l'Isle and Philippe Buache were reissued by their successor, Dezauche. The maps are colored in outline and tinted; and some are dated to 1770. Those relating to America are plate numbers I, II, III, IV, V, XIV, XV, XVI, and XVIII. Phillips 220 dates 1754-[1757] and Tooley, in *Map Collectors' Series,* Number 33, at page 33, number 100, dates [1757-1780].

[1758]

BELLIN, JACQUES NICOLAS, 1703-1772.

CARTE REDUITE DES PARTIES SEPTENTRIONALES DU GLOBE SITU-ÉES ENTRE L'ASIE ET L'AMERIQUE POUR SERVIR A L'HISTOIRE GENERALE DES VOYAGES.

[Paris, 1758.]

Map, 8¼″ high plus "Tome XV No. 4" and margins, uncolored.

Phillips 587, 588, and 586 describe the editions of *Hydrographie* with the larger maps from which this was executed. It is not in Marshall, *Clements.* Sabin 4558 describes the publication of Bellin's remarks on this map.

[1758]

GIBSON, JOHN, fl. 1750-1792.

ATLAS MINIMUS, OR A NEW SET OF POCKET MAPS . . . ENGRAVED BY J. GIBSON.

London, John Newbery [, 1758].

Thirty-twomo, 4½″ high, bound in contemporary full leather, gold-tooled.

Contains fifty-two maps called for in Index with the following numbers relating to America: 1, 2, 5, 6, and 39 through 52. Phillips 621 lists under J. Gibson and dates 1758. Maps 1 and 2 are not listed there as relating to America.

1758

BUFFIER, CLAUDE, S.J., 1661-1737.

GEOGRAFIA UNIVERSALE. . . . SESTA EDIZIONE.

Venice, Francesco Pitteri, 1758.

Twelvemo, 5⅞″ high, bound in contemporary marbled paper.

Contains nineteen uncolored maps of which these, by numbered pages, relate to America: 6, World; 7, Europe; 244, Asia; and 289, America. For the editions, including a Venice, Pitteri, "Sesta," of 1760, see Mansell, 83, 294.

1758

LOPEZ DE VARGAS MACHUCA, TOMAS, 1731-1802.

ATLAS GEOGRAPHICO DE LA AMERICA SEPTENTRIONAL Y ME-
RIDIONAL.

Madrid, Antonio Sanz, 1758.

Octavo, 5″ high, bound in contemporary full leather, gold-tooled.

Contains the thirty-eight maps listed by Phillips at 1159, all of which
relate to America. Sabin 41999 and Mansell, 341, 42, discuss.

[1758]

MOLL, HERMAN, d. 1732.

A NEW GENERALL CHART FOR THE WEST INDIES OF E WRIGHTS
PROJECTION VUL. MERCATORS CHART.

[London, William Page and J. Mount, 1758.]

Map, 17½″ high plus margins, colored in outline.

Phillips, *Maps,* page 1055, has dated 1758 as published in the *English Pilot, Fourth Book,* and the measurements are correct.

[1759]

BOWEN, THOMAS, fl. 1760-1790.

A MAP OF THE BRITISH AND FRENCH SETTLEMENTS IN NORTH
AMERICA; PART THE SECOND.

[London, 1759.]

Map, 7½″ high plus title and margins, colored.

Sellers & Van Ee 81 dates [1759], and it is after John Mitchell.

[1759?]

HOMANN, JOHANN BAPTIST, 1664-1724.

NOVA ANGLIA SEPTENTRIONALI AMERICÆ.

Nuremberg, Johann Baptist Homann [, 1759?].

Map, 19⅛″ high plus margins closely trimmed, colored.

Marshall, *Clements,* II, 430, dates [1758] and Sellers & Van Ee 806
dates "between 1759 and 1784."

[1759?]

LOTTER, TOBIAS CONRAD, 1717-1777.

PARTIE ORIENTALE DE LA NOUVELLE FRANCE.

Augsburg, Tobias Conrad Lotter [, 1759?].

Maps, 25½″ high plus margins, colored.

Sellers & Van Ee 278 dates "between 1756 and 1762," and Mansell,
342, 185, dates [175–?]. Marshall, *Clements,* I, 539, dates to [1734?]
following British Museum Map Catalogue, page 2507. This is too
early. See SEUTTER [1750] for earlier state of map and cartouche.
Two copies, one damaged at upper right affecting text at Belle Isle.

1760

THE ENGLISH PILOT. THE FOURTH BOOK. DESCRIBING THE
WEST-INDIA NAVIGATION, FROM HUDSON'S BAY TO THE RIVER
AMAZONES.

London, William and J. Mount, Thomas Page and Son, 1760.

Folio, 19″ high, bound in contemporary canvas-covered boards.

This original working copy contains the thirty-one maps called for in Phillips 1160 with the substitution noted and an additional map, number [13] from 1163, A New Mapp of the Island of St. Christophers, following page 26. Map [14] is bound upside down. In his 1960 study of the *Fourth Book,* Coolie Verner wrote that this "was the first great atlas of wholly English origin to deal exclusively with American waters." The publishing history is described there and by Tooley in *Maps and Mapmakers* at pages 60 to 62.

1760

JEFFERYS, THOMAS, 1710?-1771.

THE NATURAL AND CIVIL HISTORY OF THE FRENCH DOMINIONS IN NORTH AND SOUTH AMERICA.

London, Thomas Jefferys, 1760.

Folio, 13¾" high, bound in contemporary full leather, gold-tooled.

Eighteen uncolored maps and plans are contained in this first edition, second issue, with starred pages 129-138 but also 139-142 relating to the French effort to retake Quebec, rarely found. Also present is correction slip at page 80 in Part Two. Maps are listed in binder's directions at page 246. Sabin 35964 describes.

[1761]

[BUY DE MORNAS, CLAUD, d. 1783.]

ATLAS MÉTHODIQUE ET ELÉMENTAIRE DE GÉOGRAPHIE ET D'HISTOIRE.

[Paris, 1761.]

Folio, 13" high, bound in contemporary half leather, gold-tooled.

The engraved title page lacks names of author and imprint, but Tooley dates 1761 in his dictionary. This is the first published physical geography and is extraordinarily rare. Contains fifty-six plates with many maps of which the following relate to America: 9, World; 12, Eclipse; 23, Ombres; 28, Atlantic Ocean; 30, Geology; 38, America; 39, Poles; and 44, Winds.

[1761]

LONDON MAGAZINE.

A NEW MAP OF THE RIVER MISSISSIPPI FROM THE SEA TO BAYAGOULAS.

London, *Magazine* [, 1761].

Map, 7⅛" high plus margins and imprint, colored.

Marshall, *Clements,* II, 135, notes March 1761 as the publication date and page 120 as the location.

1762

AMERICAN GAZETTEER. . . . IN THREE VOLUMES.

London, Andrew Millar, J. and R. Tonson, 1762.

Twelvemo, 6⅞" high, bound in contemporary full leather, gold-tooled.

Contains six maps: in Volume One, America facing page xxiv and Carolina, Georgia, and Florida facing entry CAR; in Volume Two, New England, New York, and Canada facing entry GAL; and in Volume Three, West Indies facing title page, Newfoundland and Cape Breton facing entry NEW, and Pensilvania facing entry PEN.

Sabin 1090 calls this "a meritorious work," and Phillips 1161 describes a 1763 Italian translation of this, present in this collection, with many more maps.

[1762?]

[BOWEN, EMANUEL, 1700?-1767.]

A NEW CHART OF THE VAST ATLANTIC OR WESTERN OCEAN.... COURSE OF SAILING.

London, Carrington Bowles [, 1762?].

Map, 17⅝" high plus margins, colored.

Marshall, *Clements,* I, 108, has a breakdown in the alphabetical order where this map must have appeared, for MiU-C is the only location listed in Mansell, 70, 289.

[1762?]

JANVIER, JEAN.

L'AMERIQUE DIVISÉE EN SES PRINCIPAUX ETATS.

Paris, François Santini [, 1762?].

Map, 18¼" high plus margins, colored in outline in map but uncolored in cartouche.

Phillips 629 has a similar map as number 33 in *Atlas Moderne* of [1762], while Tooley dates 1772 in his dictionary. Mansell, 277, 483, supplies no dates for Janvier, and no first name, only the epithet, geographer.

1762

JANVIER, JEAN.

L'AMERIQUE DIVISÉE PAR GRANDS ETATS.

Paris, Jean Lattré, 1762.

Map, 12" high plus margins and mark, "No. 31," colored.

Phillips 629 has as number 32 in *Atlas Moderne* of [1762].

[1762]

LATTRÉ, JEAN, and
BONNE, RIGOBERT, 1727-1795.

CANADA IIE. FEUILLE ... XXXV ... B32.

[Paris, Jean Lattré, 1762.]

Map, 11½" high plus plate title, number, and margins, colored.

Sellers & Van Ee 91 dates 1762 from publication in *Atlas Moderne ou Collection,* Phillips 646. Two copies.

[1762?]

LOTTER, TOBIAS CONRAD, 1717-1777.

ATLAS GEOGRAPHICUS PORTATILIS.

Augsburg, Tobias Lobeck [, 1762?].

Octavo, 4⅜" high, bound in contemporary full leather, blind- and gold-tooled and rebacked.

Contains thirty-eight maps of which these relate to America: [1], Planisphaerium Globi; [4], Asia; [6], America; and [31], Russia. Phillips 631 assigns date, 1762?, and authorship to Tobias Lobeck but Tooley gives credit to Lotter for maps and assigns date 1762.

PASQUIER, J. J.

GEOGRAPHIE DES DAMES.

Paris, J. J. Pasquier and Louis Denis, 1762.

Thirty-twomo, 4¼" high, bound in contemporary half leather, gold-tooled.

Contains fifty-five maps of which these relate to America by page numbers: 20, New Continent; 30, North America; and 34, South America.

1762

SALMON, THOMAS, 1679-1767.

A NEW GEOGRAPHICAL AND HISTORICAL GRAMMAR. . . . EIGHTH EDITION.

London, W. Johnston, H. Woodfall, John Hinton, Richard Baldwin, Jr., William Strahan, J. Richardson, B. Law, and S. Crowder, 1762.

Octavo, 8" high, bound in contemporary full leather, gold-tooled.

Twenty-three maps are here engraved by Thomas Jefferys. The following relate to America by page numbers: 14, World; 38, Europe; 491, Africa; 542, North America; 557, South America; and 625, West Indies. Sabin 75828 includes among the various editions.

1762

RIZZI-ZANNONI, GIOVANNI ANTONIO, 1736?-1814.

ATLAS GEOGRAPHIQUE.

Paris, Jean Lattré, 1762.

Thirty-twomo, 4⅞" high, bound in contemporary full leather, gold-tooled.

Contains twenty-seven colored maps of which numbers 2, Mappe Monde; 6, North America; 7, South America; and 8, Gulf of Mexico, relate to America.

1762§

SCULL, NICHOLAS, 1687-1761.

TO THE MAYOR . . . PHILADELPHIA THIS PLAN . . . BY THE LATE. . . .

Philadelphia, Matthew Clarkson and Mary Biddle, 1762.

Maps, 16½" and 19¼" high plus margins, uncolored.

Reproductions of Sellers & Van Ee 1308, also listed with date questioned in Marshall, *Clements,* II, 360. Shipton-Mooney 9267 reproduces and dates [1762].

[1763?]

ANVILLE, JEAN BAPTISTE BOURGUIGNON D', 1697-1782.

LE FLEUVE SAINT-LAURENT REPRESENTE PLUS EN DETAIL.

[Paris, 1763?]

Map, 18¼" high plus margins, colored.

Marshall, *Clements,* I, 355, notes publication in *Atlas General* of 1743-1780 as number 26, and elsewhere, and I, 39, notes publication of an English edition in 1792.

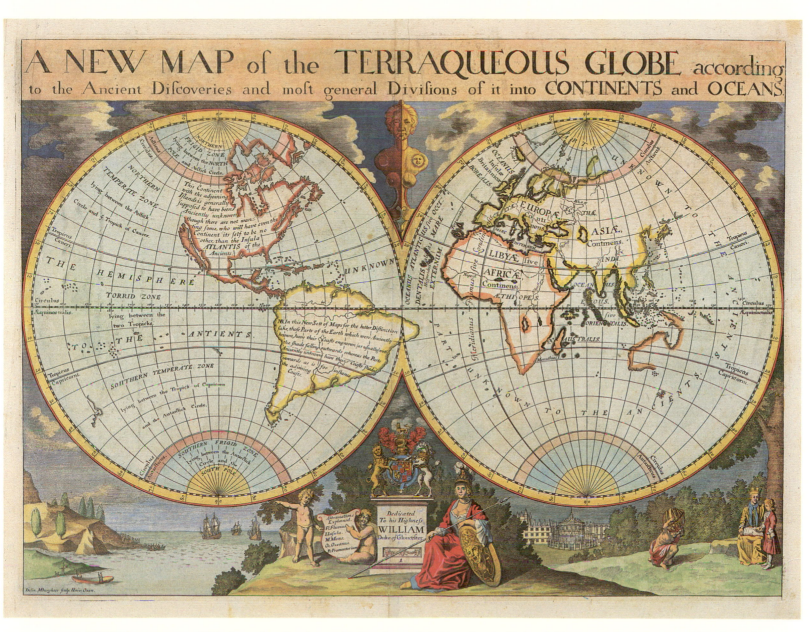

A NEW MAP of the TERRAQUEOUS GLOBE according to the Ancient Difcoveries and moft general Divifions of it into CONTINENTS and OCEANS.

1700 WELLS. NEW MAP. This elegantly colored unsophisticated map is dedicated to the Duke of Gloucester, an eleven-year-old student of Wells, teacher of geography at Oxford. They are shown at work in the lower right hand corner.

PLATE 33

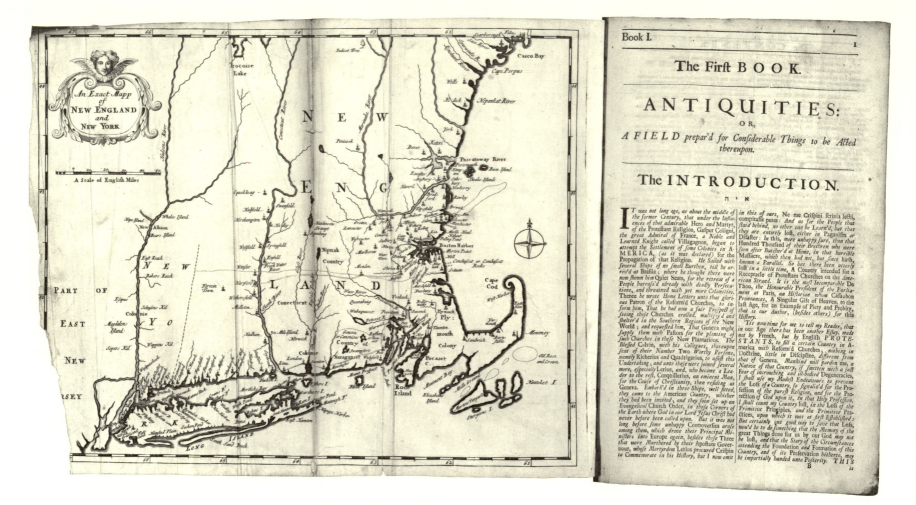

1702 MATHER. MAGNALIA. This map of New England and New York is much more rare than the text it illustrates, and it shows the settlements from Manhattan to Portland, here as Falmo, some of which had no settlers.

PLATE 34

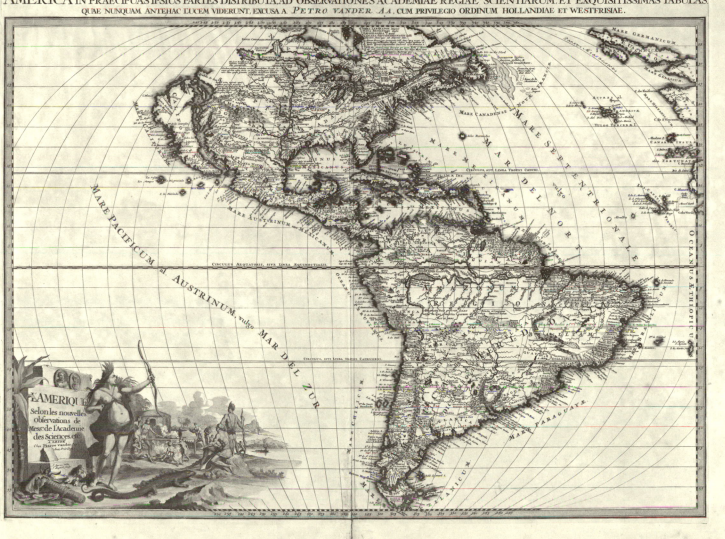

1714　AA.　AMERICA.　The superbly engraved cartouche has portraits of Columbus and Vespucci and
the depiction of the Americans grilling and eating human limbs.

PLATE 35

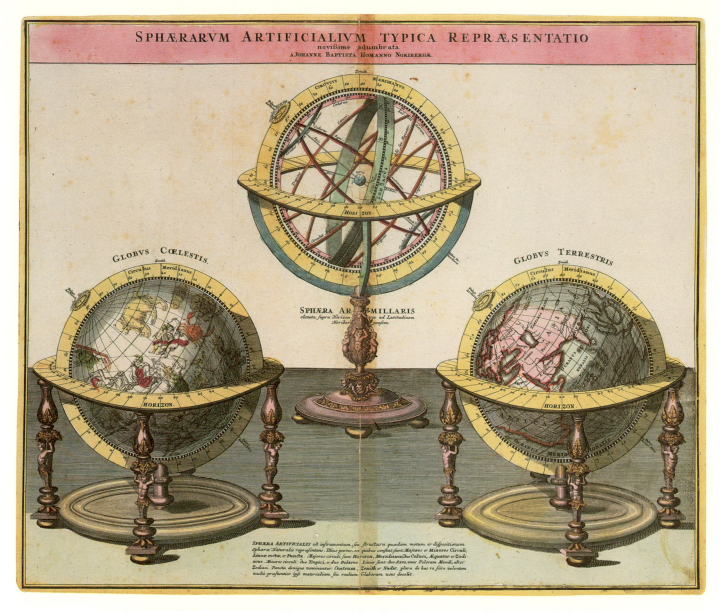

1716 HOMANN. SPHÆRARUM. Engraving depicts the three types of globes, and this collection has more than four dozen of them.

PLATE 36

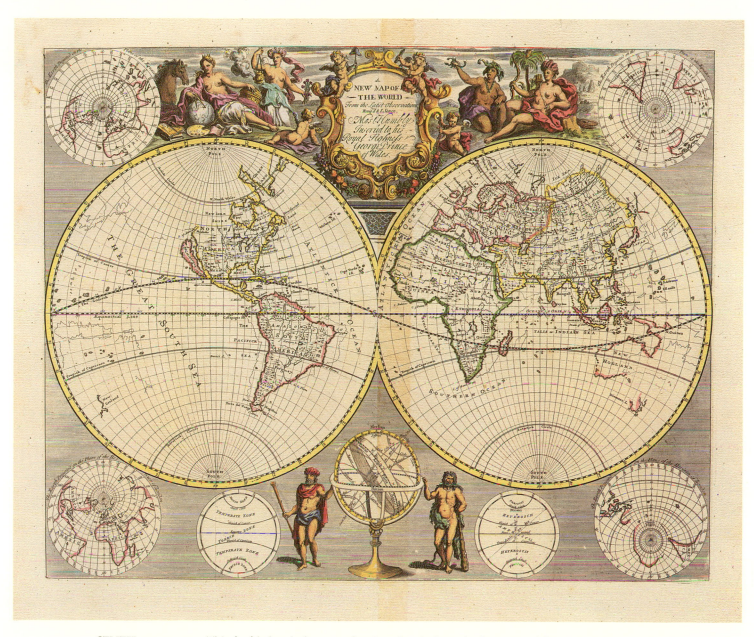

1721 SENEX. NEW MAP. This double hemisphere map has inset hemispheres in the corners. The cartouche has symbolic representations of the continents and a dedication to the Prince of Wales. The armillary sphere is flanked by heroic figures.

PLATE 37

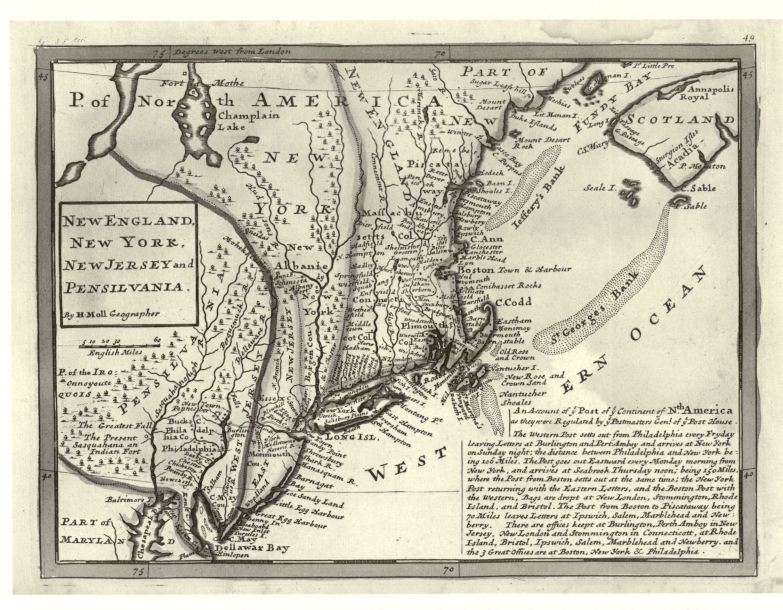

PART OF

Fort la Mothe

P. of Nor th AMERICA

Champlain Lake

NEW ENGLAND,
NEW YORK,
NEW JERSEY and
PENSILVANIA.

By H. Moll Geographer

5 10 20 30 60
English Miles

P. of the IRO
Onnoyoute
QUOIS

The Greatest Fall
The Present
Sasquahana an
Indian Fort

Baltimore T.

PART of
MARYLAND

NEW
YORK

NEW
Albanie

Chesapeak

PENSILVANIA

NEW JERSEY

WEST

EAST

Bucks C.
Phila
hia Co.

Philadelphia
Darby
Chester
Brandy Co.
Newcastle

Salem

C. May
Cou.

C. May

Dellawar Bay
Kinlopen

P. of NORTH AMERICA

NEW

New Pennes
Town
ber

Essex C.

Monmouth
Cou.

Woodland

Little Egg Harbour
Great Egg Harbour
Benny In.
Seaboard
New
Turrells I.

Shrewsbury
Shark R.
Manasquam R.
Barnagat
Bay
Shoe Sandy Land
Little Egg Harbour

New York

Connecticut R.

Massachu
setts Col.

Springfield
Westfield
Squab
Enf

Con nect
cot Col
Nors
Hadham

Middle
town
Warwick
Buta
New London

Mass ac hu
setts

Boston Town & Harbour

Con ihasset Rocks

C. Codd

Plimouth

Eastham
Monimoy
Yarmouth
stable

Old Rose
and Crown

Nantucket I.
New Rose and
Crown Sand

Nantucket
Shoales

LONG ISL.

Montang Pt.

East Hampton
South Hampton

NEW ENGLAND

Piscata
way

Dover
ook

Exeter
Hampton
Salsbury
Newbery
Rowly
Ipswich

C. Ann
Glocester
Manchester
Marble Head
Lyn

PART OF

Sugar Loaf hill

Mount
Desart

Winter H.

Kennebec

C. Porpuss

Seabeck

Baon I.
Shoales I.
Piscataway
Portsmouth

Mechias

Duke Islands

Mount Desart
Rock

Jeffery's Bank

St. Georges Bank

FUNDY BAY

Long I.
G. Passage
L. Passage

C. St. Mary

Seale I.

SCOTLAND

Annapolis
Royal

Sturgion Isles
Acadia
P. Moraton

C. Sable
F. Sable

WEST ERN OCEAN

An Account of ÿ Post of ÿ Continent of Nth America
as they were Regulated by ÿ Postmasters Genl of ÿ Post House

The Western Post setts out from Philadelphia every Fryday
leaving Letters at Burlington and Pert Amboy and arrives at New York
on Sunday night; the distance between Philadelphia and New York being 106 Miles. The Post goes out Eastward every Monday morning from
New York, and arrives at Seabrook Thursday noon; being 150 Miles.
where the Post from Boston setts out at the same time; the New York
Post returning with the Eastern Letters, and the Boston Post with
the Western, Bags are dropt at New London, Stommington, Rhode
Island, and Bristol. The Post from Boston to Piscataway being
70 Miles leaves Letters at Ipswich, Salem, Marblehead and New:
berry. There are offices keept at Burlington, Perth Amboy in New
Jersey, New London and Stommington in Connecticott, at Rhode
Island, Bristol, Ipswich, Salem, Marblehead and Newberry. and
the 3 Great Offices are at Boston, New York & Philadelphia.

1729   MOLL.   NEW ENGLAND.   The earliest postal map of the present-day United States shows the post road from Philadelphia
to Portsmouth. The text outlines the schedule and the distances.

PLATE 38

1733 POPPLE. EMPIRE. Illustration shows the rare contents leaf and the one-sheet map of this magnficent map in twenty large plates. Another set, in color, was presented to the Philadelphia Museum of Art.

PLATE 39

1730 HOMANN. PLANIGLOBII. In addition to the hemispheres representing earth and the heavens, wonderful images of such natural phenomena as volcanoes, earthquakes, tides, maelstroms, wind, and rain occupy the corners.

PLATE 40

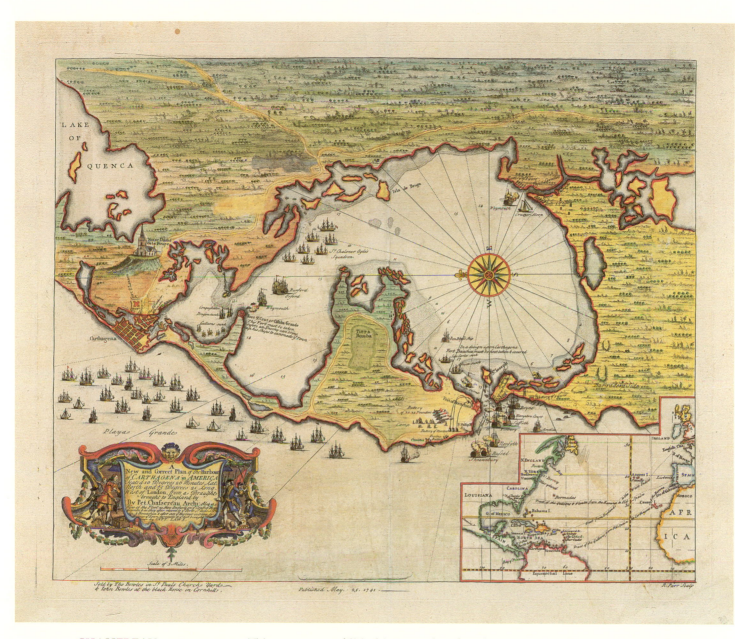

1741 CHASSEREAU. CARTHAGENA. This map was republished in 1741 altered to show the progress of Admiral Vernon's attack
on Cartagena. The inner harbor shows some of the losses of ships, and the inset map shows the routes of the treasure fleets.

PLATE 41

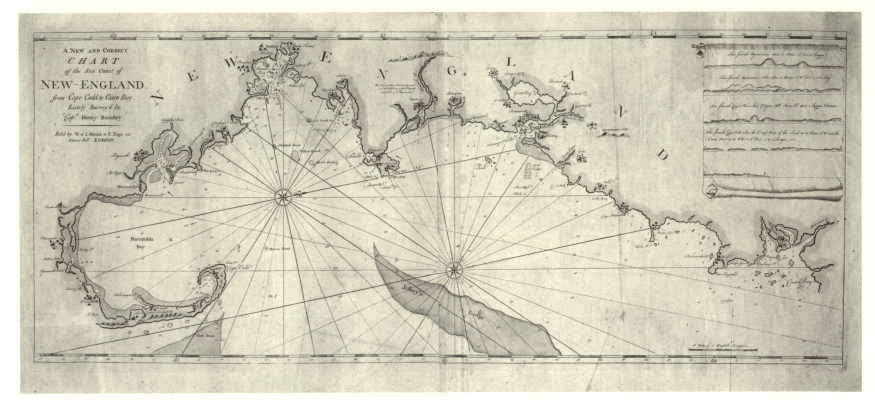

1763   BARNSLEY. NEW-ENGLAND. Chart is oriented with north to the upper right and it shows harbors, shoals, soundings, forts, and hills. It also has six profiles of landmarks from Agamenticus to Cape Cod.

PLATE 42

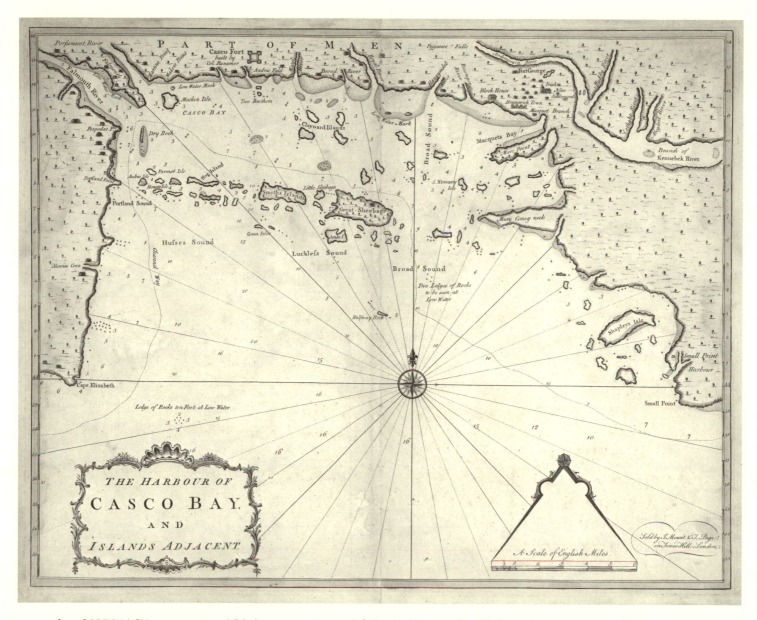

The following text labels appear on the map:

P A R T   O F   M E N

Parsumscot River

Falmouth River

Casco Fort
built by
Col. Ranamer

Andrus Field

Broad River

Pejepscoe Falls

Androscoggin River

FortGeorge

Irishm
New Settlement

Block-House

Brunswick Town

Macquet Branch

Martins Point

Macken Isle

CASCO BAY

Two Brothers

Low Water Mark

Clavoard Islands

Low Water Mark

Macquets Bay

Mare Point

Branch of Kennebek River

Porpodae P.

Dry Rock

S. Nemary Isle

Andua Isle

Parmer Isle

Houem Isle

Hog Island

Smiths Islands

Little Sleebage

Mury Coneg neck

Portland Town

Portland Sound

Great Sheebage

Green Isles

Sents I.

Hufses Sound

Luckless Sound

Broad Sound

Shapleys Isle

Channel Way

Alewae Cove

Two Ledges of Rocks to be seen at Low Water

Small Point Harbour

Halfway Rock

Cape Elizabeth

Small Point

Ledge of Rocks ten Foot at Low Water

THE HARBOUR OF
CASCO BAY.
AND
ISLANDS ADJACENT.

Sold by J. Mount & T. Page
on Tower-Hill. London.

A Scale of English Miles.

1764   SOUTHACK.   CASCO BAY.   This important map carried Southack's name for all editions between 1720 and 1760. His harshest critics suggested that destruction of Southack charts was safer than navigating by them. This may have led to their rarity.

PLATE 43

1768 BLAIR. NORTH AMERICA. One of the finest illustrations of the boundaries of the colonies extending beyond the Mississippi River and across the Great Plains, then in French and Spanish control.

PLATE 44

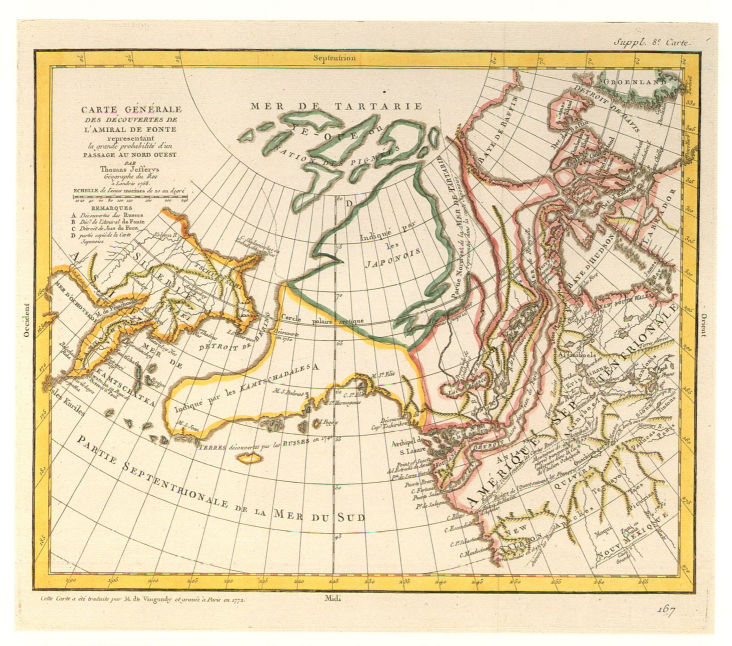

CARTE GÉNÉRALE
DES DÉCOUVERTES DE
L'AMIRAL DE FONTE
representant
la grande probabilité d'un
PASSAGE AU NORD OUEST
PAR
Thomas Jefferys
Géographe du Roi
à Londres 1768.

ECHELLE de lieues marines de 20 au degré

REMARQUES
A *Découvertes des Russes*
B *Déc.ᵗ de l'Amiral de Fonte*
C *Detroit de Jean de Fuca*
D *partie copiée de la Carte Japonoise*

Septentrion

MER DE TARTARIE

Midi

Cette Carte a été traduite par M. de Vaugondy et gravée à Paris en 1772.

167

1769 ROBERT DE VAUGONDY. ATLAS. One of the more than two hundred maps in the *Atlas Portatif,* copies of this edition are exceptionally rare. The only other copy is at the Bibliothèque Nationale and it does not have the date on the title page.

PLATE 45

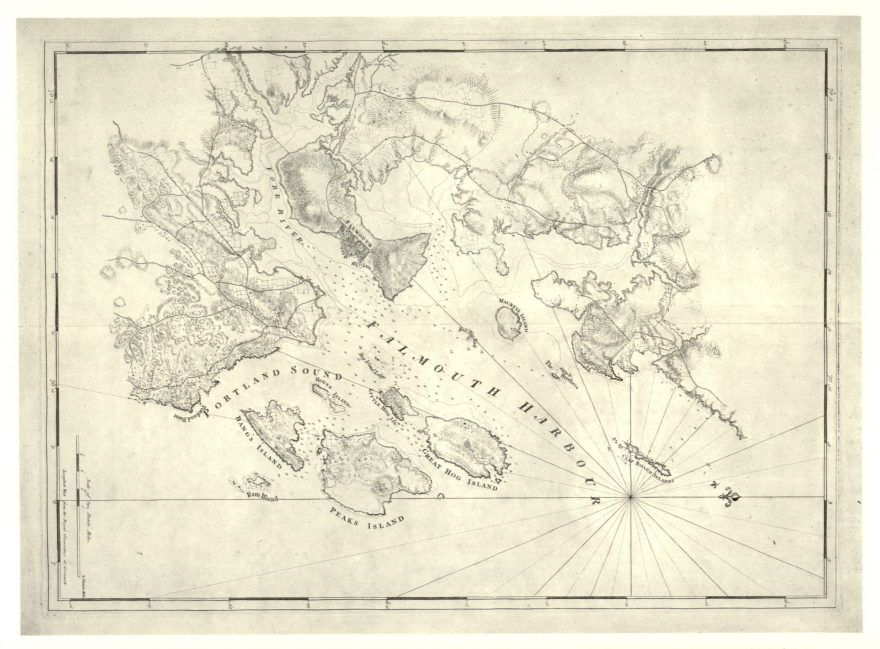

1776 DES BARRES. FALMOUTH. One of hundreds of charts and views in the *Atlantic Neptune*, the finest such collection ever published, it is typical in its alliance of the accurate and the esthetic. There are two copies of this first state in the collection.

PLATE 46

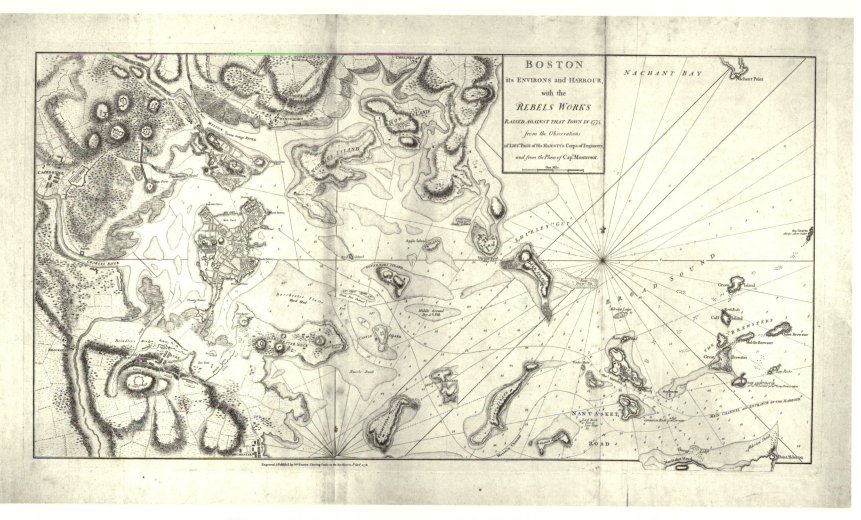

BOSTON
its ENVIRONS and HARBOUR,
with the
REBELS WORKS
RAISED AGAINST THAT TOWN IN 1775.
from the Observations
of Lieut. Page of His Majesty's Corps of Engineers,
and from the Plans of Cap.t Montresor.

1778   PAGE. BOSTON. This map of Boston is the very rare second state with the added section
showing the outer harbor, Nahant, and Nantasket.

PLATE 47

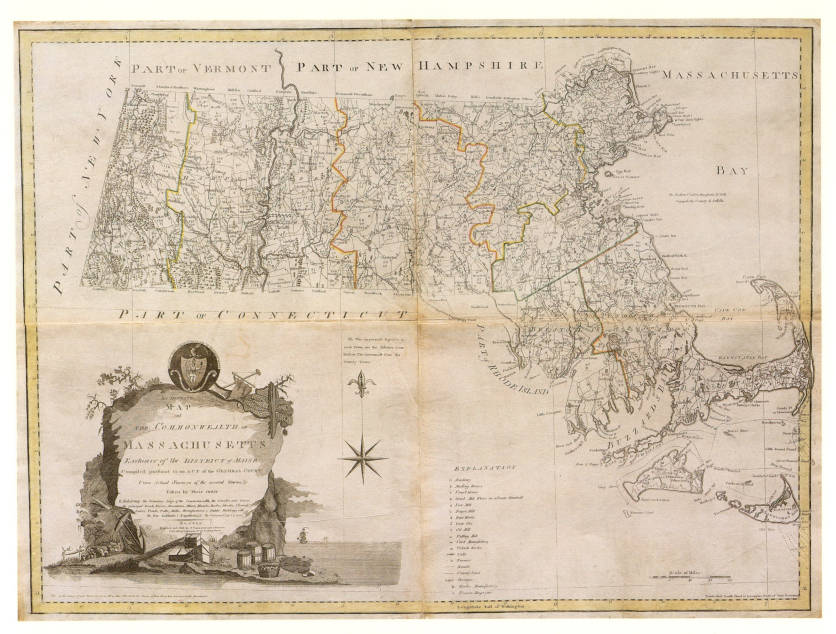

1795 CARLETON. MASSACHUSETTS. This great work of early American cartography is very rare and is printed on four sheets of English paper with watermarks dated 1794 and 1795.

PLATE 48

[1763?]

BARNSLEY, HENRY, 1742-1794.

A NEW AND CORRECT CHART OF THE SEA COAST OF NEW-ENGLAND, FROM CAPE CODD TO CASCO BAY.

London, William & John Mount and Thomas Page [, 1763?].

Map, 18⅝″ high plus margins, colored.

Marshall, *Clements,* I, 62, places at page 18 of *The English Pilot* of 1789 but Sellers & Van Ee 809 dates [1767]. Tooley's entry for Mount & Page dates from 1748 to 1755 and 1762 to 1763. Phillips 1163 notes as number [9] in the 1767 edition.

See PLATE 42

1763

BELLIN, JACQUES NICOLAS, 1703-1772.

CARTE DE L'AMERIQUE ET DES MERS VOISINES.

[Paris,] 1763.

Map, 18″ high plus binder's directions, left top, "et Tome II, No. 2," right, "Tome I, No. 2," and margins closely trimmed, colored in outline in map but full in cartouche.

Phillips, *Maps,* page 109, dates 1763 in *Petit Atlas Maritime.*

[1763?]

DURY, ANDREW, fl. 1742-1778.

A NEW, GENERAL, AND UNIVERSAL ATLAS.

London, Andrew Dury, Robert Sayer, and Carrington Bowles [, 1763?].

Thirty-twomo, 4⅝″ high, oblong, bound in contemporary full leather, gold-tooled.

Contains the thirty-nine maps called for in Phillips 634 where it is noted that maps 8, 10, and 12 show the results of the 1763 Treaty of Paris, not noted in the 1761 edition, Phillips 627. The maps relating to America are 1 and 2, World; 4, Asia; 8, North America; 9, South America; 10 and 11, Canada; and 12, West Indies. The maps are colored.

1763

IL GAZZETTIERE AMERICANO. . . . VOLUME PRIMO [-TERZO].

Livorno, Marco Coltellini, 1763.

Folio, 12″ high, bound in contemporary full leather, gold-tooled on spine.

Contains folding uncolored map of Western Hemisphere and fifteen other maps in first volume, thirteen in second, and fifteen in third. This is the first Italian edition of a translation of the *American Gazetteer* of London of 1762 with different maps. Phillips 1161 lists the Italian maps with their numbers. Also described in Sabin 26814, entered under title.

[1763]

GAZZETTIERE AMERICANO.

CARTA DELLA NUOVA INGHILTERRA NUOVA IORK, E PENSILVANIA.

[Livorno, Marco Coltellini, 1763.]

Map, 8″ high plus margins, colored.

From *Gazzettiere Americano,* a translation of the *American Gazetteer* of London, 1762, with different maps. See Phillips 1161 which has this at Volume Two, number 17. Sabin 26814 enters under *Gazzettiere,* also.

[1763]

KITCHIN, THOMAS, 1718-1784.

A NEW AND ACCURATE MAP OF THE BRITISH DOMINIONS IN AMERICA ACCORDING TO THE TREATY OF 1763.

[London, Andrew Millar, 1763.]

Map, 20¾″ high plus margins, uncolored.

Sellers & Van Ee 104 dates [1763]. Cresswell notes "an exquisite baroque cartouche which symbolizes the bucolic loveliness of North America."

1763

A NEW AND ACCURATE PLAN OF THE RIVER ST. LAWRENCE . . . QUEBEC. 1763.

[London, 1763.]

Map, 6⅞″ high plus margins and title, uncolored.

Marshall, *Clements,* II, 123, notes publication of maps of this title but different measurements in 1760, 1762, and 1766. The battle took place in 1759.

[1763?]

VANNI, VIOLANTE.

PIANO DELLA CITTA, E SOBBORGHI DI CARTAGENA.

[Livorno, Violante Vanni, 1763?]

Map, 7½″ high plus margins including "Viol. Vanni fc. Guisep. Pazzi Scriffe," colored.

Kapp 48 dates [1717] for an earlier map of similar title and 94 dates 1763 for this edition with Vanni as engraver. This appeared in *Gazzettiere Americano* by Marco Coltellini, and elsewhere.

1764

BELLIN, JACQUES NICOLAS, 1703-1772.

LE PETIT ATLAS MARITIME . . . EN CINQ VOLUMES.

[Paris,] Jacques Nicolas Bellin, 1764.

Folios, 14½″ high, bound in contemporary quarter leather, blind-tooled.

Contains five hundred and eighty colored maps. Phillips 638 lists only titles of volumes but 3508 lists all maps including the 102 in Volume One, concerning North America, and ninety in Volume Two, concerning South America, including the last three of the Azores. In Volume Three, those maps relating to America are numbers 1 and 3a; in Volume Four, numbers 1 through 6 are missing; and in Volume Five, numbers 1 and 2 are missing. Sabin 4555 calls for 575 maps and plans.

[1764?]

A MAP OF THE WHOLE CONTINENT OF AMERICA. PARTICULARLY SHEWING THE BRITISH EMPIRE . . . SINCE THE ACCESSION OF CANADA AND FLORIDA.

London, John and Carrington Bowles [, 1764?].

Map, 19¾″ high plus margins closely trimmed, colored.

Phillips, *Maps,* does not list at America, although some of the Sayer maps of similar title are present at pages 110 and 111.

1764

ROUX, JOSEPH.

CARTE DE LA MER MEDITERRANÉE EN DOUZE FEUILLES.

Marseilles, Joseph Roux, 1764.

Folio, 23″ high, bound in canvas-covered leather.

Twelve sea charts uncolored, listed in Phillips at 195, bound with FRANCE. DEPOT 1776. Mansell, 507, 185, lists but does not supply dates for Roux, only the epithet, hydrographer. Philip C. F. Smith, *The Artful Roux: Marine Painters of Marseilles,* published by the Peabody Museum of Salem in 1978, gives dates 1725-1793 and biographical sketch at pages one to four.

[1764?]

SOUTHACK, CYPRIAN, 1662-1745.

THE HARBOUR OF CASCO BAY AND ISLANDS ADJACENT.

London, John Mount & Thomas Page [, 1764?].

Map, 17″ high plus margins, colored.

See FRANCE. DEPOT 1779, for later copy of this chart from *The English Pilot.* Sellers & Van Ee 841 lists the copies and dates the chart [1755] while Marshall, *Clements,* II, 383, gives various dates. Sabin 88221 discusses this map in its many editions. Tooley's entry for J. Mount & T. Page dates 1764-1773.

See PLATE 43

1765

PLUCHE, ANTOINE, 1688-1761.

CONCORDE DE LA GÉOGRAPHIE.

Paris, Freres Estienne, 1765.

Twelvemo, 6½″ high, bound in contemporary full leather, gold-tooled.

Contains eight maps of which none relates to America.

1765

TIRION, ISAAK, 1705?-1765.

KAART VAN DE ONDERKONING SCHAPPEN VAN MEXICO EN NIEUW GRANADA IN DE SPAANSCHE WEST-INDIEN.

Amsterdam, Isaak Tirion, 1765.

Map, 11⅝″ high plus margins, uncolored.

Atlantes, Tir 4, has as number (96) in the *Hand-Atlas* of [1769?]. Depicts America from the equator north to Charleston, from Guyana to the gulf of California.

[1766?]

VARIOUS.

GUERRE DE 1755 À 1763 [spine label].

[Paris? 1766?]

Octavo, 9½″ high, bound in contemporary full leather, gold- and blind-tooled.

Contains no title page but sixty-seven maps of battles, six of which relate to America. They are numbers 2, Quebec; 12, Louisbourg; 17, Guadeloupe; 20, Quebec; 28, Martinique; and 30, Havana.

1767

CRANZ, DAVID, 1723-1777.

THE HISTORY OF GREENLAND. . . . IN TWO VOLUMES.

London, Unitas Fratrum, James Dodsley, T. Becket, P. A. de Hondt, Thomas Cadell, W. Sandby, S. Bladon, Edward and Charles Dilly, 1767.

Octavos, 8⅜″ high, bound in contemporary full leather, gold-tooled.

Contains a map of Greenland and one of the Western Coast in the first volume. Sabin 17417 calls for these two maps.

1767

THE WORLD DISPLAYED. . . . THIRD EDITION. VOL. I [-XX].

London, J. Newbery, 1767.

Octavos, 5⅜″ high, bound in contemporary full leather, gold-tooled.

Contains the following maps relating to America: Volume One, North America at Contents; Volume Three, South America at Contents; Volume Four, North America at Contents repeated, and Volume Five, "Second Edition," Philadelphia at page 20, Quebec at page 66, and Louisbourg at page 74. For an American variant, see Shipton-Mooney 29926 and 31664.

[1768]

BLAIR, JOHN, d. 1782.

A MAP OF NORTH AMERICA . . . SUPPLEMENT TO HIS TABLES OF CHRONOLOGY. . . . THOS. KITCHIN SCULPSIT.

[London, 1768.]

Map, 16½″ high plus margins and binder's direction, colored in outline.

Phillips 3305 has at number 15 and notes that *Chronology* was published in 1768. Sabin 5747 describes a later edition. Cresswell notes as "one of the finest illustrations of the proprietary grants in the Southern Colonies as the borders of Virginia, the Carolinas, and Georgia extend beyond the Mississippi River and across the Great Plains."

See PLATE 44

1768

BUFFIER, CLAUDE, S.J., 1661-1737.

GEOGRAFIA UNIVERSALE. . . . NUOVA EDIZIONE.

Venice, Francesco Pitteri, 1768.

Twelvemo, 6¼″ high, bound in contemporary full vellum.

Contains eighteen uncolored maps of which these, by numbered pages, relate to America: 8, Europe; 248, Asia; and 293, America.

1768

JEFFERYS, THOMAS, 1710?-1771.

THE GREAT PROBABILITY OF A NORTH WEST PASSAGE.

London, Thomas Jefferys, 1768.

Quarto, 10½″ high, bound in contemporary full leather, gold-tooled.

Contains three maps, one colored in outline. Sabin 28460 enters under title and discusses the disputes of authorship.

1769

ANVILLE, JEAN BAPTISTE BOURGUIGNON D', 1697-1782.

GÉOGRAPHIE ANCIENNE ABRÉGÉE. . . . NOUVELLE EDITION.

Paris, Merlin, 1769.

Folio, 22½″ high, bound in modern half leather, gold-stamped on spine.

Nine maps colored in outline, as called for in Phillips 1, none of which relates to America.

1769

FENNING, DANIEL.

A NEW AND EASY GUIDE TO THE USE OF THE GLOBES. . . . THIRD EDITION.

Dublin, James Williams, 1769.

Octavo, 6½″ high, bound in contemporary full leather, gold-stamped on spine label and blind-tooled on board edges.

Mansell, 169, 471, does not include this edition among the Fenning works.

1769

ROBERT DE VAUGONDY, DIDIER, 1723-1786.

ATLAS PORTATIF, UNIVERSEL.

Falaise, Pitel-Prefontaine, and at Paris, Panckouke, 1769.

Quarto, 8½″ high, oblong, bound in contemporary half leather, gold-tooled.

Contains 209 maps colored in outline. Those relating to America are those listed, named, and dated in Phillips 608 to which list of twenty-six maps from 184 through 209 and the world map at [2] should be added number 171, l'Afrique, 1748, which shows part of Brazil. Sabin 71862 describes a Panckouke edition and dates it [1754?].

See PLATE 45

[1770?]

BASTIONS, THOMAS.

VORSTELLUNG DER ENGLISCHEN SCHIFFE.

London, John Bowles, and Nuremberg, Homann Heirs [, 1770?].

Engraving, 19″ high plus margins, colored.

Broadside depicts six English ships using Italianate conventions of art.

Presented to the Philadelphia Maritime Museum in May 1984.

1770§

BLASKOWITZ, CHARLES, fl. 1760-1823.

A PLAN OF FALMOUTH HARBOR.

1770.

Map, 22⅞″ high plus margins, uncolored.

Facsimile of a manuscript map in the British Library.

[1770?]

LOTTER, TOBIAS CONRAD, 1717-1777.

AMSTERDAM. . . . VON MATTH. SEUTTER.

Augsburg, Tobias Conrad Lotter [, 1770?].

Map, 19⅝″ high plus margins, colored.

Inset contains a panorama of the city.

[1770?]

LOTTER, TOBIAS CONRAD, 1717-1777.

ROTTERODAMI DELINEATIO. . . . MATTH. SEUTTERI.

Augsburg, Tobias Conrad Lotter [, 1770?].

Map, 19⅝″ high plus margins, colored.

Inset contains a panorama of the city.

1770

WYNNE, JOHN HUDDLESTONE, 1743-1788.

A GENERAL HISTORY OF THE BRITISH EMPIRE. . . . IN TWO VOLUMES.

London, William Richardson and L. Urquhart, 1770.

Quartos, 8¼″ high, bound in contemporary full leather, gold-tooled.

Contains map of British North America as frontispiece of Volume One, engraved by Thomas Kitchin. Sabin 105682 discusses the publication history.

[1771?]

ANVILLE, JEAN BAPTISTE BOURGUIGNON D', 1697-1782.

A COMPLETE BODY OF ANCIENT GEOGRAPHY.

London, Robert Laurie and James Whittle over Robert Sayer [, 1771?].

Folio, 22″ high, bound in contemporary half leather, gold-tooled on spine.

Contains thirteen maps colored in outline. The title-page imprint of Sayer has been cancelled and that of his successors put in its place. Phillips 3270 states that the maps carry the Laurie & Whittle imprint and were published in 1794. These carry the Sayer imprint and were published as Phillips 3267 dated [1771?] where the maps are listed. They do not relate to America.

BOUGAINVILLE, Louis Antoine, Comte de, 1729-1811.

A VOYAGE ROUND THE WORLD. . . . TRANSLATED FROM THE FRENCH BY JOHN REINHOLD FORSTER.

London, J. Nourse and Thomas Davies, 1772.

Quarto, 10⅛" high, bound in contemporary full leather, gold-tooled.

Contains five maps, two of which relate to America: Route Map facing page 1 and Straits of Magellan facing page 127.

CREPY, Chez.

PLAN DE PARIS ET DE SES FAUBOURGS EN . . . 1765.

Paris, Chez Crepy, 1772.

Map, 20" high plus margins and title, uncolored.

On verso is a map of Lisbon, see description at LE ROUGE 1756.

[1772?]

LOTTER, Tobias Conrad, 1717-1777.

BELGICA FOEDERATA COMPLECTENS SEPTEM PROVINCIAS. . . . MATTHÆUS ALBRECHT LOTTER SCULPSIT.

Augsburg [, 1772?].

Map, 18½" high plus margins, colored.

Phillips 3513 describes the *Atlas Novus* of [1772?] where this is number [31].

ROBERT DE VAUGONDY, Didier, 1723-1786.

CARTE GÉNÉRALE DES DÉCOUVERTES DE L'AMIRAL DE FONTE . . . PASSAGE AU NORD OUEST PAR . . . JEFFERYS . . . 1768.

Paris, Didier Robert de Vaugondy, 1772.

Map, 11⅜" high plus imprint line, "Cette Carte a été traduite par M. de Vaugondy et gravée à Paris en 1772," and plate numbers and margins, colored in outline.

The measurements called for in Marshall, *Clements,* I, 468, do not agree. Streeter 3779 gives measurements of paper while Wagner, *Cartography,* 637, gives measurements of plate marks and indicates a "set also issued in smaller form." Phillips 1195 gives publishing history as part of Diderot's Encyclopaedia.

[1772]

ROBERT DE VAUGONDY, Didier, 1723-1786.

CARTE DE LA CALIFORNIE SUIVANT I LA CARTE MANUSCRITE . . . 1604. II SANSON 1656. III DE L'ISLE . . . 1700. IV LE PERE KINO . . . 1705. V LA SOCIÉTÉ DES JÉSUITES . . . 1767.

Paris [, Didier Robert de Vaugondy, 1772].

Map, 11½" high plus "Suppl. 5e Carte 164" and margins, uncolored.

This is the map that finally put to rest the California as an Island controversy, and it is also one of the first known thematic maps on a historical subject. See Tooley, California, 100. Streeter 3779 gives measurements of paper while Wagner, *Cartography,* 637, gives measurements of plate marks and indicates a "set also issued in smaller form." Phillips 1195 gives publishing history as part of Diderot's Encyclopaedia.

[1773?]

SAYER, ROBERT, 1725-1794.

A MODERN MAP OF BUCKINGHAMSHIRE . . . W. PALMER SCULP.

London, for Carrington Bowles and for Robert Sayer [, 1773?].

Map, 9¾″ high plus imprint and margins, colored.

1774

DUNN, SAMUEL, d. 1794.

NORTH AMERICA AS DIVIDED AMONGST THE EUROPEAN POWERS.

London, Robert Sayer, 1774.

Map, 12″ high plus plate numbers 39 and margins, colored in outline.

Sellers & Van Ee 131 notes only upper plate number.

1774

JEFFERYS, THOMAS, 1710?-1771.

[A MAP OF THE MOST INHABITED PART OF NEW ENGLAND, TOP HALF ONLY.]

London, Thomas Jefferys, 1774.

Map, 20¼″ high plus margins, one copy colored in two separate sheets; the other colored in full and joined, making width 38½″.

Sellers & Van Ee 797 describes, and page 173 illustrates, the complete map.

1774

LOTTER, TOBIAS CONRAD, 1717-1777.

GLOBUS TERRESTRIS . . . GLOBUS COELESTIS.

Augsburg, Tobias Conrad Lotter, 1774.

Engraving, 19⅛″ high plus margins, colored.

1774

REED, JOHN, fl. 1774-1785.

AN EXPLANATION OF THE MAP OF . . . PHILADELPHIA.

Philadelphia, Nicholas Brooks, 1774.

Folio, 9″ high, bound in contemporary paper wrapper, rebacked.

This is an excellent copy of a very rare book. Shipton-Mooney 13564 notes that the map is not included and Sabin 68555 notes that the map "was issued separately."

1775§

COSTA, J. DE.

A PLAN OF THE TOWN AND HARBOR OF BOSTON. . . . C. HALL SC.

London, J. de Costa, 1775.

Map, 14½″ high plus margins and new title, colored.

Facsimile of the original in the John Carter Brown Library published by Henry Stevens, Son & Stiles in 1911. Tooley at Costa points out that this is the "earliest battle plan of the War for Independence." Sellers & Van Ee 900 also lists.

JEFFERYS, THOMAS, 1710?-1771.

THE AMERICAN ATLAS: OR, A GEOGRAPHICAL DESCRIPTION OF THE WHOLE CONTINENT. . . . ENGRAVED ON FORTY-EIGHT COPPER-PLATES.

London, Robert Sayer and John Bennett, 1775.

Folio, 22″ high, bound in half leather on modern boards, goldtooled on original rehinged spine.

Contains the maps called for at Phillips 1165, twenty-two on twentynine sheets, colored in outline. Streeter entry 72 points out that Phillips's count of twenty-three maps was a counting error. Phillips sheet numbers 17, 18, and 19 are here 19, 17, and 18. Sabin 35953 includes this edition.

JEFFERYS, THOMAS, 1710?-1771.

AN EXACT CHART OF THE RIVER ST. LAURENCE.

London, Robert Sayer, 1775.

Map, 23¼″ high plus imprint and margins, colored in outline.

Sellers & Van Ee 233 describes the fourth state and notes publication in Kitchin's *General Atlas,* Sabin 38021.

JEFFERYS, THOMAS, 1710?-1771.

THE VIRGIN ISLANDS FROM ENGLISH AND DANISH SURVEYS.

London, Robert Sayer, 1775.

Map, 16″ high plus margins, colored.

Facsimile of which Sellers & Van Ee 1982 notes that it is from the "West-India atlas, plate 3 [i.e. 26]."

MONTRESOR, JOHN, 1736-1799.

A MAP OF THE PROVINCE OF NEW YORK WITH PART OF PENSILVANIA, AND NEW ENGLAND.

London, Andrew Dury, 1775.

Map, 56½″ high plus margins and "P. Andrews Sculp," colored, in two sheets.

Sellers & Van Ee 1066 notes its occasional publication in Faden's *North American Atlas.*

ROCQUE, JOHN, fl. 1734-1762.

A COLLECTION OF PLANS OF THE PRINCIPAL CITIES OF GREAT BRITAIN AND IRELAND.

London, Andrew Dury [, 1775?].

Thirty-twomo, 4⅝″ high, oblong, bound in contemporary full leather, gold-tooled.

See DURY, NEW, GENERAL, AND UNIVERSAL ATLAS [1763?] "to which this is designed as a Second Volume." None of the colored maps and plans listed in the Catalogue relates to America.

[1775]

SOUTHACK, CYPRIAN, 1662-1745.

A MAP OF THE COAST OF NEW ENGLAND, FROM STATEN ISLAND.

London, John Mount, Thomas Page & William Mount [, 1775].

Map, 23⅝″ high plus margins, uncolored.

Marshall, *Clements*, II, 388, dates [1744?] and [1789]. Phillips 1164 has as number [8] in the *English Pilot* edition of 1775. Sabin 88221 includes this map.

1775[-1781]

APRÈS DE MANNEVILLETTE, JEAN BAPTISTE NICOLAS DENIS D', 1707-1780.

LE NEPTUNE ORIENTAL, DÉDIÉ AU ROI.

Paris, Demonville, and at Brest, Malassis, 1775[-1781].

Folio, 22½″ high, bound in contemporary full leather with gold-tooled green boards and spine.

Contains sixty-seven maps and two plates of headlands called for in Phillips 3167. Only map numbered 7 relates to America, Plan de la Baye et du Port de Rio-Janiero.... 1751. See SUPPLEMENT 1781.

1776

DES BARRES, JOSEPH FREDERICK WALLET, 1722-1824.

[CAPE ELIZABETH TO MERRYMEETING BAY.]

[London,] Joseph Frederick Wallet Des Barres, 1776.

Map, 29″ high plus margins, uncolored.

Atlantic Neptune, Sabin 3606, has at Volume Three, page 15, and Marshall, *Clements,* I, 273, also mentions publication in *Charts of the Coast* in London in 1778. Sellers & Van Ee 855 confirms. This is an early state without cartouche and without shore and shoals information.

[1776?]

DES BARRES, JOSEPH FREDERICK WALLET, 1722-1824.

FALMOUTH HARBOR.

[London, Joseph Frederick Wallet Des Barres, 1776?]

Map, 29¼″ high plus margins, uncolored.

Atlantic Neptune, Sabin 3606, has at Volume Three, page 14. Sellers & Van Ee 863 lists ten copies of this first state. See G. N. D. Evans for a biography of Des Barres. Two copies are present.

See PLATE 46

1776

DES BARRES, JOSEPH FREDERICK WALLET, 1722-1824.

[GOULDSBOROUGH TO MOOSE HARBOR, MAINE.]

[London,] Joseph Frederick Wallet Des Barres, 1776.

Map, 28⅞″ high plus margins, uncolored, in three sheets.

Atlantic Neptune, Sabin 3606, has at Volume Three, page 9, and Marshall, *Clements,* I, 275, also mentions publication in *Charts of the Coast* in London in 1778. Sellers & Van Ee 866 confirms. This is an early impression.

[1776]

HOLLAND, Samuel, 1728-1801.

THE SEAT OF ACTION BETWEEN THE BRITISH AND AMERICAN FORCES . . . LONG ISLAND.

[London, Robert Sayer and John Bennett, 1776.]

Map, 17⅜″ high with no margins and imprint missing, colored.

Marshall, *Clements,* I, 429, has the missing imprint information as does Sellers & Van Ee 1146.

1776

JEFFERYS, Thomas, 1710?-1771.

THE AMERICAN ATLAS: OR, A GEOGRAPHICAL DESCRIPTION OF THE WHOLE CONTINENT . . . FORTY-NINE COPPER-PLATES.

London, Robert Sayer and John Bennett, 1776.

Folio, 22″ high, bound in contemporary half leather, gold-tooled on modern spine.

Has thirty maps on forty-nine sheets, colored in outline, all on a large scale and mostly carried out by the surveyors of the colonies from 1762 to 1776. Phillips 1166 lists contents including insertions not present here. Sabin 35953 lists the editions.

[1776?]

LOTTER, Mathias Albrecht, 1741-1810.

CARTE NOUVELLE DE L'AMERIQUE ANGLOISE . . . SAVOIR LE CANADA . . . LES TREIZE PROVINCES UNIES . . . AVEC LA FLORIDE.

Augsburg, Mathias Albrecht Lotter [, 1776?].

Map, 23½″ high plus margins, colored.

Sellers & Van Ee 141 dates [1776?] and notes that it appeared in Tobias Conrad Lotter, *Atlas* of 1778. Two copies.

[1776?]

[MANUSCRIPT MAP OF VOYAGE OF SHIP ANNA, WILLIAM SMITH, MASTER, FROM PHILADELPHIA TO ENGLAND.]

Map, 8″ high plus margins.

Presented to the Philadelphia Maritime Museum in May 1984.

[1776]

MAP OF THE PROGRESS OF HIS MAJESTY'S ARMIES IN NEW YORK, DURING THE LATE CAMPAIGN.

London, *Gazette* [, 1776].

Map, 7⅝″ high plus margins, colored.

Marshall, *Clements,* II, 38, also mentions publication in *Gentleman's Magazine,* XLVI, 605, published in December of 1776.

1776

RATZER, Bernard.

. . . PLAN OF THE CITY OF NEW YORK. . . . T. KITCHIN, SCULPT.

London, Thomas Jefferys and William Faden, 1776.

Map, upper half only, 23¾″ high plus margins, uncolored.

Stokes, *Iconography,* I, 341, and plate 41, describe as the second state. Sellers & Van Ee 1107 does not discuss state. Marshall, *Clements,* II, 301, mentions state in three of the four copies.

SAYER, ROBERT, 1725-1794, and
BENNETT, JOHN, d. 1787.

THE AMERICAN MILITARY POCKET ATLAS . . . OF THE BRITISH COLONIES.

London, Robert Sayer and John Bennett [, 1776].

Octavo, 9″ high, bound in contemporary half leather, gold-stamped.

This was known at the Holster Atlas, for it was made for the use of mounted officers. Contains the six folding colored maps called for in Phillips 1206. Sabin lists as 1147 and also dates [1776].

1776

SAYER, ROBERT, 1725-1794, and
BENNETT, JOHN, d. 1787.

THE THEATRE OF WAR IN NORTH AMERICA.

London, Robert Sayer and John Bennett, 1776.

Map, 16¼″ high plus title at top margin closely trimmed and text and imprint at bottom margin, colored in outline.

Sellers & Van Ee 144 notes that this is the first state and does not give an author. The map uses such sources as Popple, Mitchell, and Evans.

[1777?]

BOWEN, THOMAS, fl. 1760-1790.

A NEW & ACCURATE MAP OF NORTH AMERICA; DRAWN FROM THE MOST AUTHENTIC MODERN MAPS.

[London, 1777?]

Map, 10⅜″ high plus imprint, "Engraved for Middleton's Complete System of Geography," and margin closely trimmed, colored in outline.

Sellers & Van Ee 1737 dates the geography [1777-1779]. In the collection are two copies, one without imprint.

1777

HOMANN HEIRS.

AMERICA SEPTENTRIONALIS A DOMINO D'ANVILLE.

Nuremberg, Homann Heirs, 1777.

Map, 18″ high plus margins, colored in outline in map but uncolored in cartouche.

Sellers & Van Ee 69 describes this second state with date advanced from 1756 and boundaries altered. It appears in *Atlas Geographicus Major*.

1777

SALMON, THOMAS, 1679-1767.

THE MODERN GAZETTEER. . . . TENTH EDITION.

Edinburgh, P. Anderson, 1777.

Octavo, 6⅞″ high, bound in contemporary full leather, gold-stamped.

Of the seven maps listed on the title page, these relate to America: World facing title page, Europe facing page [5], Asia facing page [7], Africa facing page [15], North America facing page [17], and South America facing page [19]. Sabin 75824 lists earlier editions.

1777 §

SAUTHIER, Claude Joseph.

A MAP OF THE PROVINCES OF NEW-YORK AND NEW-JERSEY.

Augsburg, Mathias Albrecht Lotter, 1777.

Map, 40¼″ high plus margins, colored.

Reproduction of Marshall, *Clements,* II, 344, where dimensions are listed as 15″ x 22″. Mansell, 522, 111, lists "size, when joined, 28½ x 21⅜ inches."

1777

SAUTHIER, Claude Joseph.

A TOPOGRAPHICAL MAP OF THE NORTHN. PART OF NEW YORK ISLAND.

London, William Faden, 1777.

Map, 18⅜″ high plus margins and imprint, colored.

Sellers & Van Ee 1160 refers to description at 1159, and Marshall, *Clements,* II, 344, refers to Phillips, *Maps,* page 526. Mansell, 522, 112, refers to Faden's battle plans atlas where this is number 6.

[1777]

SCULL, Nicholas, 1687-1761, and
HEAP, George, 1715?-1752.

A MAP OF PHILADELPHIA AND PARTS ADJACENT.

[London, *Magazine,* 1777.]

Map, 13⅜″ high with margins.

When it was first published in 1752, this map by the Penn family's Surveyor General was used to promote an attractive image and encourage settlement in Pennsylvania. This edition was published in London to show the readers of *The London Magazine* the most vital theater of war then in America.

1778

FRANCE. Depot de la Marine.

CARTE DE LA BAYE ET RIVIERE DE DELAWARE. . . . CARTE DE L'ENTRÉE DE LA RIVIERE D'HUDSON . . . PAR ORDRE DE M. DE SARTINE.

Paris, Depot, 1778.

Map, 23″ high plus margins including at bottom, "Petit Sculp, Prix Trois Livres," uncolored.

Sellers & Van Ee 1365 enters under Joshua Fisher for left-hand map and does not include right-hand map. Marshall, *Clements,* I, 157 and 164, notes both maps, and Phillips 1211 has as numbers [20] and [21].

1778

FRANCE. Depot de la Marine.

CARTE RÉDUITE DES CÔTES ORIENTALES DE L'AMERIQUE SEPTENTRIONALE CONTENANT PARTIE DU NOUVEAU JERSEY . . . LA GEORGIE. . . . PAR ORDRE DE M. DE SARTINE.

Paris, Depot, 1778.

Map, 22¾″ high plus margins, "Gravé par Petit," and price.

Marshall, *Clements,* I, 187, notes publication in *Hydrographie,* II, number [62], and elsewhere. Phillips 590 has also and 1211 has as numbers [1-2] in the *Neptune.*

1778

HOMANN HEIRS.

CARTE GEOGRAPHIQUE DES PROVINCES NEU YORK ET NEU JERSEY.

Nuremberg, Homann Heirs, 1778.

Map, 14⅛″ high plus margins with title, colored in outline.

Top half only is present.

[1778?]

JANVIER, JEAN.

MAPPE MONDE OU DESCRIPTION DU GLOBE TERRESTRE.

Paris, François Santini [, 1778?].

Map, 18½″ high plus margins, colored in outline in maps but full in cartouche.

On the two hemispheres are traced the tracks of the great explorers. Phillips 629, dated 1762, has an earlier map of similar title as number 1, and thus indicates the first appearance of Janvier's world map. Phillips 647 lists this title in a 1776-1784 atlas published in Venice by Giuseppe Antonio Remondini in 1776[-1784], *Atlas Universel*.

1778

KITCHIN, THOMAS, 1718-1784.

PART OF THE COUNTIES OF CHARLOTTE AND ALBANY IN THE PROVINCE OF NEW YORK; BEING THE SEAT OF WAR.

London, for Robert Baldwin "at the Rose Pater Noster Row," 1778.

Map, 9⅞″ high plus margins and imprint, and "For the London Magazine 1778," colored.

Marshall, *Clements*, I, 495, dates [1778] and Sellers & Van Ee 1078 follows.

1778

MIDDLETON, CHARLES THEODORE.

A NEW AND COMPLETE SYSTEM OF GEOGRAPHY. . . . VOL. I [-II in one volume].

London, John Cooke, 1778.

Folio, 14″ high, bound in modern half leather, gold-stamped.

Contains the following maps related to America: World by Thomas Bowen 1778 facing page xxviii, World by Thomas Bowen facing page 5, and Asia facing page 6 in Volume One, and West Indies facing page 468, North America facing page 486, and Atlantic Ocean facing page 488 in Volume Two. Mansell, 382, 582, lists the editions.

1778

PAGE, THOMAS HYDE, 1746-1821.

BOSTON ITS ENVIRONS AND HARBOUR.

London, William Faden, 1778.

Map, 17⅞″ high plus margins and imprint, uncolored.

Verso has note "very rare state with added section," from the Kenneth Roberts sale. Sellers & Van Ee 913 describes this second state.

See PLATE 47

RATZER, Bernard.

THE PROVINCE OF NEW JERSEY . . . SECOND EDITION.

London, William Faden, 1778.

Map, 30¾″ high plus margins, colored.

Facsimile by the New Jersey Historical Society in 1962. Sellers & Van Ee 1238 describes the 1777 edition and 1239 discusses the alterations for the 1778 edition.

1778

ROBERTSON, William, 1721-1793.

L'HISTOIRE DE L'AMÉRIQUE. . . . TOME PREMIER [-SECOND].

Paris, Panckoucke, 1778.

Quartos, 9⅝″ high, bound in nineteenth-century half leather, gold-stamped.

Volume One contains at end two folding maps, Carte du Golfe du Mexico and Carte de l'Amérique Méridionale, and Volume Two contains at end two folding maps, Carte du Mexique and Carte des Pays . . . depuis Panama jusqu'à Guayaquil, and an engraving.

[1778]

[ZATTA, Antonio, fl. 1757-1797.]

L'ACADIA, LE PROVINCIE DI SAGADAHOOK E MAIN . . . CONNECTI-CUT.

[Venice, Antonio Zatta, 1778.]

Map, 12½″ high plus margins and title, colored in outline.

Marshall, Clements, II, 523, has as number 42 in Volume Four of

Atlante Novissimo of 1775-1779, Sabin 106276, and as number 7 in Le Colonie Unite of 1778, Sellers & Van Ee 163.

[1778-1780]

FRANCE. Depot de la Marine.

NEPTUNE AMERICO-SEPTENTRIONAL. . . . DEPUIS DE GROEN-LAND INCLUSIVEMENT, JUSQUES ET COMPRIS LE GOLFE DU MEXIQUE.

[Paris, Depot, 1778-1780.]

Folio, 27¾″ high, bound in contemporary marbled paper over boards and spine, gold-tooled leather title panel on spine.

Twenty-seven maps are contained in this earliest French Neptune. Phillips 1121 lists and numbers twenty-six maps which are present here bound in this order: 1, 2, 5, 6, 7, 8, 17, 9, 10, 11, 12, 13, 14, 15, 16, 17 repeated, 18, 19, 20, 21, 22, 23, 24, 25, 26, 3, and 4. Sabin 52337 quotes Rich's comment that this has "very beautiful charts of the coast."

1778[-1792]

LE ROUGE, George Louis, fl. 1740-1780.

ATLAS AMERIQUAIN SEPTENTRIONAL. . . . TRADUIT DES CARTES. . . . PAR LE MAJOR HOLLAND, EVANS, SCULL, MOUZON, ROSS . . . &C.

Paris, George Louis Le Rouge, 1778[-1792].

Folio, 21½″ high, bound in contemporary marbled boards.

Has the frontispiece engraved after West's painting of Penn's Treaty with the Indians and twenty-six maps, colored in outline, following Jefferys's Atlas of 1776. The engraved title page has a table of maps which neither Phillips 1212 nor this item follows, for each has substitutions. Here as number 4 is Theatre de la Guerre, 1777. This atlas lacks Phillips sheet number 3 of 1792 and number 23 of 1778, and Phillips sheet numbers 19, 20, 21, and 22 are here 21, 22, 19, and 20. Sabin 40141 lists under Le Rouge and 35954 lists under Jefferys. Contains the Le Rouge edition of the Mitchell map.

1778-1807

FADEN, WILLIAM, 1750-1836.

GENERAL ATLAS [binder's title on spine].

[London,] William Faden, 1778-1807.

Folio, 23½″ high, bound in contemporary half leather, gold-tooled.

Contains the fifty-four maps called for on the printed Contents page plus 53*, South America with its Political Divisions, of 1806. The maps correlate closely with those listed in LeGear 6010 under different numbers with later edition substitutions for numbers 5, 16, 23, 24, 25, and elsewhere. Those relating to America are the first five and the last seven maps.

1779

DES BARRES, JOSEPH FREDERICK WALLET, 1722-1824.

A CHART OF DELAWARE BAY, WITH SOUNDINGS . . . BY CAPT. SIR ANDREW SNAPE HAMMOND.

[London,] Joseph Frederick Wallet Des Barres, 1779.

Map, 30½″ high plus margins, colored.

Sellers & Van Ee 1367 describes this map, which originally appeared in *Atlantic Neptune*, Sabin 3606.

[1779?]

DES BARRES, JOSEPH FREDERICK WALLET, 1722-1824.

[COAST OF SOUTH CAROLINA AND GEORGIA FROM STONO RIVER TO INLET ST. MARY.]

[London, 1779?]

Map, 29½″ high plus margins, uncolored.

Phillips 1198 has this as map 56 of Volume Three of the *Atlantic Neptune*, Sabin 3606, copy number 1 there. Marshall, *Clements*, I, 272, notes two of first state as maps 166 and 167 of Stevens, *Notes*, and dates [c. 1779]. This is the second state without the inset plan of the siege of Savannah as described in Sellers & Van Ee 1594.

1779

FRANCE. DEPOT DE LA MARINE.

PLAN DE LA BAIE ET DU HAVRE DE CASCO . . . PAR . . . CYPRIAN SOUTHACK . . . PAR ORDRE DE M. DE SARTINE.

[Paris,] Depot, 1779.

Map, 16″ high plus margins, uncolored.

Sellers & Van Ee 843 points out that "anchorages in the English edition were mistakenly interpreted by the French copyist as symbols for currents."

1779

SAUTHIER, CLAUDE JOSEPH.

A CHOROGRAPHICAL MAP OF THE PROVINCE OF NEW YORK . . . BY ORDER OF . . . TRYON.

London, William Faden, 1779.

Map, 72⅞″ high plus margins, colored, on three sheets.

Sellers & Van Ee 1070 also notes its occasional publication in Jefferys's *American Atlas,* Sabin 35953.

1779-1788

ZATTA, ANTONIO, fl. 1757-1797.

ATLANTE NOVISSIMO TOMO I [-IV].

Venice, Antonio Zatta, 1779-1788.

Folios, 15½″ high, bound in contemporary half leather, gold-tooled.

Phillips 650 dates 1779-1788 and lists the maps relating to America in Volume One: numbers 6, 7, 8, 9, 14, 15, 53, 54, 55, 56, 57, 58, 59, 60, 61, 62, 63, 64, 65, 66, 67, and 68, to which should be added number 11. The maps are colored in outline but full in cartouches. Sabin 106276 lists the maps by volumes.

1779-1785

ZATTA, ANTONIO, fl. 1757-1797.

ATLANTE NOVISSIMO [in four volumes].

Venice, Antonio Zatta, 1779-1785.

Contains 216 double-page maps, colored in outline in maps but full in cartouches, of which twenty-six relate to America. They are listed in Phillips at 650 and 651. Sabin has at 106276. Not seen.

Presented to Cabrini College in honor of Mr. and Mrs. Raymond Green.

[1780]

BONNE, RIGOBERT, 1727-1795.

ATLAS DE TOUTES LES PARTIES CONNUES.

[Geneva, J. L. Pellet, 1780.]

Quarto, 10¼″ high, bound in contemporary half leather, gold-tooled.

Contains fifty maps of which twenty-five relate to America. They are listed in Phillips 652 where this atlas is dated [1780].

[1780]

BONNE, RIGOBERT, 1727-1795.

CARTE DE LA PARTIE NORD DES ETATS UNIS.

[Geneva, 1780.]

Map, 8½″ high plus margins and plate marks and "Liv. XVII et XVIII. No. 47," colored in outline.

Marshall, *Clements,* I, 99, dates [1780], as does Phillips 652, Raynal's *Atlas* of Geneva, where this is number 47.

1780

GUTHRIE, WILLIAM, 1708-1770.

A NEW SYSTEM OF MODERN GEOGRAPHY. . . . NEW EDITION. . . . MAPS ENGRAVED BY MR. KITCHIN.

London, Charles Dilly and George Robinson, 1780.

Quarto, 11″ high, bound in contemporary full leather, blind-tooled, rebacked.

Contains twenty maps of which the following relate to America: World facing page 1, North America facing page 631, British Dominions facing page 657, West Indies facing page 703, and South America facing page 727. Sabin 29327 lists the editions.

1781

APRÈS DE MANNEVILLETTE, Jean Baptiste Nicolas Denis D', 1707-1780.

SUPPLÉMENT AU NEPTUNE ORIENTAL.

Paris, Demonville, and at Brest, Malassis, 1781.

Folio, 22½″ high, bound in contemporary full leather with gold-tooled green boards and spine.

Contains the eighteen maps called for in Phillips 3168 none of which relates to America. See NEPTUNE ORIENTALE 1775.

[1781?]§

ESNAUTS & RAPILLY.

CARTE DE LA PARTIE DE LA VIRGINIE OU L'ARMÉE COMBINÉE . . . LE 19 OCTBRE. 1781.

Paris, Esnauts & Rapilly [, 1781?].

Map, 17⅝″ high plus margins and imprint, colored.

Facsimile published by the Naval Historical Foundation in 1945 from a map in the Library of Congress, dated [1781] by Phillips at page 1132 in the list of maps, and 1782 by Tooley at page 195 of the dictionary. Sellers & Van Ee 1462 dates [1781?].

1782

EXPILLY, Jean Joseph Georges, Abbé d', 1719-1793.

LE GEOGRAPHE MANUEL. . . . NOUVELLE EDITION.

Paris, Couturier Fils and Onfroy, 1782.

Octavo, 5⅜″ high, bound in contemporary full leather, gold-tooled.

Contains five maps of which two relate to America: [1], Mappemonde, and [5], New World.

[1782]

MILLAR, George Henry.

VARIOUS PLANS AND DRAUGHTS OF CITIES, TOWNS, HARBOURS. . . . NEW-YORK. . . . BOSTON. . . . PHILADELPHIA. . . . CHARLES TOWN, SOUTH CAROLINA. . . . HAVANNA.

[London, Alexander Hogg, 1782.]

Map, 12⅜″ high at platemarks including imprint "Engraved for Millar's New Complete & Universal System of Geography," plus margins, colored.

Mansell, 384, 9, lists this as the first edition.

[1782?]

WRIGHT, George, 1740-1783.

WRIGHT'S NEW IMPROVED CELESTIAL GLOBE.

London, William Bardin [, 1782?].

Globe, 13″ diameter, on base of four pillars.

A celestial globe dated [1782?] by Yonge at page 79.

1783

COLSON, NATHANIEL.

THE MARINER'S NEW CALENDAR.

London, Mount and Page, 1783.

Quarto, 7⅝″ high, bound in contemporary full leather covered with ugly plastic coating.

[1783]

FIELDING, JOHN.

A MAP OF THE UNITED STATES OF AMERICA, AS SETTLED BY THE PEACE OF 1783.

[London, John Fielding, 1783.]

Map, 8¼″ high plus margins, colored in outline.

Sellers & Van Ee 755 notes this having appeared in Volume Four of *European Magazine* of 1783, although the date of publication on the map appears to be 1785 and may be the one in Marshall, *Clements,* I, 350. Phillips, *Maps,* page 864, gives page location in the *Magazine.* Mansell, 172, 11, supplies no dates for Fielding.

1783

FIELDING, JOHN.

NORTH AMERICA INCLUDING THE UNITED STATES AND THEIR BOUNDARIES, AGREEABLE TO THE PEACE OF 1783.

London, John Fielding, 1783.

Map, 4½″ high plus imprint in very narrow margins, colored in outline in map but full in cartouche.

Cartouche has portraits of Washington and Franklin. Marshall, *Clements,* I, 350, has the companion, Map of the Powers, of the same dimensions, from Andrews, *History of the War* of London 1785.

[1784]§

BUELL, ABEL, 1742-1822.

A NEW AND CORRECT MAP OF THE UNITED STATES . . . AGREE-ABLE TO THE PEACE OF 1783.

New Haven, Abel Buell [, 1784].

Map, 16½″ high plus margins, colored in outline in map but full in cartouche.

Facsimile published by American Heritage as the first American map of the United States. On verso is a description of map of which Wheat & Brun describe states at 109 and 110.

1784§

LATTRÉ, JEAN.

CARTE DES ETATS-UNIS DE L'AMERIQUE.

Paris, Jean Lattré, 1784.

Map, 21½″ high plus imprints, printed in color.

Facsimile published by R. R. Donnelley from the original in the Newberry Library. This first French map of the United States is dedicated to Franklin. Phillips, *Maps,* has at page 864, and Sellers & Van Ee 750 describes it briefly. The pamphlet by Lester Cappon accompanying the facsimile has an extended discussion.

MORSE, JEDIDIAH, 1761-1826.

GEOGRAPHY MADE EASY. BEING A SHORT, BUT COMPREHENSIVE SYSTEM.

New Haven, Meigs, Bowen & Dana [, 1784].

Octavo, 6⅛″ high, bound in modern paper wrapper.

Contains the world map facing the title page but missing the map of the United States. Shipton-Mooney 18615 calls for the two plates as does Sabin 50936 where this is the first in the list of many editions.

[1785]

ATTACK OF THE REBELS UPON FORT PENOBSCOT IN THE PROVINCE OF NEW ENGLAND.

[London, 1785.]

Map, 14½″ high plus margins and imprint.

Sellers & Van Ee 839 notes publication in Jefferys's *General Topography,* Sabin 35962, as number [109] and card in collection notes imprint "for the Continuation (after Tindal's) of Rapin's History of England published as the Act directs Dec. 18, 1785." Not seen except in photograph.

Presented to the Maine State Museum.

1785

BARDIN, WILLIAM, fl. 1782-1800.

THE CELESTIAL GLOBE.

London, William Bardin, 1785.

Globe, 9″ diameter on four-footed base.

A celestial globe described by Yonge at page 6.

[1785?]

BONNE, RIGOBERT, 1727-1795.

L'EMPIRE DE LA CHINE D'APRES L'ATLAS CHINOIS.

Paris, Jean Lattré [, 1785?].

Map, 12¼″ high plus margins, colored.

1785

FENNING, DANIEL.

A NEW AND EASY GUIDE TO THE USE OF THE GLOBES. . . . FIFTH EDITION WITH LARGE CORRECTIONS AND IMPROVEMENTS.

London, S. Crowder, 1785.

Twelvemo, 6¾″ high, bound in contemporary full leather with modern spine, boards gold-tooled on edges.

Contains engraving by T. K. Powell of the two hemispheres as frontispiece and nine other plates, of which the following relate to America: Asia at page 20, Africa at page 24, North America at page 31, South America at page 37, and Terrestrial Globe at page 47.

1785

ROBERT DE VAUGONDY, Didier, 1723-1786.

ETATS-UNIS DE L'AMERIQUE SEPTENTRIONALE AVEC LES ISLES . . . SUPPLÉMENT À L'ATLAS DE. . . .

Paris, Antoine Boudet, 1785.

Map, 18¾″ high plus margins, colored in outline in map but uncolored in cartouche.

Sellers & Van Ee 761 notes this as appearing in the *Atlas Universel* of 1799, but it appeared from 1785 until as late as 1810. Karpinski, *Bibliography of the Printed Maps of Michigan,* item 103, discusses.

1786

AMERICAN PHILOSOPHICAL SOCIETY.

TRANSACTIONS.

Philadelphia, Robert Aitken, 1786.

Quarto, 9½″ high, bound in contemporary full leather, gold-stamped.

Contains Benjamin Franklin's Letter to Mr. Alphonsus le Roy at Paris and his Chart of The Gulf Stream facing page 315. Shipton-Mooney 19465 calls for five folding plates.

1786

FRANCE. Depot de la Marine.

CARTE GÉNÉRALE DE L'OCÉAN ATLANTIQUE OU OCCIDENTAL, DRESSÉE AU. . . . [sixth edition].

Paris, Depot, 1786.

Map, 24″ high plus price and margins, colored.

1786

HOMANN HEIRS.

NEUE UND VOLLSTAENDIGE POSTKARTE DURCH GANZ DEUTSCHLAND.

Nuremberg, Homann Heirs, 1786.

Folio, 9⅛″ high, bound in contemporary marbled paper over boards, as issued.

Map in sixteen parts colored in outline and with the small-scale reduction.

1786

KEULEN, Gerard Hulst, d. 1801.

NIEUWE PASKAART VAN HET ZUIDELYKSTE GEDEELTE DER NOORD ZEE.

Amsterdam, Gerard Hulst Keulen, 1786.

Map, 32″ high plus margins, uncolored.

Atlantes, IV, 276-281, discusses the confused genealogy of the Van Keulens. The charts follow on pages 370 through 402.

1787

CARY, John, 1754?-1835.

CARY'S NEW AND CORRECT ENGLISH ATLAS: BEING A NEW SET OF COUNTY MAPS.

London, John Cary, 1787.

Folio, 13″ high, bound in contemporary full leather, gold-tooled.

Phillips 5207 describes the 1793 edition of forty-seven maps as here, colored, none of which relates to America. See Skelton on county atlases.

1787

DELAMARCHE, Charles François, 1740-1817.

GLOBE DRESSÉ PAR M. ROBERT DE VAUGONDY.

Paris, 1787.

Globe, 9½″ diameter on walnut base.

A terrestrial globe described by Yonge at page 24.

1787

DEZAUCHE, J. A.

CARTE DE FRANCE . . . DEPUIS 1589. JUSQU'EN 1610.

Paris, J. A. Dezauche, 1787.

Map, 17¾″ high plus margins, colored.

1787

JEFFERSON, Thomas, 1743-1826.

NOTES ON THE STATE OF VIRGINIA.

London, John Stockdale, 1787.

Octavo, 7¾″ high, bound in modern half leather, gold-stamped.

Contains the map called for on title page, A Map of the Country between Albemarle Sound and Lake Erie. Sabin 35896 has a discussion of the publication history. The first American edition of 1788 is Shipton-Mooney 21176.

[1787-1810?]

[BOWEN, Thomas, fl. 1760-1790.]

A NEW & ACCURATE MAP OF NORTH AMERICA WITH THE NEWLY DISCOVERED ISLANDS.

[London, 1787-1810?]

Map, 10¼″ high plus "Engraved for Bankes's New System of Geography" and margins, uncolored.

Sellers & Van Ee 756 dates another of the Bankes maps at [178?] while Marshall, *Clements*, I, 111, dates at [1787-1810?] as does Phillips 665 where this is number [1] in Volume Two.

1788

BOWEN, Thomas, fl. 1760-1790.

A NEW & ACCURATE CHART OF THE WESTERN OR ATLANTIC OCEAN.

[London,] Thomas Bowen, 1788.

Map, 8⅜″ high plus "Engraved for Bankes's New System of Geography Published by Royal Authority" and margins, uncolored.

Phillips 665 has as number [2] in Volume Two.

1788

GUTHRIE, William, 1708-1770.

A NEW GEOGRAPHICAL, HISTORICAL, AND COMMERCIAL GRAMMAR. . . . MAPS, ENGRAVED BY MR. KITCHIN. . . . ELEVENTH EDITION.

London, Charles Dilly and George G. and J. Robinson, 1788.

Octavo, 8½" high, bound in contemporary full leather, gold-stamped.

The Directions on page 10 call for twenty maps of which the following relate to America: World facing title page (damaged), North America facing page 777, West Indies facing page 822 (torn), and South America facing page 839. In addition there is a map of new discoveries facing page 867. Sabin 29327 lists the many editions including this.

1788-1798

ROBERTSON, WILLIAM, 1721-1793.

THE HISTORY OF AMERICA. . . . IN THREE VOLUMES. . . . FIFTH EDITION.

London, A. Strahan, Thomas Cadell, and J. Balfour, 1788-1796.

Octavos, 8¼" high, bound in contemporary full leather, gold-stamped.

Contains these maps related to America, in Volume One, South America facing page 1 and Gulf of Mexico facing last page, and in Volume Two, Mexico facing page 1 and Panama to Guayaquil facing last page. There are no maps in Volume Three nor in Books Nine and Ten published in 1796. Sabin 71973 lists the editions as does Mansell, 498, 211.

1789

BONNE, RIGOBERT, 1727- 1795, and
DESMAREST, NICOLAS, 1725-1815.

ATLAS ENCYCLOPÉDIQUE [volume one of two].

Padua, 1789.

Quarto, 11¾" high, bound in contemporary full leather, gold-tooled.

The Paris edition of 1787-1788 is described at Phillips 666 and 667 where he lists maps relating to America as numbers 20, 21, 22, 23, 24, 25, 26, 30, and 31, to which should be added number 28.

[1789]

[BONNE, RIGOBERT, 1727-1795.]

CARTE DU DUCHÉ DE VALOIS ET DU COMTÉ DE SENLIS.

[Paris, 1789.]

Map, 9⅛" high plus "Perrier del et sculp. Macquet scrip" and margins, uncolored.

1789

CADELL, THOMAS, 1742-1802.

MAP OF SWITZERLAND MARKED WITH THE ROUTES OF THE FOUR TOURS. . . . 1776 . . . 1786 BY THE REVD. WILLM. COXE. . . . W. PALMER SCULP. ISLINGTON.

London, Thomas Cadell, 1789.

Map, 20½" high plus margins closely trimmed, uncolored except for routes.

1789

MORSE, JEDIDIAH, 1761-1826.

THE AMERICAN GEOGRAPHY [the first edition].

Elizabeth, Shepard Kollock, 1789.

Quarto, 7¾″ high, bound in contemporary full leather, gold-stamped.

Contains Map of the States of Virginia . . . Florida, facing the Introduction, and Map of the Northern and Middle States, facing page 33, as called for in Shipton-Mooney 21978. Sabin 50924 lists the editions of which this is the first in the list.

[1790]

CHURCHMAN, JOHN, 1753-1805.

TO GEORGE WASHINGTON . . . THIS MAGNETIC ATLAS OR VARIATION CHART IS HUMBLY INSCRIBED.

[Philadelphia, 1790.]

Map, 24½″ high at plate mark plus margins, colored.

Published as frontispiece in his *Magnetic Atlas.* Wheat & Brun 6 describes in detail. Shipton-Mooney 22406 dates 1790 for the book.

Presented to the Philadelphia Maritime Museum in May 1984.

1790

HARRISON, JOHN.

A PARTICULAR MAP OF THE AMERICAN LAKES, RIVERS &C. PAR LE SR. D'ANVILLE.

London, John Harrison, 1790.

Map, 20″ high plus margins, uncolored.

This is from D'Anville's *Atlas* published in London in 1792, at page 23.

1790

LOWNDES, WILLIAM.

GEOGRAPHY FOR YOUTH. . . . FOURTH EDITION.

London, William Lowndes, 1790.

Twelvemo, 7¼″ high, bound in contemporary full leather, gold-stamped.

Contains four maps related to America: World as frontispiece, Asia facing page 153, North America facing page 227, and South America facing page 267. Mansell, 343, 500, supplies no dates for Lowndes, only the epithet, bookseller.

1790

MORSE, JEDIDIAH, 1761-1826.

GEOGRAPHY MADE EASY: BEING AN ABRIDGEMENT OF THE AMERICAN GEOGRAPHY. . . . SECOND EDITION.

Boston, Isaiah Thomas and Ebenezer T. Andrews, 1790.

Octavo, 7¾″ high, bound in contemporary full leather, gold-tooled.

Contains the eight maps called for in the Directions to the Bookbinder, of which these relate to America: World facing title page; Earth facing page 15; United States facing page 37; South America facing page 250; Europe facing page 262; and Africa facing page 310. Shipton-Mooney 22681 calls for eight plates while the New Haven [, 1784], edition, Shipton-Mooney 18615, calls for two plates. Sabin 50936 lists the editions.

1790-1792

CASSINI, Giovanni Maria, fl. 1788-1805.

GLOBO TERRESTRE DELINATIO. GLOBO CELESTE.

Rome, Presso la Calcografa, 1790-1792.

Globes, 14″ diameter, on four-footed bases.

A pair of globes.

1791

HOOPER, Samuel, fl. 1770-1793.

AN INDEX MAP TO THE ANTIQUITIES OF SCOTLAND.

London, Samuel Hooper, 1791.

Map, 17½″ high plus imprint and margins, colored.

Tooley entry for Hooper mentions publication of his work on Scotland.

1791

MORSE, Jedidiah, 1761-1826.

GEOGRAPHY MADE EASY: BEING AN ABRIDGEMENT OF THE AMERICAN GEOGRAPHY. . . . THIRD EDITION, CORRECTED.

Boston, Samuel Hall, 1791.

Octavo, 7″ high, bound in contemporary full leather, gold-stamped.

Contains the eight maps called for in the Directions to the Bookbinder and Shipton-Mooney 23579, of which these relate to America: World facing title page; Earth facing page 15; United States facing page 37; South America facing page 250; Europe facing page 262; and Africa facing page 310. Sabin 50936 lists the editions.

1792

CARY, John, 1754?-1835.

CARY'S TRAVELLER'S COMPANION, OR, A DELINEATION OF THE TURNPIKE ROADS OF ENGLAND AND WALES.

London, John Cary, 1792.

Thirty-twomo, 4⅜″ high, oblong, bound in contemporary full leather, gold-tooled.

Although the engraved title page has 1791, each of the forty-three maps colored in outline is dated 1792. Phillips 4012 notes only twenty-two maps.

1792§

ELWE, Jan Barend.

MAPPE MONDE OU DESCRIPTION DU GLOBE.

Amsterdam, Jan Barend Elwe, 1792.

Map, 11¼″ high plus margins, colored.

Facsimile of the map which *Atlantes* El 2 lists as number (3).

1792

GIBSON, John, fl. 1750-1792.

ATLAS MINIMUS, OR A NEW SET OF POCKET MAPS. . . . NEW EDITION.

London [, Emanuel Bowen], 1792.

Thirty-twomo, 4⅜″ high, bound in contemporary paper wrapper.

Contains fifty-two maps. Phillips 676 lists as relating to America numbers 1, World; 5, North America; 6, South America; 39, Nova Scotia; 40, New England; 41, New York and Pensilvania; 42, Pensilvania, Maryland and Virginia; 43, United States; 44, Carolina; 45, Newfoundland; 46, Cape Breton; 47, West Indies; 48, Canada; 49, Mexico; 50, Brazil; 51, Paraguay; and 52, Peru. To these should be added number 2, Europe, which shows Greenland above Norway.

1792

LINNERHJELM, GUSTAV FREDERIC, 1757-1819.

LANDS WÄGARNE GENOM SÖDRA DELEN AF SWERIGE.

[Stockholm?] Herrar Lands Hösdingarnes, 1792.

Map, 25⅝″ high, with margins including imprint, colored.

The map is cut into twenty parts and backed on linen for folding.

1792

MORSE, JEDIDIAH, 1761-1826.

THE AMERICAN GEOGRAPHY. . . . WITH TWO SHEET MAPS. . . . THIRD EDITION.

Dublin, John Jones, 1792.

Octavo, 8″ high, bound in contemporary full leather, gold-stamped.

Contains the Map of the States of Virginia . . . Florida, facing title page and the Map of the Northern and Middle States facing page 33, both engraved for this edition. Sabin 50924 lists the editions.

1792

STOCKDALE, JOHN, 1729-1814.

A MAP OF THE NORTHERN AND MIDDLE STATES.

[London,] John Stockdale, 1792.

Map, 12½″ high plus margins and "Engraved for [1794 London edition of Jedidiah] Morse's Geography. . . . Engraved by G. Allen Sadlers Wells Row, Islington," uncolored.

Marshall, *Clements,* II, 409, also notes publication in Pictet's *Tableau de la Situation* in Paris in 1795, Volume One, page 246.

[1793]

CARLETON, OSGOOD, 1742-1816.

THE DISTRICT OF MAIN FROM THE LATEST SURVEYS O. CARLETON DELIN.

[Boston, 1793.]

Map, 10⅝″ high plus margins, uncolored.

Published in Jedidiah Morse, *The American Universal Geography,* Shipton-Mooney 25847, opposite page 345. See Wheat & Brun 168.

[1793]

CARLETON, OSGOOD, 1742-1816.

A MAP OF PENSYLVANIA WITH PART OF THE ADJACENT STATES.

[Philadelphia, 1793.]

Map, 7⅛″ high, uncolored.

Wheat & Brun 438 notes publication in Morse's *American Universal*

Geography, I, facing 469. Shipton-Mooney 25847 calls for eleven maps.

Presented to the Pennsylvania Historical and Museum Commission in November 1981.

1793

CARY, JOHN, 1754?-1835.

BUCKINGHAMSHIRE.

London, John Cary, 1793.

Map, 10¼″ high plus imprint and margins, colored.

Phillips 5207 describes the *English Atlas* of 1793 with forty-seven maps.

1793

IMLAY, GILBERT, 1754?-1828?

A TOPOGRAPHICAL DESCRIPTION OF THE WESTERN TERRITORY OF NORTH AMERICA. . . . SECOND EDITION.

London, John Debrett, 1793.

Octavo, 7¾″ high, bound in modern half leather, gold-tooled.

Contains a map of the Western Territories, one of the Rapids of the Ohio, and one of Kentucky. Sabin 34355 calls for two maps, a plan, and a table. Mansell, 265, 138, lists editions.

1793

MORSE, JEDIDIAH, 1761-1826.

THE AMERICAN UNIVERSAL GEOGRAPHY. . . . IN TWO PARTS.

Boston, Isaiah Thomas and Ebenezer T. Andrews, Isaiah Thomas in Worcester, Berry, Rogers & Berry in New York, H. and P. Rice in Philadelphia, and W. P. Young in Charleston, 1793.

Contains the eleven maps called for in the Directions to the Bookbinder facing the Introduction, of which these relate to America: World facing title page; Northern and Middle States facing page 309; Maine facing page 345; Pennsylvania facing page 469; Virginia, North Carolina, etc., facing page 532; South America facing page 642, West Indies facing page 666; Asia facing page 384 in second volume along with Africa facing page 484. Shipton-Mooney 25847 calls for the eleven maps, eight in Volume One and three in Volume Two. Sabin 50926 lists the editions.

1793

PERKS, WILLIAM.

THE YOUTH'S GENERAL INTRODUCTION TO GEOGRAPHY. . . . SECOND EDITION.

London, George G. and J. Robinson, 1793.

Octavo, 8⅛″ high, bound in contemporary full leather, gold-stamped.

Of the twenty-eight maps called for on the title page and listed in Directions on page viii, these relate to America: two maps of World facing title page, North America facing page 333, West Indies facing page 343, and South America facing page 345. This work is not found in any bibliography of Americana except Mansell at 451, 60, where this edition is described.

CAREY, MATHEW, 1760-1839.

A GENERAL ATLAS FOR THE PRESENT WAR.

Philadelphia, Mathew Carey, 1794.

Folio, 15″ high, bound in contemporary marbled paper boards with printed paper label on front cover.

This is "the first known atlas published in the United States" in the words of Wheat & Brun in their bibliography, where this atlas is number 77. There are seven maps including one of American interest, that of the West Indies, which Phillips 6003 lists as number 7. Shipton-Mooney 26471 also calls for seven maps and Sabin 10858 has later editions.

GUTHRIE, WILLIAM, 1708-1770.

A NEW SYSTEM OF MODERN GEOGRAPHY. . . . IN TWO VOLUMES. . . . FIRST AMERICAN EDITION.

Philadelphia, Mathew Carey, 1794.

Folio, 10¼″ high, bound in contemporary full leather, gold-tooled.

The Preface contains a long and important critical essay on the merit of the work and speaks of the need for those new maps included in a separate atlas, and Shipton-Mooney 27077 and 28782 call for forty-seven maps there. Sabin 29327 lists the editions.

JEFFERYS, THOMAS, 1710?-1771.

THE COAST OF WEST FLORIDA AND LOUISIANA.

London, William Laurie & James Whittle, 1794.

Map, 18⅝″ high plus margins and title, colored.

Marshall, *Clements,* I, 469, describes the Sayer 1775 edition of this map first printed in the 1750s.

MORSE, JEDIDIAH, 1761-1826.

THE AMERICAN GEOGRAPHY. . . . NEW EDITION.

London, John Stockdale, 1794.

Quarto, 11¼″ high, bound in contemporary paper, rebacked.

Contains the twenty-five maps called for on the title page. Phillips 1361 lists those maps and points out that "while this work can not be regarded as an atlas, it contains a collection of the earliest maps of the states in the union." Sabin 50924 lists the editions.

MORSE, JEDIDIAH, 1761-1826.

GEOGRAPHY MADE EASY: BEING AN ABRIDGMENT OF THE AMERICAN UNIVERSAL GEOGRAPHY. . . . FOURTH EDITION, ABRIDGED, CORRECTED AND ENLARGED BY THE AUTHOR.

Boston, Isaiah Thomas and Ebenezer T. Andrews, 1794.

Octavo, 6⅞″ high, bound in contemporary full leather, gold-tooled.

Contains the nine maps called for in the Directions to the Bookbinder at page 432, of which these relate to America: World facing title page; United States facing page 67; Europe facing page 312; and Africa facing page 393. Shipton-Mooney 27351 reproduces these nine maps and Sabin 50936 lists the editions.

1794

PLOWDEN, FRANCIS PETER, 1749-1829.

A SHORT HISTORY OF THE BRITISH EMPIRE, FROM MAY 1792 TO ... 1793.

Philadelphia, Mathew Carey, 1794.

Quarto, 8″ high, bound in contemporary full leather, gold-stamped.

Shipton-Mooney 27529 notes that no map is included.

[1794-1799]

HEATHER, WILLIAM, fl. 1790-1812.

EAST INDIA PILOT.

London, William Heather [, 1794-1799].

Presented to the Philadelphia Maritime Museum in May 1982.

1795

CAREY, MATHEW, 1760-1839.

CAREY'S AMERICAN ATLAS.

Philadelphia, Mathew Carey, 1795.

Folio, 14¾″ high, bound in contemporary half leather, blind-tooled.

This is the first American atlas printed in the United States and it contains twenty-one maps listed in Phillips 1172, all of which relate to America. Shipton-Mooney 28390 enters under title. Sabin 10855 mentions twenty maps and one chart.

1795

CAREY, MATHEW, 1760-1839.

THE GENERAL ATLAS FOR CAREY'S EDITION OF GUTHRIE'S GEOGRAPHY.

Philadelphia, Mathew Carey, 1795.

Folio, 17¾″ high, bound in contemporary half leather.

Contains forty-five maps as listed in Phillips 683 which is for Carey's *General Atlas* of 1796. Those relating to America are numbers 1 and 23 through 45 of which all but numbers 1, 42, and 43 are new in this edition. Shipton-Mooney 47370 notes that the "only copy cannot be reproduced," making this copy extremely rare. Sabin 10858 mentions the American edition of Guthrie. Cresswell says that "this is the largest copy I have ever seen: huge margins on the folding maps, light impressions, but all first states."

[1795]

CARLETON, OSGOOD, 1742-1816.

AN ACCURATE MAP OF THE COMMONWEALTH OF MASSACHUSETTS EXCLUSIVE OF THE DISTRICT OF MAIN.

Boston, Osgood Carleton and John Norman [, 1795].

Map, 34⅝″ high plus margins, colored in outline in map, in four sheets.

Wheat & Brun 214 dates [1795] and cites only two locations in America. Shipton-Mooney does not include under Carleton nor under title.

See PLATE 48

[1795]

CARLETON, OSGOOD, 1742-1816.

AN ACCURATE MAP OF THE DISTRICT OF MAINE.

Boston, Osgood Carleton, John Norman, and William Norman [, 1795].

Map, 53⅝″ high plus margins, colored in outline.

Shipton-Mooney 28391 dates [1795], for Carleton was only selling maps in that year. Wheat & Brun 170 describes the range of dates from 1790 through 1799. Not seen.

Presented to the Maine State Museum.

[1795]§

CARLETON, OSGOOD, 1742-1816.

A MAP OF THE DISTRICT OF MAINE.

[Boston, Isaiah Thomas and Ebenezer Andrews, 1795.]

Map, 16⅜″ high plus margins, uncolored.

Facsimile of the John Carter Brown Library copy from Sullivan's *History of Maine,* Shipton-Mooney 29589, where it is a folding map. Marshall, *Clements,* I, 144, gives the measurements as 20½″ x 16½″.

[1795]

DWIGHT, NATHANIEL, 1770-1831.

A SHORT BUT COMPREHENSIVE SYSTEM OF THE GEOGRAPHY. . . . SECOND CONNECTICUT EDITION.

Hartford, Barzillai Hudson and George Goodwin, Isaac Beers of New Haven, B. Talmadge of Litchfield, Timothy C. Green of New London, and Andrew Huntington of Norwich [, 1795].

Octavo, 6⅜″ high, bound in contemporary half leather.

The two maps engraved by Amos Doolittle relate to America, one facing page 10, Eastern Continent, and the other facing page 143, Western Continent, in Shipton-Mooney 28607. In addition to this edition, Shipton-Mooney, I, 236, lists those of Boston, Albany, Hartford, and, at 28609, a questionable date of [1802] for the Philadelphia edition.

1795

FORTIN, JEAN, 1750-1831.

ATLAS CÉLESTE DE FLAMSTEED. . . . TROISIEME EDITION.

Paris, Charles François Delamarche, 1795.

Quarto, 8¾″ high, bound in contemporary half leather, gold-stamped.

Contains thirty celestial charts.

[1795]

GILLING, W.

A NEW GENERAL ATLAS OF THE WORLD.

London, W. Gilling [, 1795].

Folio, 16½" high, bound in nineteenth-century half leather with contemporary boards, gold-tooled.

Contains thirty-eight colored maps listed on leaf following title page, plus map of world bound as frontispiece. Those relating to America are frontispiece map and numbers 27, 28, 29, and 30. Mansell, 200, 219, lists the only copy, that at Princeton, dated [18—?].

1795

KITCHIN, THOMAS, 1718-1784.

A GENERAL ATLAS, DESCRIBING THE WHOLE UNIVERSE . . . FROM THE LAST EDITION OF D'ANVILLE AND ROBERT [DE VAUGONDY].

London, Robert Laurie and James Whittle, 1795.

Folio, 21½" high, bound in modern half leather with contemporary boards, blind- and gold-stamped.

Thirty-seven maps are listed on the title page and are present, colored in outline. Phillips 3529 lists those maps of which the following relate to America: 1, 2, 25, 26, 32, 33, 34, 35, 36, and 37. Sabin 38021 describes the 1773 edition.

1795

PEACOCK, W.

A COMPENDIOUS GEOGRAPHICAL AND HISTORICAL GRAMMAR.

London, W. Peacock, 1795.

Octavo, 5" high, bound in contemporary full leather, gold-stamped.

Of the maps present, the following relate to America: World facing title page and United States facing page 295. Mansell, 118, 200, has the editions entered under title.

1795

THE PROVINCE OF MAINE, FROM THE BEST AUTHORITIES 1795.

[New York, John Reid, 1796.]

Map, 14⅜" high plus margins, uncolored.

Published in John Reid, *The American Atlas,* as number 5 of the twenty maps called for in Shipton-Mooney 31078. Wheat & Brun 176 discusses two editions.

1795

SCOTT, JOSEPH.

THE UNITED STATES GAZETTEER.

Philadelphia, Francis and R. Bailey, 1795.

Octavo, 6⅝" high, bound in contemporary full leather, gold-stamped.

The nineteen maps called for on the title page are present, bound in alphabetically. Shipton-Mooney 29476 provides no dates for Scott, using instead the epithet, geographer, to distinguish from Joseph Scott, importer. Mansell, 534, 182, lists the editions of this first gazetteer of the United States.

1795

SMITH, CHARLES, 1768-1808.

UNIVERSAL GEOGRAPHY MADE EASY.

New York, Wayland & Davis, 1795.

Octavo, 5⅜" high, bound in contemporary full leather, gold stamped.

Contains five maps of which those related to America are the frontispiece map of the World and maps facing these pages: 21, Europe showing Greenland as an island above Norway which is similar to map in GIBSON, ATLAS MINIMUS 1792; 133, United States, and 172, South America. Shipton-Mooney 29521 calls for seven maps.

1795

SULLIVAN, JAMES, 1744-1808.

THE HISTORY OF THE DISTRICT OF MAINE.

Boston, Isaiah Thomas and Ebenezer T. Andrews, 1795.

Octavo, 8″ high, bound in contemporary full leather, gold-tooled.

Contains the map by Osgood Carleton called for on the title page and in Shipton-Mooney 29589. Sabin 93499 discusses the map.

[1795]

TANNER, BENJAMIN.

CHINA, DIVIDED INTO ITS GREAT PROVINCES.

[Philadelphia, 1795.]

Map, 13″ high at neat lines plus lines and margins and "Engraved for Carey's American Edition of Guthrie's Geography improved," uncolored.

The earliest American map of China, Wheat & Brun 880, State I, 1795. Shipton-Mooney 27077 and 28782 call for forty-seven maps in the two volumes.

Presented to the Philadelphia Maritime Museum in May 1984.

[1795]

WALKER, JOHN, 1759-1830.

[AN ATLAS OF THE GLOBE.]

[London, 1795.]

Octavo, 8½″ high, bound in contemporary half leather, gold-tooled.

Contains twenty-five maps of which the first two, the last three, and number 19 (plate XXV) relate to America; plates I, VII, XXV, XXVIII, XXIX, and XXX. Phillips 689 describes the Dublin edition of 1797 and points out that the "maps and plates are like those in Walker's 'Universal Gazetteer' and 'Elements of Geography'."

1795

WINTERBOTHAM, WILLIAM, 1763-1829.

AN HISTORICAL GEOGRAPHICAL . . . VIEW OF THE AMERICAN UNITED STATES. . . . IN FOUR VOLUMES.

London, J. Ridgway, H. D. Symonds, and D. Holt of Newark, 1795.

Quartos, 8¼″ high, bound in contemporary half leather, gold-stamped.

Those maps relating to America by volume are:

I United States, J. Russell, 1794, facing page 157, United States, 1783, facing page 175,

II Northern States facing page 1, Middle States facing page 282,

III Southern States facing page 1,
Washington facing page 69,
Kentucky facing page 125,
Lystra facing page 141,
Franklinville facing page 144,

IV South America facing page 119, and
West Indies facing page 228.

This is Sabin 104832. Shipton-Mooney 31647 reproduces the New York 1796 edition.

1796

BARROW, JOHN, 1764-1848.

A CHART . . . TRACK AND SOUNDINGS OF THE LION, THE HINDOSTAN AND TENDERS FROM TURON-BAY.

London, George Nicol, 1796.

Map, 27½″ high plus margins and "Engraved by B. Baker," uncolored.

Presented to the Philadelphia Maritime Museum in May 1984.

1796

BARROW, JOHN, 1764-1848.

A GENERAL CHART . . . TRACK OF THE LION AND HINDOSTAN FROM ENGLAND TO THE GULPH OF PEKIN IN CHINA.

London, George Nicol, 1796.

Map, 22½″ high plus margins and "J. Barrow del't." and "B. Baker sculp't," uncolored.

Presented to the Philadelphia Maritime Museum in May 1984.

1796

BROOKES, RICHARD.

BROOKES' GENERAL GAZETTEER ABRIDGED.

London, B. Law, etc., 1796.

Twelvemo, 7″ high, bound in contemporary full leather, gold-stamped on morocco spine label.

Contains six maps of which those relating to America are the World as frontispiece and maps of North and South America facing entry AME.

1796

CAREY, MATHEW, 1760-1839.

CAREY'S AMERICAN POCKET ATLAS.

Philadelphia, Lang and Ustick for Mathew Carey, 1796.

Twelvemo, 6½″ high, bound in contemporary full leather with modern spine.

Contains nineteen maps of America, listed in Phillips 1364 where he points out that they are engraved by "W. Barker, J. H. Seymour, A. Doolittle." Shipton-Mooney 30161 notes that no copy located has the imprint called for by Evans. Sabin 10856 has this as the first in the list of editions.

1796

FLAVEL, JOHN, 1630?-1691.

NAVIGATION SPIRITUALIZED.

Newburyport, Edmund M. Blunt, 1796.

Quarto, 7⅛″ high, bound in contemporary half leather.

A spiritual work for sailors originally published in London in 1663 and reproduced in a 1726 American edition at Shipton-Mooney 2742 and for this edition at 30428.

[1796]

HARRIS, CYRUS.

PENNSYLVANIA DRAWN FROM THE BEST AUTHORITIES.

[Boston,] Isaiah Thomas and Ebenezer T. Andrews [, 1796].

Map, 7⅝″ high plus margins, uncolored.

Wheat & Brun 446 notes publication in Morse's *American Universal Geography,* third edition, I, facing 533. Shipton-Mooney 30824 calls for eighteen maps.

Presented to the Pennsylvania Historical and Museum Commission in November 1981.

1796

MORSE, JEDIDIAH, 1761-1826.

ELEMENTS OF GEOGRAPHY. . . . SECOND EDITION, CORRECTED.

Boston, Isaiah Thomas and Ebenezer T. Andrews, Isaiah Thomas in Worcester, S. Campbell in New York, Mathew Carey in Philadelphia, Thomas, Andrews and Butler in Baltimore, 1796.

Octavo, 5⅜″ high, bound in contemporary half leather.

Contains two maps called for on title page and in Shipton-Mooney 30826, World as frontispiece and United States facing page 74. Sabin 50935 lists the editions.

1796

MORSE, JEDIDIAH, 1761-1826.

GEOGRAPHY MADE EASY: BEING AN ABRIDGEMENT OF THE AMERICAN UNIVERSAL GEOGRAPHY. . . . FIFTH EDITION, CORRECTED.

Boston, Isaiah Thomas and Ebenezer T. Andrews, Isaiah Thomas in Worcester, S. Campbell in New York, Mathew Carey in Philadelphia, and Thomas, Andrews and Butler in Baltimore, 1796.

Octavo, 6⅞″ high, bound in contemporary full leather, gold-stamped.

Contains the nine maps called for in the Directions to the Bookbinder at page iv, and in Shipton-Mooney 30827, of which these relate to America: World facing title page; United States facing page 67, Europe facing page 312; and Africa facing page 393. Sabin 50936 lists the editions.

1796

PAYNE, JOHN, fl. 1800.

UNIVERSAL GEOGRAPHY. . . . IN TWO VOLUMES.

London, J. Johnson and B. Crosby, and at New York, Rogers and Berry, 1796.

The maps relating to America in Volume One are World in Introduction, Pacific Ocean at page 524, World at page 560, and Discoveries at page 593, and in Volume Two are North America at page 645, United States at page 664, West Indies at page 692, and South America at page 723. Cresswell notes that "of the geographies and general histories then published, this is one of the more lovely due to the engraving quality and appreciation of botany." The American editions of Payne's work appear at Shipton-Mooney 34316, 38199, and 36047.

1797

MALHAM, JOHN, 1747-1821.

THE NAVAL GAZETTEER; OR, SEAMAN'S COMPLETE GUIDE. . . . FIRST AMERICAN EDITION. IN TWO VOLUMES.

Boston, Samuel Etheridge for William Spotswood and Joseph Nancrede, 1797.

Quartos, 8¼″ high, bound in modern cloth, stamped.

The following maps in Volume One relate to America: World facing title page, East Coast of North America facing page 30, West Coast of North America facing page 30, South America facing page 30, and West India Islands facing page 515. Shipton-Mooney 32415 calls for seventeen maps. Sabin 44119 also has the second edition.

1797

MORSE, JEDIDIAH, 1761-1826.

THE AMERICAN GAZETTEER [first edition].

Boston, Samuel Hall, Isaiah Thomas and Ebenezer T. Andrews, Ebenezer Larkin; Hugh Gaine and Ten Eyck and S. Campbell in New York; Mathew Carey and William Young in Philadelphia; Websters and Thomas, Andrews and Penniman in Albany; and Thomas, Andrews and Butler in Baltimore; 1797.

Octavo, 8⅜″ high, bound in contemporary full leather, rebacked.

Contains the seven maps called for in the Directions to the Binder at end, and reproduced in Shipton-Mooney 32509, of which these relate to America: North America facing title page; South America facing entry AMB; Western Georgia facing entry GEO; Northern United States facing entry NEW; Southern United States facing entry SPL; and West Indies facing entry TEU. Sabin 50923 lists the editions.

1798

F., W., OF WARWICK.

AN INTRODUCTION TO THE USE OF THE GLOBES.

Warwick, H. Sharpe for J. Johnson of London, 1798.

Octavo, 7″ high, bound in contemporary full leather, gold-tooled by Sharpe of Warwick.

Mansell does not have under author or title, but 165, 124, at F., W., refers to William Field, 1768-1851, an antiquarian of Warwick, whose publications are at 171, 633.

1798

GIBSON, JOHN, fl. 1750-1792.

ATLAS MINIMUS UNIVERSALIS.

London, William Faden, 1798 [dated on engraved title page].

Twenty-fourmo, 5⅛″ high, oblong, bound in contemporary full leather, gold-tooled.

Contains fifty-five maps including maps 20 and 31 dated 1804. The following relate to America: 12, 13, 14, 15, 16, 17, 38, 45, 50, 51, 52, 53, and 54. Phillips 690 has only map 21 dated 1804 and only nine relating to America. He dates this at 1798.

1798

GIBSON, JOHN, fl. 1750-1792.

ATLAS MINIMUS. . . . NEW EDITION.

Philadelphia, Mathew Carey, 1798.

Octavos, 5″ high, bound in contemporary full leather, gold-stamped.

Contains forty-one maps, of which Phillips 691 lists numbers 5 and 6 as relating to America, to which should be added number 1 and three maps not called for in Index, numbers 39, 40, and 41. Shipton-Mooney 33794 enters under Gibson, James, and reproduces the maps. Two copies present.

1798§

HILLS, JOHN, fl. 1777-1817

THIS PLAN OF THE CITY OF PHILADELPHIA AND ITS ENVIRONS. . . . MAY 30TH 1796.

Philadelphia, John Hills, 1798.

Map, 24" high plus margins, uncolored.

Facsimile published by the Society of Colonial Wars in the Commonwealth of Pennsylvania in 1959, following republication by Samuel L. Smedley in 1881 by photolithography by Thomas Hunter using a London 1798 engraving by John Cooke of Hendon for John and Josiah Boydell, "Published 1st January, 1798." Shipton-Mooney 32253 gives no dates for Hills but reproduces map.

1798

MORSE, JEDIDIAH, 1761-1826.

AN ABRIDGEMENT OF THE AMERICAN GAZETTEER.

Boston, Isaiah Thomas and Ebenezer T. Andrews, Ebenezer Larkin; Isaiah Thomas in Worcester; Thomas, Andrews and Penniman in Albany; and Thomas, Andrews and Butler in Baltimore, 1798.

Contains the map of North America as a frontispiece in Shipton-Mooney 34143. Sabin 50922 lists the editions.

1798

MORSE, JEDIDIAH, 1761-1826.

ELEMENTS OF GEOGRAPHY. . . . THIRD EDITION, IMPROVED.

Boston, Isaiah Thomas and Ebenezer T. Andrews, Isaiah Thomas in Worcester, Thomas, Andrews and Penniman in Albany, Thomas, Andrews and Butler in Baltimore, 1798.

Octavo, 5½" high, bound in contemporary half leather.

Contains two maps called for on title page, World as frontispiece and United States facing page 36, reproduced in Shipton-Mooney 34145. Sabin 50935 lists the editions.

[1799?]

[DELAMARCHE, CHARLES FRANÇOIS, 1740-1817.]

[ARMILLARY SPHERE.]

[Paris, 1799?]

Sphere, 9" diameter, on a round base.

In his appraisal of the fifty-nine globes in the collection, Donald Cresswell assigned this globe to Delamarche on stylistic grounds and dated it ca. 1790s, and Pedley has done work on this subject.

1799

GOLDBACH, Christian Friedrich, 1763-1811.

NEUESTER HIMMELS-ATLAS ZUM GEBRAUCHE FÜR SCHUL- UND AKADEMISCHEN UNTERRICHT.

Weimar, 1799.

Octavo, 9¾″ high, bound in contemporary half leather with engraved label on front cover.

Contains fifty-six celestial charts. Tooley dates 1803 in his dictionary, and Mansell notes only four copies.

1799

WILLIAMS, Jonathan, 1750-1815.

THERMOMETRICAL NAVIGATION.

Philadelphia, Robert Aitken, 1799.

Quarto, 8¾″ high, bound in nineteenth-century half leather.

Contains folding map of the Gulf Stream and is reproduced in Shipton-Mooney 25040.

1799-1800

DELAMARCHE, Charles François, 1740-1817.

GLOBE TERRESTRE . . . AN. 8.

Paris, 1799-1800.

Globe, 9″ diameter, on single-pillar base.

A terrestrial globe described by Yonge at page 24. By the French Republican Calendar, Year VIII ran from September 23, 1799, to September 22, 1800.

1800

ADAMS, George, 1750-1795.

ASTRONOMICAL AND GEOGRAPHICAL ESSAYS. . . . FOURTH EDITION.

Philadelphia, "Whitehall: Printed for" William Young, 1800.

Quarto, 8⅜″ high, bound in modern half leather, gold-tooled.

Contains engraved frontispiece related to America and fifteen numbered plates of which numbers VII, IX, and XII relate to America. Shipton-Mooney 36756 reproduces sixteen folding plates.

1800

ADAMS, George, 1750-1795.

AN ESSAY ON THE USE OF THE CELESTIAL AND TERRESTRIAL GLOBES. . . . FOURTH EDITION.

Philadelphia, "Whitehall: Printed for" William Young, 1800.

Quarto, 8⅝″ high, bound in contemporary full leather, gold-tooled.

Contains three plates, the first of which relates to America. Shipton-Mooney 36757 calls for two plates.

CARY, JOHN, 1754?-1835, and
CARY, WILLIAM, 1759-1825.

> CARY'S NEW TERRESTRIAL GLOBE.
>
> London, John and William Cary, 1800.
>
> Globe, 12″ diameter on stand.

CARY, JOHN, 1754?-1835, and
CARY, WILLIAM, 1759-1825.

> CARY'S NEW CELESTIAL GLOBE.
>
> London, John and William Cary, 1800.
>
> Globe, 12″ diameter on stand.

CARY, JOHN, 1754?-1835, and
CARY, WILLIAM, 1759-1825.

> CARY'S NEW CELESTIAL GLOBE ON WHICH ARE CORRECTLY LAID DOWN UPWARDS OF 3300 STARS.
>
> London, John and William Cary, 1800.
>
> Globe, 12″ diameter, on tripod base.

Yonge describes this at page 17.

OXHOLM, PETER LOTHARIUS VON, 1753-1827.

> CHARTE OVER DEN DANSKE OE ST. JAN I AMERICA.
>
> Copenhagen, Peter Lotharius von Oxholm, 1800.
>
> Map, 13½″ high overall, uncolored.

Facsimile published by the Virgin Islands Agency, Eastern National Park and Monument Association. Sabin 58042 and 58043 notes his work on the Danish West Indies, and Mansell, 436, 355 and 356, lists his publications including this map engraved by G. N. Angelo.

Select References

————•————

Index of Mapmakers and Geographers

SELECT REFERENCES

Atlantes Cornelis Koeman, *Atlantes Neerlandici: Bibliography of Terrestrial, Maritime and Celestial Atlases and Pilot Books, Published in the Netherlands up to 1880.* Amsterdam, Theatrum Orbis Terrarum, 1967 [Volume I]-1971 [Volume V].

British Museum *Catalogue of the Printed Maps, Plans, and Charts in the British Museum.* London, British Museum, 1885.

Cumming, British William P. Cumming, *British Maps of Colonial America.* Chicago, University of Chicago Press, 1974.

Cumming, Southeast William P. Cumming, *The Southeast in Early Maps, With an Annotated Check List of Printed and Manuscript Regional and Local Maps.* Chapel Hill, University of North Carolina Press, 1962.

Discovering New World *Discovering the New World, Based on the Works of Theodore de Bry.* Edited by Michael Alexander. New York, Harper & Row, 1976.

Evans, Des Barres Geraint N. D. Evans, *Uncommon Obdurate: The Several Public Careers of J. F. W. Des Barres.* Salem, Peabody Museum, 1969.

Harrisse B.A.V. Henry Harrisse, *Bibliotheca Americana Vetustissima: A Description of Works Relating to America . . . 1492-1551.* New York, George P. Philes, 1866.

Kapp Kit S. Kapp, "The Early Maps of Colombia up to 1850." *Map Collectors' Circle,* Number 77, 1971.

Koeman, Sea Cornelis Koeman, *The Sea on Paper: The Story of the Van Keulens and Their 'Sea-Torch.'* Amsterdam, Theatrum Orbis Terrarum, 1972.

LeGear Clara Egli LeGear, *A List of Geographical Atlases in the Library of Congress with Bibliographical Notes (A Continuation of Four Volumes by Philip Lee Phillips).* Washington, Government Printing Office, 1958 [Volume 5]-1973 [Volume 7].

Mansell *The National Union Catalog Pre-1956 Imprints: A Cumulative Author List Representing Library of Congress Printed Cards and Titles Reported by Other American Libraries.* London, Mansell Publishing, 1968 [Volume 1]-1980 [Volume 685] and Supplement 1980 [Volume 686]-1981 [Volume 754].

Maritime *National Maritime Museum Catalogue of the Library: Atlases & Cartography.* London, Her Majesty's Stationery Office, 1971.

Marshall, Clements Douglas W. Marshall, *Research Catalog of Maps of America to 1860 in the William L. Clements Library University of Michigan Ann Arbor.* Boston, G. K. Hall & Company, 1972.

Miller C. William Miller, *Benjamin Franklin's Philadelphia Printing 1728-1766: A Descriptive Bibliography.* Philadelphia, American Philosophical Society, 1974.

Pedley Mary Sponberg Pedley, "The Subscription List of the 1757 Atlas Universel: A Study in Cartographic Dissemination." *Imago Mundi,* 31, 66-77.

Phillips   Philip Lee Phillips, *A List of Geographical Atlases in the Library of Congress with Bibliographical Notes.* Washington, Government Printing Office, 1909 [Volumes I and II], 1914 [Volume III], and 1920 [Volume IV].

Phillips, Maps Philip Lee Phillips, *A List of Maps of America in the Library of Congress Preceded by a List of Works Relating to Cartography.* Washington, Government Printing Office, 1901.

STC   *A Short-Title Catalogue of Books Printed in England, Scotland, & Ireland ... 1475-1640.* Compiled by A. W. Pollard and G. R. Redgrave. London, Bibliographical Society, 1926 & 1976.

Sabin   Joseph Sabin, *Bibliotheca Americana. A Dictionary of Books Relating to America, from its Discovery to the Present Time.* Begun by Joseph Sabin, continued by Wilberforce Eames and Completed by R. W. G. Vail for the Bibliographical Society of America. New York, 1868 [Volume I]-1936 [Volume XXIX].

Schwartz and   Seymour I. Schwartz and Ralph E. Ehrenberg, *The
Ehrenberg   Mapping of America.* New York, Harry N. Abrams, Inc., 1980.

Sellers & Van Ee John R. Sellers and Patricia Molen Van Ee, *Maps and Charts of North America and the West Indies 1750-1789.* Washington, Government Printing Office, 1981.

Shipton-Mooney Clifford K. Shipton and James E. Mooney, *National Index of American Imprints Through 1800: The Short-Title Evans.* Worcester, American Antiquarian Society and Barre Publishers, 1969.

Shirley   Rodney W. Shirley, *The Mapping of the World: Early Printed World Maps 1472-1700.* London, Holland Press, 1984.

Skelton, County R. A. Skelton, "County Atlases of the British Isles
Atlases   1579-1850: A Bibliography." *Map Collectors' Circle,* Numbers 9, 14, 41, 49, and 63 [1964-1970].

Skelton, Maps   R. A. Skelton, *Decorative Printed Maps of the 15th to 18th Centuries.* London, Staples Press, 1952.

Stevenson   Edward Luther Stevenson, *Terrestrial and Celestial Globes: Their History and Construction.* New Haven, Yale University Press for the Hispanic Society of America, 1921.

Stokes   Isaac Newton Phelps Stokes, *The Iconography of Manhattan Island, 1498-1909; Compiled from Original Sources and Illustrated by Photo-Intaglio Reproductions of Important Maps, Plans, Views, and Documents in Public and Private Collections.* New York, Robert H. Dodd, 1915 [Volume I]-1928 [Volume VI].

Streeter   *The Celebrated Collection of Americana Formed by the Late Thomas Winthrop Streeter.* New York, Parke-Bernet Galleries Inc., 1966 [Volume 1]-1969 [Volume 7].

Thomas   Isaiah Thomas, *The History of Printing in America with a Biography of Printers & an Account of Newspapers.* Second Edition. Worcester, American Antiquarian Society Transactions, 1874.

Tooley,   Ronald Vere Tooley, "Printed Maps of America." *Map
America   Collectors' Circle,* Numbers 68, 69, 80, 96, 106 [1971-1974].

Tooley,
California

Ronald Vere Tooley, "California as an Island: A Geographical Misconception Illustrated by 100 Examples from 1625 to 1770. *Map Collectors' Circle,* Number 8 [1964].

Tooley,
Dictionary

Ronald Vere Tooley, *Tooley's Dictionary of Mapmakers.* Tring, Map Collector Publications, 1979.

Tooley, Maps

Ronald Vere Tooley, *Maps and Map-makers.* London, B. T. Batsford Ltd., 1952.

Van Eerde

Katherine S. Van Eerde, *John Ogilby and the Taste of His Times.* Folkestone, Dawson, 1976.

Wheat & Brun

James Clements Wheat and Christian F. Brun, *Maps and Charts Published in America Before 1800: A Bibliography.* New Haven, Yale University Press, 1969.

Yonge

Ena L. Yonge, *A Catalogue of Early Globes Made Prior to 1850 and Conserved in the United States.* New York, American Geographical Society, 1968.

INDEX OF MAPMAKERS AND GEOGRAPHERS

This guide is to the date assigned to the item in the catalogue, without inclusion of brackets, question marks, or continuations, and without reference to the number of items in any year. For example, Ortelius 1570 refers to five maps and two atlases.

AA, Pieter van der, 1707, 1714, 1730

ADAMS, George, 1800

ALINGHAM, William, 1703

ALLARD, Carel, 1695

ALLEN, George S., 1792

ANSON, George, 1751

ANDREWS, P., 1775

ANVILLE, Jean Baptiste Bourguignon d', 1700, 1727, 1746, 1763, 1769, 1771, 1777, 1790, 1795

APIAN, Peter, 1520

APRÈS DE MANNEVILLETTE, Jean Baptiste Nicolas Denis d', 1775, 1781

ARIAS, Montano Benito, 1571

BACON, Francis, 1648

BAKER, Benjamin, 1796

BALDWIN, Richard, Jr., 1755

BANKES, Thomas, 1787, 1788

BARDIN, William, 1785

BARKER, William, 1796

BARNSLEY, Henry, 1755

BARROW, John, 1796

BASTIONS, Thomas, 1770

BAYER, Johann, 1603

BEHAIM, Martin, 1492

BELLIN, Jacques Nicolas, 1700, 1747, 1751, 1753, 1754, 1755, 1758, 1763, 1764

BENNETT, John, 1775, 1776

BEREY, Claude Auguste, 1688

BERLINGHIERI, Francesco di Nicola, 1482

BERTELLI, Fernando, 1565

BERTIUS, Petrus, 1618, 1629

BICKHAM, George, 1747

BIDDLE, Mary, 1762

BION, Nicolas, 1700

BLAEU, Cornelis, 1640

BLAEU, Joan, 1635, 1640, 1654, 1662, 1665, 1668, 1700

BLAEU, Willem, 1602, 1603, 1606, 1612, 1619, 1630, 1635, 1636, 1640, 1645, 1650, 1660, 1662, 1668

BLAIR, John, 1768

BLASKOWITZ, Charles, 1770

BLOME, Richard, 1670, 1688

BONNE, Rigobert, 1762, 1780, 1785, 1789

BORDONE, Benedetto, 1528

BOUGAINVILLE, Louis Antoine, Comte de, 1772

BOUGUEREAU, Maurice, 1594

BOULENGER, Jean, 1620

BOWEN, Emanuel, 1740, 1744, 1747, 1748, 1752, 1759, 1762, 1777, 1778, 1787, 1788, 1792

BOYDELL, John and Josiah, 1797

BRAUN, George, 1572, 1575

BROOKES, Richard, 1796

BROUCKNER, Isaac, 1749

BRY, Theodore de, 1588, 1590, 1597, 1609

BUACHE, Philippe, 1700, 1740, 1745, 1757

BUELL, Abel, 1784

BUFFIER, Claude, 1758, 1768

BURGHERS, Michael, 1700

BUY DE MORNAS, Claud, 1761

CADELL, Thomas, 1789

CAMDEN, William, 1607, 1610, 1695

CAREY, Mathew, 1794, 1795, 1796, 1798

CARLETON, Osgood, 1793, 1795

CARTIER, Jacques, 1556

CARY, John, 1787, 1792, 1793, 1800

CARY, William, 1800

CASSINI, Giovanni Maria, 1790

CELLARIUS, Christophorus, 1703

CHAMPLAIN, Samuel de, 1612, 1616, 1677

CHASSEREAU, Pierre, 1741

CHATELAIN, Henry Abraham, 1705, 1719

CHIAVES, Hieronymus, 1584

CHILMEAD, John, 1639

CHURCH, Benjamin, 1716

CHURCHMAN, John, 1790

CLARKE, Robert, 1614

CLARKSON, Matthew, 1762

CLUVER, Philip, 1616, 1629, 1659

COLSON, Nathaniel, 1783

COLTELLINI, Marco, 1763

COOKE, John, 1797

CORDIER, Louis, 1674

CORONELLI, Vincenzo Maria, 1695, 1706

COSTA, J. de, 1775

COVENS, Johannes, 1700, 1722, 1730, 1734,
    1740, 1741, 1745

CRANZ, David, 1767

CREPY, Chez, 1772

CRESPY, Jean, 1688

CURSON, Henry, 1706

CUSHEE, Richard, 1731

CUTLER, Nathaniel, 1728

DANCKERTS, Justus, 1696

DELAHAYE, Guillaume Nicolas, 1746, 1753

DELAMARCHE, Charles François, 1787, 1795,
    1799

DES BARRES, Joseph Frederick Wallet, 1776, 1779

DESMAREST, Nicolas, 1789

DEZAUCHE, J. A., 1757, 1787

DIDEROT, Denis, 1770

DONCKER, Hendrik, 1689

DOOLITTLE, Amos, 1795, 1796

DOUGLASS, William, 1755

DONIS, Nicolaus, 1482

DOPPELMAYR, Johann Gabriel, 1742

DRAYTON, Michael, 1612

DUDLEY, Robert, 1646

DUNN, Samuel, 1774

DURELL, Philip, 1740

DURY, Andrew, 1763, 1775

DU SAUZET, Henri, 1734

DU VAL, Pierre, 1677, 1684

DWIGHT, Nathaniel, 1795

EIMMART, Georg Christopher, 1705

ELWE, Jan Barend, 1792

ESNAUTS & RAPILLY, 1781

EVANS, Lewis, 1755, 1776, 1778

EXPILLY, Jean Joseph Georges, Abbé d', 1782

FADEN, William, 1775, 1776, 1777, 1778, 1779,
    1798

FAVOLI, Hugo, 1585

FENNING, Daniel, 1769, 1785

FER, Nicolas de, 1697, 1702, 1705, 1717

FERGUSON, James, 1754

FIELD, William, 1798

FIELDING, John, 1783

FISHER, Joshua, 1778

FISHER, William, 1677

FLAMSTEED, John, 1795

FLAVEL, John, 1796

FORTIN, Jean, 1795

FOSTER, John, 1677

FOX, Luke, 1635

FRANCE, Depot de la Marine, 1751, 1753, 1754,
    1755, 1778, 1779, 1786

FRANKLIN, Benjamin, 1755, 1784

FRANQUELIN, Jean Baptiste Louis, 1714

FREITAG, Gerard, 1630

GASTALDI, Giacomo, 1548, 1571

GASTALDO, Jacopo, 1548, 1571

GERRITSZ, Hessel, 1630, 1633

GIBSON, Edmund, 1695

GIBSON, John, 1758, 1792, 1798

GIGANTE, Joannes Michael, 1630

GILLING, W., 1795

GIRAULT, Simon, 1592

GOLDBACH, Christian Friedrich, 1799

GOOS, Pieter, 1639, 1666, 1667, 1676

GRAVELOT, Hubert François Bourguignon, 1746

GREGORY, John, 1671

GRIJP, Dirck, 1676

GUERARD, Jean, 1634

GUTHRIE, William, 1780, 1788, 1794, 1795

HAKLUYT, Richard, 1582, 1589

HALL, C., 1775

HALL, Ralph, 1637

HALLEY, Edmund, 1710

HAMMOND, Capt. Sir Andrew Snape, 1779

HARRIS, Cyrus, 1796

HARRIS, John, 1721, 1744

HARRISON, John, 1790

HEAP, George, 1777

HEATHER, William, 1794

HENNEPIN, Louis de, 1698

HEYLIN, Peter, 1677

HEYNS, Pieter, 1585
HILLS, John, 1798
HINTON, John, 1757
HOCKER, Johann Ludwig, 1734
HOGENBERG, Frans, 1570, 1572, 1575
HOLLAND, Samuel, 1776, 1778
HOLME, Thomas, 1689
HOMANN, Johann Baptist or Heirs, 1700, 1703, 1710, 1716, 1728, 1730, 1741, 1742, 1746, 1755, 1759, 1770, 1777, 1778, 1786
HONDIUS, Henricus, 1632, 1633, 1670, 1671
HONDIUS, Jodocus, 1606, 1610, 1611, 1618, 1633, 1636, 1637, 1676
HONTER, Jan Coronensis, 1549
HOOPER, Samuel, 1791
HUES, Robert, 1639
HUSKE, John, 1755
HUTCHINSON, E[dward?], 1753

IMLAY, Gilbert, 1793
IRIE (HEIMA), Kobayashi (Shimbei), 1750
IZACKE, Richard, 1677

JACOBSZ, Theunis, 1668
JAILLOT, Alexis-Hubert, 1674, 1692, 1737
JANSSON, Jan, 1630, 1632, 1636, 1639, 1650, 1652, 1676, 1696, 1730
JANVIER, Jean, 1762, 1778
JEFFERSON, Thomas, 1787
JEFFERYS, Thomas, 1755, 1760, 1762, 1768, 1772, 1774, 1775, 1776, 1778, 1779, 1785, 1794
JENKINS, Anthony, 1570

JODE, Cornelis de, 1593
JODE, Gerard de, 1578
JOHNSTON, Thomas, 1753
JOKEN, Nisuikawa, 1708
JOUTEL, Henry, 1714

KAI TSU SHOU KOU, 1708
KEERE, Pieter van den, 1593, 1617
KEULEN, Gerard Hulst, 1786
KEULEN, Johannes van, 1680, 1683, 1695, 1710, 1715
KINO, Eusebio Francisco, S.J., 1770
KIP, William, 1607
KITCHIN, Thomas, 1755, 1763, 1768, 1770, 1775, 1776, 1778, 1780, 1788, 1795
KOEHLER, Johan David, 1720

LAET, Joannes de, 1630, 1633
LAFRERI, Antonio, 1566
LAHONTAN, Louis Armand, Baron de, 1703
LANGENES, Barent, 1609, 1618
LASSO, Bartolomeo, 1603
LATTRÉ, Jean, 1762, 1784, 1785
LAUNAY, Carl Ludwig, 1738
LAWS, William, 1741
LEMAU DE LA JAISSE, 1733
LE ROUGE, George Louis, 1756, 1778
LESLIE, Charles, 1740
LETH, Hendrik de, 1742
LINDE, Luca di, 1655
LINNERHJELM, Gustav Frederic, 1792
LINSCHOTEN, Jan Huygen van, 1605

L'ISLE, Guillaume de, 1700, 1722, 1730, 1740, 1745, 1750, 1752, 1757, 1770
LOBECK, Tobias, 1762
LOPEZ DE VARGAS MACHUCA, Tomas, 1758
LOTTER, Mathias Albrecht, 1772, 1776, 1777
LOTTER, Tobias Conrad, 1740, 1750, 1759, 1762, 1770, 1772, 1774, 1776
LOWNDES, William, 1790

MAGER, Johann Georg, 1716
MAJOR, [Joyn?], 1746
MALHAM, John, 1797
MALLET, Alain Manesson, 1686
MARCI, Adolph Frederik, 1744
MARTYR, Peter d'Angieri, 1533
MATHER, Cotton, 1702
MELA, Pomponius, 1582
MENDEZ, Didaco, 1584
MERCATOR, Gerard, 1590, 1595, 1606, 1633, 1636, 1637, 1639
MERCATOR, Michael, 1595
MERCATOR, Rumold, 1595
MERIAN, Matthaus, 1671
METEREN, Emmanuel van, 1598
METIO, Adrian, 1630
MEURS, Jacob van, 1662, 1671
MIDDLETON, Charles Theodore, 1778
MILLAR, George Henry, 1782
MISSY, Jean Rousset de, 1742
MITCHELL, John, 1700, 1755, 1759, 1776, 1778
MOLL, Herman, 1690, 1695, 1700, 1709, 1715, 1719, 1723, 1729, 1734, 1739, 1755, 1758

The text of this volume was composed in Linotype Garamond No. 3
and printed letterpress at The Shagbark Press, South Portland, Maine.
The illustrations were printed by offset lithography at
Meriden-Stinehour Press, Meriden, Connecticut.
Bound by Acme Bookbinding Company,
Charlestown, Massachusetts.

Produced in an edition of 1,250 copies:
750 for the Smith family and, with emendations,
500 for the Library of the University of Southern Maine.